T0259980

Lecture Notes in Computer Science   9153

Commenced Publication in 1973
Founding and Former Series Editors:
Gerhard Goos, Juris Hartmanis, and Jan van Leeuwen

More information about this series at http://www.springer.com/series/7408

Gabriele Taentzer · Francis Bordeleau (Eds.)

Modelling Foundations and Applications

11th European Conference, ECMFA 2015
Held as Part of STAF 2015
L'Aquila, Italy, July 20–24, 2015
Proceedings

 Springer

Editors
Gabriele Taentzer
Universität Marburg FB Mathematik
Marburg
Germany

Francis Bordeleau
Ericsson Canada Inc
Ottawa
Canada

ISSN 0302-9743   ISSN 1611-3349   (electronic)
Lecture Notes in Computer Science
ISBN 978-3-319-21150-3   ISBN 978-3-319-21151-0   (eBook)
DOI 10.1007/978-3-319-21151-0

Library of Congress Control Number: 2015943444

LNCS sublibrary: SL2 – Programming and Software Engineering

Springer Cham Heidelberg New York Dordrecht London

Printed on acid-free paper

Springer International Publishing AG Switzerland is part of Springer Science+Business Media
(www.springer.com)

Foreword

Software Technologies: Applications and Foundations (STAF) is a federation of a number of leading conferences on software technologies. It provides a loose umbrella organization for practical software technologies conferences, supported by a Steering Committee that provides continuity. The STAF federated event runs annually; the conferences that participate can vary from year to year, but all focus on practical and foundational advances in software technology. The conferences address all aspects of software technology, from object-oriented design, testing, mathematical approaches to modeling and verification, model transformation, graph transformation, model-driven engineering, aspect-oriented development, and tools.

STAF 2015 was held at the University of L'Aquila, Italy, during July 20–24, 2015, and hosted four conferences (ICMT 2015, ECMFA 2015, ICGT 2015 and TAP 2015), a long-running transformation tools contest (TTC 2015), seven workshops affiliated with the conferences, a doctoral symposium, and a project showcase (for the first time). The event featured six internationally renowned keynote speakers, a tutorial, and welcomed participants from around the globe.

This was the first scientific event in computer science after the earthquake that occurred in 2009 and affected L'Aquila. It is a small, and yet big step towards the grand achievement of restoring some form of normality in this place and its people.

The STAF Organizing Committee thanks all participants for submitting and attending, the program chairs and Steering Committee members for the individual conferences, the keynote speakers for their thoughtful, insightful, and engaging talks, the University of L'Aquila, Comune dell'Aquila, the local Department of Human Science, and CEA LIST for their support: *Grazie a tutti!*

July 2015   Alfonso Pierantonio

Preface

The 11th European Conference on Modelling Foundations and Applications (ECMFA 2015) was organized by the Universitá degli Studi dell'Aqulia, Italy, and held during July 22–23, 2015.

Model-based engineering (MBE) is an approach to the design, analysis, and development of software and systems that relies on exploiting high-level models and computer-based automation to achieve significant boosts in both productivity and quality. The ECMFA conference series is dedicated to advancing the state of knowledge and fostering the industrial application of MBE and related approaches. Its focus is on engaging the key figures of research and industry in a dialog that will result in stronger and more effective practical application of MBE, hence producing more reliable software based on state-of-the-art research results.

In 2015, the Program Committee received 54 submissions. Each submission was reviewed by at least three Program Committee members. The committee decided to accept 13 papers, nine papers for the Foundations Track and four papers for the Applications Track, resulting in an overall acceptance rate of 32 %. Papers on a wide range of MBE aspects were accepted, including topics such as aspect-oriented modeling, model management, model transformation, advanced meta-modeling, UML modeling tools, and domain-specific modeling w.r.t. energy consumption and cloud-based systems.

We thank Arend Rensink and Sam Nicander for their enlightening keynote talks at ECMFA 2015. Furthermore, we are grateful to all the Program Committee members for providing their expertise and quality while reviewing the submitted papers. Their helpful and constructive feedback to all authors is most appreciated. We thank the ECMFA Steering Committee members for their advice and help. We also thank all authors who submitted papers to ECMFA 2015.

July 2015

Gabriele Taentzer
Francis Bordeleau

Organization

Program Committee

Shaukat Ali	Simula Research Laboratory, Norway
Behzad Bordbar	University of Birmingham, UK
Francis Bordeleau	Ericsson, Canada
Goetz Botterweck	Lero, University of Limerick, Ireland
Marco Brambilla	Politecnico di Milano, Italy
Jean-Michel Bruel	IRIT, France
Jordi Cabot	Inria-École des Mines de Nantes, France
Michel Chaudron	Gothenburg University, Sweden
Federico Ciccozzi	Mälardalen University, Sweden
Benoit Combemale	IRISA, Université de Rennes 1, France
Diarmuid Corcoran	Ericsson AB, Sweden
Marco Di Natale	Scuola Superiore SantAnna, Italy
Juergen Dingel	Queen's University, Canada
Maged Elaasar	NASA's Jet Propulsion Laboratory, USA
Gregor Engels	University of Paderborn, Germany
Sebastien Gerard	CEA, LIST, France
Martin Gogolla	University of Bremen, Germany
Jeff Gray	University of Alabama, USA
Esther Guerra	Universidad Autónoma de Madrid, Spain
Oystein Haugen	SINTEF, Norway
Reiko Heckel	University of Leicester, UK
Gert Johansson	Combitech AB, Sweden
Maximilian Koegel	EclipseSource Munich, Germany
Dimitris Kolovos	University of York, UK
Thomas Kuehne	Victoria University of Wellington, New Zealand
Vinay Kulkarni	Tata Consultancy Services, India
Philip Langer	EclipseSource, Austria
Roberto Erick Lopez-Herrejon	Johannes Kepler University, Austria
Ralf Lämmel	Universität Koblenz-Landau, Germany
Pierre-Alain Muller	Université de Haute-Alsace, France
Ileana Ober	IRIT - Universite de Toulouse, France
Daniel Ratiu	Siemens Corporate Technology, Munich, Germany
Charles Rivet	Zeligsoft, Canada
Bernhard Rumpe	RWTH Aachen University, Germany
Houari Sahraoui	Université de Montréal, Canada
Rick Salay	University of Toronto, Canada

Ina Schaefer	Technische Universität Braunschweig, Germany
Bernhard Schaetz	TU München, Germany
Andy Schürr	TU Darmstadt, Germany
Harald Störrle	Danmarks Tekniske Universitet, Denmark
Gabriele Taentzer	Philipps-Universität Marburg, Germany
Francois Terrier	CEA, LIST, France
Juha-Pekka Tolvanen	MetaCase, Finland
Antonio Vallecillo	Universidad de Málaga, Spain
Mark Van Den Brand	Eindhoven University of Technology, The Netherlands
Pieter Van Gorp	Eindhoven University of Technology, The Netherlands
Manuel Wimmer	Vienna University of Technology, Austria
Steffen Zschaler	King's College London, UK

Additional Reviewers

Abdeen, Hani
Arifulina, Svetlana
Batot, Edouard
Benomar, Omar
Bousse, Erwan
Burgueño, Loli
Bürdek, Johannes
Chitchyan, Ruzanna
Corley, Jonathan
Corradini, Andrea
Dajsuren, Yanja
Degueule, Thomas
Fazal-Baqaie, Masud
García, Jokin
Greifenberg, Timo
Grieger, Marvin
Hamann, Lars
Heim, Robert

Heindorf, Stefan
Hilken, Frank
Hölzl, Florian
Kanstren, Teemu
Karasneh, Bilal
Kowal, Matthias
Leblebici, Erhan
Lity, Sascha
Mengerink, Josh
Plotnikov, Dimitri
Scandariatto, Riccardo
Sedlmeier, Matthias
Seidl, Christoph
Teufl, Sabine
Verhoeff, Tom
von Wenckstern, Michael
Weckesser, Markus

Contents

Model Management and Transformation

Energy Consumption Analysis and Design of Energy-Aware WSN Agents in fUML

Luca Berardinelli[1,3], Antinisca Di Marco[1,2], Stefano Pace[1,2(✉)],
Luigi Pomante[1,2], and Walter Tiberti[1,2]

[1] Dipartimento DISIM, University of L'Aquila, L'Aquila, Italy
[2] Center of Excellence DEWS, University of L'Aquila, L'Aquila, Italy
{berardinelli,dimarco,pace,pomante}@univaq.it
[3] Business Informatics Group, Vienna University of Technology, Wien, Austria
wtuniv@gmail.com

Abstract. Wireless Sensor Networks (WSN) are nowadays applied to a wide set of domains (e.g., security, health). WSN are networks of spatially distributed, radio-communicating, battery-powered, autonomous sensor nodes. WSN are characterized by scarcity of resources, hence an application running on them should carefully manage its resources. The most critical resource in WSN is the nodes' battery.

In this paper, we propose model-based engineering facilities to analyze the energy consumption and to develop energy-aware applications for WSN that are based on Agilla Middleware. For this aim i) we extend the Agilla Instruction Set with the new **battery** instruction able to retrieve the battery Voltage of a WSN node at run-time; ii) we measure the energy that the execution of each Agilla instruction consumes on a target platform; and iii) we extend the Agilla Modeling Framework with a new analysis that, leveraging the conducted energy consumption measurements, predicts the energy required by the Agilla agents running on the WSN. Such analysis, implemented in fUML, is based on simulation and it guides the design of WSN applications that guarantee low energy consumption. The approach is showed on the Reader agent used in the WildFire Tracker Application.

Keywords: fUML · Model-driven analysis · Tool support · WSN

1 Introduction

A Wireless Sensor Network (WSN) consists of spatially distributed autonomous sensors that cooperate in order to accomplish a task. Sensor nodes are small, low-cost, wireless and battery-powered devices. They can be easily deployed to monitor several environmental parameters and they create large-scale flexible architectures. Sensors can be distributed everywhere and they enable different applications such as domotics, disaster relief, alternate reality game.

This work is supported by the EU-funded VISION ERC project (ERC-240555), the Christian Doppler Forschungsgesellschaft and the BMWFJ, Austria.

© Springer International Publishing Switzerland 2015
G. Taentzer and F. Bordeleau (Eds.): ECMFA 2015, LNCS 9153, pp. 1–17, 2015.
DOI: 10.1007/978-3-319-21151-0_1

The growing request for applications running on WSN showing high quality, demands for suitable design and analysis approaches, that consider non-functional properties already in an early development stage to guarantee the fulfillment of non-functional requirements. Model-based engineering facilitates an early analysis of non-functional properties based on design models. In this respect, UML and its profiles can be chosen as the primary design notation and analysis-specific languages suitable for model-based analysis. The complexity brought by the required set of model-based methodologies, notations and tools may hinder the adoption of UML-based approaches in the WSN domain. The specific nature of sensors complicates the development of applications, because the quality of the services they provide is influenced by several factors like network availability, battery levels. Despite this, a WSN must continue providing its services as long as possible, and with the best effort trying to guarantee network longevity. Traditionally, WSN applications have been developed by with a code-and-fix approach, that is by directly programming nodes with the use of low level primitives. This approach, neglecting design and quality validation phases, results in not structured, hard to maintain code with the risk of missing non-functional requirements and compromising the system usability. Indeed, the system's non-functional properties must be considered as earlier as possible in the system life-cycle to guarantee their fulfillment.

In this work, we propose model-based engineering facilities to analyse the energy consumption and to develop energy-aware applications for WSN that are based on Agilla Middleware. For this aim i) we extend the Agilla Instruction Set with the new `battery` instruction able to sense at run-time the battery of a WSN node; ii) we measure the energy that the execution of each Agilla instruction consumes on a target platform; and iii) we extend the Agilla Modeling Framework (AMF)[1,2] with a new analysis that, leveraging on the conducted energy consumption measurements, predicts the energy required by the Agilla agents running on the WSN. AMF is an executable model library we implemented to model and analyze Agilla based applications running on WSN. It permits to conveniently design agent-based software applications and to carry out its analysis upon the execution of the corresponding UML model. It exploits the recently introduced Foundational UML (fUML) standard that provides a formal semantics of a subset of UML enabling the execution of UML models.

The paper is organized as follows: Section 2 describes the new version of Agilla middleware we implemented; Section 3 shows the process of measurement of the energy consumption of Agilla instructions; Section 4 introduces the used case study; Section 5 illustrates the Agilla Modeling Framework we implemented and its new energy consumption analysis; Section 6 shows the application of the new energy; Section 7 illustrates related work and Section 8 comments the main advantages of our approach; Finally, Section 9 concludes the paper.

2   Agilla v2.0: Energy-Aware Middleware

With the introduction of TinyOS 2.x (TOS2, 2005), that is not compatible with the older TinyOS versions (TinyOS 1.x, TOS1), there is no possibility to exploit some of the old reference applications. Agilla [3] is one of these applications, that allows creating, migrating and destroying software agents on WSN nodes at run-time, without service interruption. To continue working with Agilla we needed to perform a porting of the original Agilla to TinyOS 2.x. Such a porting, called Agilla2.0, was also released to the TinyOS community and it allows to exploit increased reliability of TinyOS2.x and new sensor node technologies (i.e. those not supported by TinyOS1.x), in particular the Memsic IRIS node[1].

Agilla2.0 is fully ISA-compatible with the old version, hence it is possible to execute all the old Agilla applications. To re-use the timing and performance analysis defined in [1,2] also for Agilla2.0/TOS2.x, we performed once again the measurement of the execution time of each single Agilla2.0 instruction. The techniques used in [1] were partially adapted by exploiting a free-running HW counter to timestamp start and end times of each instruction. Such timestamps have been then collected and used to evaluate offline (in order to be as less as possible intrusive in the code behavior) the average execution time for each instruction and other statistical information. The AMF framework hence contains all the information needed to execute timing and performance analysis both in case of Agilla1/TinyOS1 and in case of Agilla2.0/TOS2.x.

In order to also provide an effective run-time support to energy analysis and WSN lifetime estimation, the Agilla2 ISA has been extended by means of a new instruction (i.e. battery) that is able to provide information about the current battery voltage of a node to an agent. This made Agilla2.0 energy-aware.

The battery instruction provides voltage information with a precision of 100 mV. Technically, the new instruction reads data from the ADC and puts it on the top of the agent stack after some processing. Final measurement unit is 100 mV for each unit of the stacked integer value (e.g. a value 33 represents 3.3V).

The ISA extension has followed the procedure reported in the original Agilla website[2]. In the following the main issues are described with some details.

VoltageC Module - Memsic IRIS nodes can obtain information about the voltage by means of the VoltageC TOS2 module. Since the power supply voltage is attached to a dedicated ADC channel, this module is able to retrieve it easily. It uses a split-phase command called read() that retrieves voltage data in term of ADC divisions. Such data is then converted by means of the formula 1. It is a conversion formula from ADC divisions to the real voltage value, where we just added the 10 factor and -36 in order to adjust the offset. The formula takes into account the features of the IRIS ADC[3]:

$$V = 10 * [(1100 * 1024)/read()] - 36 \qquad (1)$$

where: i) the 10 factor is used to convert from Volt to Volt/10 (decivolt); ii) the 1100 value refers the internal reference voltge of iris motes; iii) the 1024 value is the number of ADC steps (10 bit resolution); iv) read() is the actual value read via VoltageC module; v) The 36 (360mV) value is an offset adjustment needed to obtain a correct value.

OPBatteryM Module. By following the standard procedure to extend the Agilla2 ISA, we created a module called OPBatteryM, that contains all the instructions needed to read and process the voltage value (as described above). Such a module is also related to a configuration called OPBatteryC that we inserted in the *opcodes* Agilla2.0 directory. Moreover, it makes use of all the interfaces needed to perform its work: previously cited VoltageC and also all the Agilla2.0 modules that allow to interact with Agilla2.0 main elements (e.g. stack, context, tuple space, etc.). Finally, to be fully usable in the Agilla2.0 MW, the module provides an implementation of the interface BytecodeI. The main code related to the execution of a new instruction in the Agilla2.0 MW context can be found in the execute command of such an interface. In fact, such a command stops the Agilla2 agent execution and starts the split-phase operation needed to read the voltage. When the read is done, the value is processed and then passed to the Agilla2.0 code that writes it on the top the stack (interface OPStackI). Finally, the agent execution is resumed. To conclude ISA extension, the Agilla2.0 Agent Injector should be able to identify the new instruction. For this, we modified the related Java code by inserting `battery` and associating to it a unique opcode. In this way, the OPBatteryM module can be properly exploited when the `battery` instruction is detected.

Time Measurements of the `Battery` Instruction. The code related to `battery` instruction is nothing more than an ADC read, same as the `sense` instruction, for example. So, its execution time can be estimated as equal to the one of the `sense` instruction. Code debugging and time measurements have confirmed the validity of this assumption.

3   Energy Consumption Measurements of Agilla Instructions

The concept of low-power is strictly related to WSN since their invention. For this, one of the main goals of this work is to improve the power-awareness of adopted devices and related software. Considering the previously described Agilla2.0, we needed an analysis to consider the energy consumption issues related to the adoption of such a middleware. In particular, starting from Agilla2.0 instructions' execution times, we estimated their energy consumption. For this, we decomposed each instruction into several basic operations and, for each of them, we measured the power involved on IRIS nodes as detailed below. Finally, by combining the energy consumption of basic operations and the timing information, we estimated the consumption of each Agilla2.0 instruction.

In order to estimate the energy consumption, we adopted the milli Ampere per hour (mAh) metric. Such metric is very useful, since it is directly related to information provided for some commercial batteries. So, by knowing timing information for each instruction and decomposing each of them in basic operations, we have measured the power related to each basic operation and we have combined them with their duration to obtain mAh estimations. In particular, the considered basic operations are the following ones: i) microprocessor processing, ii) radio RX/TX, and iii) leds ON/OFF. To measure power consumption associated to basic operation, we exploited the experimental setup shown in Figure 1. By means of the voltage measured on R_TEST ($1.2ohm$) we evaluated the power by using an oscilloscope.

To associate measured current to the basic operations, we created a proper Agilla2.0 agent with the following 5-phases behavior (10 seconds for phase): *i)* microprocessor activity only, *ii)* microprocessor and led activities, *iii)* radio ON in reception mode, *iv)* radio ON/OFF switching, and *v)* periodic radio transmission. Finally, we could estimate mAh consumption for each Agilla2.0 instruction.

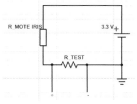

Fig. 1. Energy measurement experimental setup

3.1   Battery Behavior Analysis

Once estimated Agilla2.0/IRIS energy consumption, some considerations about commercial batteries behaviours have to be made in order to be able to use consumption data in a correct way. In particular, nominal mAh could be affected by operating conditions (e.g. temperature, humidity, etc.). So, in order to be able to estimate the energy status of a node, we analyzed some info about AA batteries normally used to power WSN nodes [4]. In particular, for IRIS nodes, we need two AA batteries, for a total of about 3V. Then, by means of some stress tests with different reference voltages, we identified a critical threshold of 1.7 V under which the node is no more active. Once under such voltage, only a nominal voltage (3V-3.3V) followed by a reset allows the node to start working again. Moreover, we identified four operational zones:

- more than 3V (up to 3.3V): ideal conditions.
- 3V-2.8V: good conditions.
- 2.8V-2.4V: still working but with some warning.
- Under 2.4V: serious warning.

The last zone, considering the information reported in [4], represents a point in which energy consumption analysis could no more be representative of a real operative condition due to a possible very fast batteries failure. It is worth noting that this means that, also if the available mAh have not been totally used, it is not possible to make reliable assumptions about their availability in a short period. Maybe it could be better to change the batteries, if possible, or to consider using the node only for non critical activities.

4   Case Study

In this paper we reuse and extend the Wildfire Tracking Application (WTA), an existing case study originally described in [3] and already adopted in our previous work [1,2]. The WTA software is deployed on a WSN distributed into a region that is prone to fires. It must detect a fire and determine its perimeter. Figure 2 shows the high-level behavior of the application.

The original WTA is composed by three Agilla agents. The *Reader* agent runs on all the WSN nodes and is programmed to sense the temperature at regular time intervals of 1/8 of second. The readings are sent to the Base Station (BS). A *Forwarder* agent, running on the BS, forwards the sensed values up to the PC, where the temperature level is evaluated. Once a fire has been detected, a *Tracker* agent is injected from the PC into the WSN, through the BS, in order to dynamically determine the perimeter of the fire.

Fig. 2. The WTA App

In this paper, we carry out the energy analysis of two variants of the `Reader` agent by extending the original version (Figure 3) with battery awareness capability through our new `battery` instruction (battery-aware reader, `baReader`, Figure 4). The Agilla code of both agents, `Reader` and `baReader`, consists of Agilla instructions (e.g., `pushc`) that are grouped in tasks (e.g., `BEGIN`, depicted as small gray nodes in the control flow graph. By default, the Agilla middleware executes tasks sequentially by scheduling the next tasks after the latest

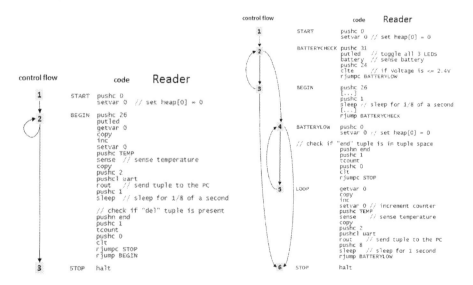

Fig. 3. The standard Reader (`Reader`)   **Fig. 4.**   The   battery-aware   Reader (`baReader`)

instruction of the previous one. However, goto-like instructions such as `rjump` and `rjumpc` allow (un)conditional relative jumps [3].

This `Reader` version is programmed to `sense` the temperature at regular time intervals of 125 ms (default waiting time of `sleep` in task `BEGIN`) and to send it (`rout`) to the BS. Since `Reader` is not `battery`-aware, no further actions are taken in case of low battery level.

The `baReader` version is extended with a battery-level check (`BATTERYCHECK` task) before sensing the temperature. In case of low voltage (lower or equal to 2.4 Volts), the execution jumps to the `BATTERYLOW` task, from where a `LOOP` task is entered, where the same actions as the `BEGIN` task are executed (a counter is incremented, and the temperature is sensed and sent to the PC) but with a lower frequency.

Finally, both `Reader` and `baReader` agents can stop their execution by checking the presence of a *del* entry in the Tuple Space (in `BEGIN` and `BATTERYLOW` tasks, respectively). If found, both `Reader` and `baReader` agents jump to the `STOP` task where the `halt` instruction is executed.

5   The Agilla Modeling Framework

The Agilla Modeling Framework (AMF)[4] is part of a model-driven, tool-supported approach (see Figure 5) to design and analyze Agilla applications [3] suitably modeled through the Foundational UML (fUML) [5], a new standard of the Object Management Group (OMG) that defines the operational semantics of a (strict) UML subset.

Figure 5 sketches the fUML-driven approach supported by AMF. Artifacts (*fUML Model* and *Analysis Results*) and functionalities (*Parsing, Instruction Semantics Simulation, Trace Generation, Timing Analysis, Performance Analysis, Energy Analysis*) are depicted as rectangles and rounded boxes, respectively, while dashed arrows connect functionalities and related artifacts with labels detailing their relationships.

The AMF nature is two-fold. On the one hand AMF is a *fUML model library*, i.e., a model consisting of reusable classes and activities for fUML models representing Agilla applications as created by the *Users*. On the other hand, AMF is also a *tool* whose analysis algorithms are *implemented* (i.e., modeled)

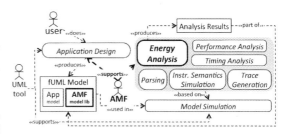

Fig. 5. Actors, functionalities and artifacts in AMF

through executable UML activities and *Analysis Results* are saved as slot values [6] within the same executable *fUML Model*.

---

[4] http://sealabtools.di.univaq.it/tools.php

The remainder of this section provides a brief background on fUML and AMF design choices, then describes the new *Energy Consumption Analysis* capability. The other AMF capabilities (parsing, instruction semantics simulation, trace generation, timing and performance analyses) are described in our previous works [1, 2].

5.1   The Foundational UML and AMF Design Choices

fUML[5] defines the operational semantics of a strict UML subset (cf. Figure 7a) that includes Classes, Common Behaviors, Activities, and Actions. Neither heavy (e.g., metamodel changes) nor lightweight extensions (e.g., UML profiles) are required. fUML enables the execution of UML models including Classes with their own Structural (i.e., attributes) and BehavioralFeatures (i.e., operations). Behavioral specifications (i.e., operations' body) are modeled through Activities.

The fUML standard goes along with a Java-based reference implementation of an fUML virtual machine (fUML VM)[5], to simulate fUML models. Free open source and commercial UML modeling tools exist that embed this reference implementation within their modeling environments, like Papyrus[6] and Magic-Draw[7]. We adopted the latter, in conjunction with its plug-in Cameo Simulation Toolkit, as modeling and simulation environment (i.e., UML tool in Figure 5).

Figure 7b shows an excerpt of the user-defined fUML Model for the Reader agent. Its structure and behavior are modeled through composition of Classes and hierarchical Activities, respectively. The AMF Model Library helps the structural modeling of Agilla applications. It includes:

- An abstract, hierarchical structure of classes (AppComp, AgentComp, TaskComp, InstrComp). User-defined fUML Model of Agilla applications are modeled with classes and proper *Generalization* relationships. (e.g., the Reader agent and its own START, BEGIN, and STOP tasks).
- A set of 74 concrete InstrComp classes (e.g., pushc, cf. Figure 7c) covering the whole Agilla instruction set [3], including a new class for the battery instruction.

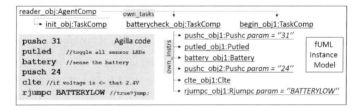

Fig. 6. baReader agent instance model at simulation time

[5] http://fuml.modeldriven.org

[6] www.papyrusuml.org/

[7] www.nomagic.com/products/magicdraw.html

At simulation time, the fUML VM generates a so-called *instance model* and ignores the non-executable part (e.g., Sequences, Statemachines, Deployments or annotations [7]). InstanceSpecifications, Links, and Slots elements are generated within the instance model as counterparts of Classes, Associations and Properties, respectively.

The execution of fUML Activities then reads, adds, deletes, and modifies elements of the instance model. Figure 6 shows a graph-like excerpt of the Reader agent instance where InstanceSpecification (e.g., reader_obj) and Links (e.g., own_tasks) are depicted as nodes and arrows, respectively.

The behavioral specification of an `AgentComp` comprises a layered set of fUML Activities representing i) the flow of tasks (e.g., START, BEGIN, and STOP, cf. Activity Level 1 in Figure 7b), ii) the flow of instructions for each task (cf. Level 2 in Figure 7b) and, iii) AMF algorithms like the Energy Analysis (cf. Level 3 in Figure 7b). The AML user is in charge of modeling the task flow from scratch. On the contrary, the instruction-level flow is built by dragging and dropping instruction actions (e.g., `halt`) from the library and, if needed, manually add parameters through typed pins (e.g., 26:`String` for pushc)[6]. Such actions transparently invokes further nested fUML activities realizing instruction semantics and AMF analysis algorithms (cf. Level 3 in Figure 7c).

The AMF Instruction Semantics Simulation is in charge of traversing an agent's instance model and collecting instruction-specific slot values for the sake of Timing, Performance and Energy Consumption Analyses.

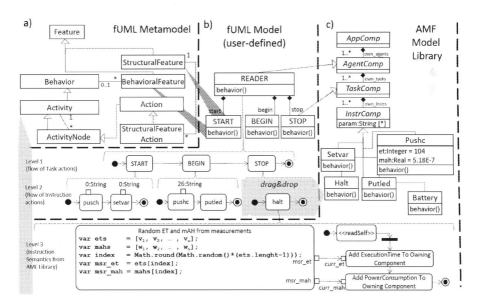

Fig. 7. Modeling with fUML and the AML Library

In [1] we modeled and implemented[8] the timing analysis algorithm which collects and sums slot values corresponding to measured instruction execution times (e.g., the *et* default value of `pushc` in Figure 7c). In [2] we further enhanced AMF with a First Come First Served (FCFS) scheduling policy required by the Performance Analysis capability to generate additional timed properties like waiting (*wt*), and completion times (*ct*). Similar to the timing analysis algorithm, all these timed properties (*ets*, *wts*, *cts*), stored as slot values in the Agent's instance model, are collected during the instruction semantics simulation to finally obtain performance indices (e.g., response time) from fUML models of Agilla agents.

In this paper, we enrich AMF with the Energy Consumption Analysis capability by reusing the same algorithm design. AMF collects the measured energy consumption of each Agilla Instruction while traversing the instance model during the fUML model simulation (see Figure 8a).

Figure 7c shows a generic energy consumption analysis algorithm as executed during the `behavior()` operations of each InstrComp instance. In particular, a `Random ET and mAh from measurements` JavaScript snippet [9] randomly selects a couple of values v_i and w_i for et and mah, respectively, from two arrays of n measurements and adds them to the corresponding partial sums saved as slots of the owning `TaskComp` instances. A similar activity calculate the execution time and power consumption of an `AgentComp` instance from partial sums stored in the owned `TaskComp` ones.

6   Energy Consumption Analysis

The analysis work flow is shown in Figure 8a. We analyzed the energy consumption of `Reader` and `baReader` agents in three different scenarios (Sc). In each scenario, we simulate the fUML model of both `Reader` and `baReader` agents, in isolation, from the beginning (i.e., the execution of the first Agilla instruction, `pushc`, see Figures 3 and 4) up to the end (i.e., the first execution of the `halt` instruction of the `STOP` task). Each simulation run corresponds to the execution occurrence shown in the sequence diagram in Figure 8b[10]. The three different simulation scenarios Sc1, Sc2, and Sc3, differs from the agent's `sleep` time between two consecutive `sense` and dispatch (`rout`) of temperature to the base station (BS). By default, a `sense 1` instruction hibernates an agent for 125 milliseconds. In our scenarios Sc1, Sc2, and Sc3, we hibernate the agent for 30, 60, and 120 seconds. This behaviors are implemented by setting the `sleep` parameter to 240, 480, and 960, respectively. At the modeling level, setting such scenarios consists in i) saving distinct fUML models for both `Reader` and `baReader` for a total of six artifacts (e.g., .mdzip files using MagicDraw), ii) opening each model and updating the integer *value specification* [6] of the `sleep` action (imported from the Agilla InstructionSet in the AMF model library) within the containing

---

[8] AMF is a tool directly designed in fUML realizing the motto "the model is the code".

[9] Set as body of a UML Opaque action.

[10] Both state machine and sequence diagram are not part of the fUML model and it is used for explanation purposes.

BEGIN task action, and iii) starting the model simulation which repeat the agent simulation for a user-defined number of runs (see Figure 8).

Figure 9 shows the analysis results. Minimums, maximums, and averages of the energy consumption for both Reader and baReader agents have been calculated through AMF by executing the corresponding fUML model. Each scenario has been executed 100 times.

As expected, the baReader agent saves energy (from $38,37\%$ in Sc1 up to $43,22\%$ in Sc3, see Figure 9) w.r.t. the battery unaware Reader one. However, focusing on analysis results of the same reader version in different scenarios, we observe that the energy consumption is almost the same, i.e., it is invariant w.r.t.

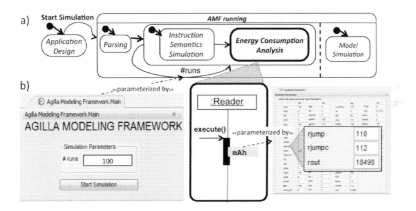

Fig. 8. Energy consumption analysis work flow

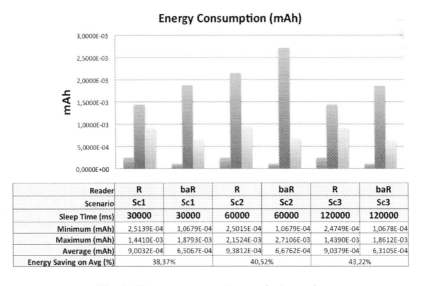

Reader	R	baR	R	baR	R	baR
Scenario	Sc1	Sc1	Sc2	Sc2	Sc3	Sc3
Sleep Time (ms)	30000	30000	60000	60000	120000	120000
Minimum (mAh)	2,5139E-04	1,0679E-04	2,5015E-04	1,0679E-04	2,4749E-04	1,0678E-04
Maximum (mAh)	1,4410E-03	1,8793E-03	2,1524E-03	2,7106E-03	1,4390E-03	1,8612E-03
Average (mAh)	9,0032E-04	6,5067E-04	9,3812E-04	6,6762E-04	9,0379E-04	6,3105E-04
Energy Saving on Avg (%)	38,37%		40,52%		43,22%	

Fig. 9. Energy consumption analysis results

to the sensing frequency. It may be caused by the busy wait of the `sleep` instruction which does not turn off but only hibernates the agent then causing a lower, but not null, energy consumption while waiting for resuming the agent behavior. As a consequence, the longer is the busy wait (i.e., greater is the `sleep` integer parameter), the higher is the energy required to complete the execution of the `sleep` instruction. In addition, we also observe a lower difference among minimums and maximums of the `baReader` version w.r.t. the corresponding results for the `Reader` version in all scenarios. These results are caused, on the one hand, by the greater complexity of the `baReader` version whose execution may generate longer control flows (e.g., more loops) thus requiring more energy to their completion. On the other hand, it may be caused by the limited number of simulation runs (100) for the proposed scenarios. Even if, as already experienced in our previous works [1,2,8], we are limited by the current scalability problem of the fUML virtual machine which it is not optimized for simulation-based analysis [9], our approach is promising since we are able to integrate several non-functional analyses in a single tool. This will open to an easy and consistent multi-dimensional analyses environment where trade-off analysis are possible. Moreover, since we do not move from different modeling notations and analysis tools, we are sure that the results of the analyses refer to the same software system. Instead when we move to different modeling notations and tools, this warranty is obtained if it is proved that the provided M2M transformation does not change the modelled system. Up to day this proof is not provided for most of the transformation in literature, but it is leaved to intuition. Finally, in literature, we can find some example of multi-dimensional analysis environment, such as Palladio [10], using proprietary modeling notations. Differently from them, we do not use own notations, but UML that is a standard de-facto modeling language hence the impact of AMF is wider and more general.

7   Related Work

fUML - In this work, that directly stems from [1] as well as in [7] and [11], we pursue a similar goal but aiming at a tighter integration between fUML and analysis methodologies. In particular, we showed in [7] and [11] how performance analysis can be conducted on annotated fUML models by generating and analyzing traces compliant with a fUML runtime metamodel [12]. Tool support is provided through a Java-based Eclipse plug-in that suitably interacts with the fUML VM during its execution. In [1] and in this subsequent work, we further emphasize the role and importance of fUML by directly designing (that is, implementing) the analysis tool as a fUML model library.

In [1,7,11] and in this work as well, the expected benefits of directly utilizing the execution of UML models for carrying out model-based analysis are twofold: *(i)* the costly translation of UML models into formal languages dedicated to specific analysis purposes is avoided and, hence, *(ii)* the implementation and maintenance of supporting analysis tool sets is eased significantly. With AMF approach presented in this paper, we offer both of these benefits and showcased them by developing a performance analyzer that implements an analysis method directly on UML models for WSN applications. A translation of UML models into an analysis model can now be omitted and it is not necessary to use additional external tools for analysis purposes.

In [13], the authors present a behavioural design solution for WSN, abstracting the complicated dynamic aspects of WSN software systems through the concept of activity-driven states. This provides the programmer with concrete design elements that can be directly mapped to the constructs of target programming languages opening towards more accurate verification and validation of software systems for WSNs. Differently from [13], our approach gives the possibility to design software for WSN with fUML and to map it to the Agilla target language and provides functional, timing, performance and energy analyses on the UML models via simulation.

Romero and Ferreira propose an MDA-based approach applied to the domain of space real-time software for sake of code generation and schedulability analysis [14]. In their approach platform independent models and test cases are specified using fUML activities. Non-functional properties are annotated on the activities using the UML profile MARTE. However, for carrying out the schedulability analysis, fUML activities are translated into AADL models [15].

Benyahia et al. [16] evaluate how well the current fUML semantics supports the formalization of concurrent and temporal semantic aspects which is required for the design and analysis of real-time embedded systems. They illustrate how the standard fUML execution model, as well as the fUML VM, have to be extended for this purpose to explicitly incorporate a *scheduler* into fUML that, at each step of the model execution, determines the activity node to be executed next according to certain scheduling policies (e.g., first-in-first-out (FIFO)). The same limitation has been addressed by Abdelhalim et al. [17]. In contrast to Benyahia et al. [16], they do not propose an extension of the standard fUML execution model but rather present a model-based framework that translates fUML activities into communicating sequential processes (CSP) for performing a deadlock analysis detecting possible scenarios leading to deadlocks which are provided as UML sequence diagrams.

Energy Analysis - In [18], a Model-Driven approach is used to separately model the software architecture of a WSN, the low-level hardware specification of the WSN nodes and the physical environment where nodes are deployed in. The framework can use these models to generate executable code to analyze the energy consumption of the modeled application. The last three approaches aim at evaluating the quality of the WSN application (that is, its performance for the first two and the energy consumption for the last one). Instead, our approach aims at performing non-functional analysis, including energy analysis, on the models with no model-weaving processes. We also generate the executable code, ready to be deployed and run on a node.

In [19], the authors first break down the energy consumption for the components of a typical sensor node, and they discuss the main directions to energy conservation in WSNs. Then, they present a systematic and comprehensive taxonomy of the energy conservation schemes. This work guided us through the step of integrating in the framework an energy consumption analysis for Agilla agents. In [20], the authors propose an energy-efficient MAC protocol for WSNs, so they save energy at lower level, while we save energy at the application level.

The authors of [21] formulate the energy consumption and study their estimated lifetime based on a clustering mechanism with varying parameters related to the sensing field (e.g., size and distance). They provide numerical analysis and results of the energy consumed by the WSN and the WSN's lifetime, but they only consider energy consumed in communication, without taking into account energy consumed in data processing, etc. Further, their analysis is generic and does not take into account differences between different hardware platforms. With our approach, instead, we take into account the energy consumed by every single instruction of an agent, and the energy consumption of each instruction is evaluated in the specific hardware platform where it is executed. So, when changing the platform, the energy consumption value may vary also, if the hardware has got different characteristics. In general, great research effort is focused on optimizing protocols and clustering schemes for performance and energy saving, but there's a very poor work on designing and generating good applications for WSNs, from performance and energy viewpoint. This is instead our research direction: We design, simulate and analyze Agilla-based WSN applications, in order to automatically obtain application code that meets the non-functional constraints.

8 Discussion

It is worth noting that, in this paper, we are extending the analysis capabilities of AMF with the intent of showing the suitability of fUML for i) the design and analysis of WSN applications, and ii) the design of more and more complex analysis tools as fUML model libraries, at the same time. In accordance with our background and research goals, we primarily focus on assessing the exploitation of fUML and related technologies in the WSN and extra-functional analysis domains. We consider AMF and, more in general, the underlying fUML-driven approach proposed in this paper, an initial as well as a first practical evaluation of the impact that fUML and its related technologies may have i) on expectations from UML practitioners and ii) on future research directions in MDE [22,23]. With this work, we show that both the design and analysis of WSN as well as tool development are feasible activities with fUML. While pursuing our goals, we experienced both opportunities and limitations related to the usage of fUML.

fUML is a young OMG standard, published on February 2011. It makes a strict (and then easier to learn) subset of UML executable. By leveraging their current background in UML, both researchers and practitioners can already adopt it for their specific purposes. At the time of writing, the (positive or negative) impact of fUML on daily modeling activities still have to be assessed (e.g., [23] was concluded in July 2011). fUML promotes model reuse through executable model libraries, like AMF, and it may be compared to a new programming language that, however, still suffers from the lack of an adequate support in term of built-in libraries. In AMF, for example, we had to model from scratch common auxiliary data structures like queue and stack. The modeling effort required to create executable model libraries may then be high. For example, fUML activities are much more detailed than non-executable ones and so far usually disregarded details, like input/output pins, have to be systematically modeled to allow a correct execution. Being aware of this, we worked on AMF for its users to simplify the modeling of agents' control flows.

In addition, still few UML modeling tools exist that provide plug-ins that support the simulation of their models. We choose MagicDraw and its plug-in Cameo Simulation Toolkit to support the modeling and simulation tasks in AMF. However, being fUML models also valid UML models, such artifacts may be exchanged among any UML modeling tools supporting common serialization formats (e.g., XMI and Eclipse UML).

In this work, we are adopting fUML to design, from scratch, an analysis tool. From [1] on, the AMF executable model is growing fast to support its new functionalities, including also possibly heavy computational tasks, like performance analysis is. It is worth noting that AMF can be seen as a layered tool infrastructure and all the AMF functionalities run within an hosting UML Modeling environment which, in turn, run on atop a Java Virtual Machine. This layered infrastructure may cause scalability issues for analysis tools, like AMF, running on the topmost layer. In this work, we mainly focused on promoting MDE approaches in the WSN domain using fUML as the only modeling and simulation notation. Assessing the maturity level of fUML and its underlying technology for such a challenge task is out of scope of this paper and left for future work.

9   Conclusion

AMF is an ongoing work that spread MDE methodologies and tools in the Wireless Sensor Network domain. We developed a model-driven approach that allows both modeling and multiple analysis (timing, performance and energy consumption) of software for WSN nodes running the Agilla mobile agents-based middleware. We adopted fUML, a strict executable UML subset, as design notation for AMF users and as well as development language for AMF itself. We provided modeling guidelines to AMF users in order to obtain an executable specification directly in UML, without the need of learning ad-hoc notations and tools. In this respect, thanks to its fUML native compatibility with UML, our approach is tool-supported by construction and can leverage many existing, industrial-strength UML-based tools. We simulated different fUML models representing two (un)aware variants of a reader agent in three different scenarios by feeding the analysis with measured data obtained from a real Agilla execution platform. For this purpose, we extended both the Agilla middleware and the corresponding AMF model library with a new `battery` instruction.

As future research goals, we plan to improve the design and scalability of existing analysis algorithms in fUML and to combine them in trade off analyses.

References

1. Berardinelli, L., Di Marco, A., Pace, S., Marchesani, S., Pomante, L.: Modeling and timing simulation of agilla agents for WSN applications in executable UML. In: Balsamo, M.S., Knottenbelt, W.J., Marin, A. (eds.) EPEW 2013. LNCS, vol. 8168, pp. 300–311. Springer, Heidelberg (2013)
2. Berardinelli, L., Di Marco, A., Pace, S.: fUML-driven design and performance analysis of software agents for wireless sensor network. In: Avgeriou, P., Zdun, U. (eds.) ECSA 2014. LNCS, vol. 8627, pp. 324–339. Springer, Heidelberg (2014)
3. Fok, C.L., Roman, G.C., Lu, C.: Agilla: A mobile agent middleware for self-adaptive wireless sensor networks. ACM Trans. Auton. Adap. 4(3), 16 (2009)
4. A Comparison of Primary Battery Performance using a Solartron 7150plus Multimeter. http://www.drkfs.net/bestbattery.htm
5. OMG. Semantics of a foundational subset for executable UML models (2011)
6. OMG. UML, Superstructure, Version 2.4.1 (2011)
7. Berardinelli, L., Langer, P., Mayerhofer, T.: Combining fUML and profiles for non-functional analysis based on model execution traces. In: QoSA (2013)
8. Berardinelli, L., Cortellessa, V.: fUML-driven performance analysis through the moses model library. In: ACES-MB, MoDELS, pp. 34–43 (2014)
9. Tatibouet, J., Cuccuru, A., Gérard, S., Terrier, F.: Principles for the realization of an open simulation framework based on fuml (wip). In: Proc. of the Symposium on Theory of Modeling & Simulation-DEVS Integrative M&S Symposium, p. 4. Society for Computer Simulation International (2013)
10. Brosig, F., Meier, P., Becker, S., Koziolek, A., Koziolek, H., Kounev, S.: Quantitative evaluation of model-driven performance analysis and simulation of component-based architectures. IEEE Trans. Software Eng. 41(2), 157–175 (2015)
11. Fleck, M., Berardinelli, L., Langer, P., Mayerhofer, T., Cortellessa, V.: Resource contention analysis of service-based systems through fUML-driven model execution. In: Proc. of NiM-ALP, p. 6 (2013)
12. Mayerhofer, T., Langer, P., Kappel, G.: A runtime model for fUML. In: Proc. of the Int'l Workshop on Models@run.time (MRT 2012) at MODELS (2012)
13. Taherkordi, A., Eliassen, F., Johnsen, E.B.: Behavioural design of sensor network applications using activity-driven states. In: Int'l Workshop on Soft. Eng. Sensor Network App. (SESENA), pp. 13–18 (2013)
14. Romero, A.G., Ferreira, M.G.V.: An approach to model-driven architecture applied to space real-time software. In: Proc. of the Int'l Conf. on Space Op. (2012)
15. Feiler, P.H., Gluch, D.P.: Model-based engineering with AADL: An introduction to the sae architecture analysis & design language. Addison-Wesley (2012)
16. Benyahia, A., Cuccuru, A., Taha, S., Terrier, F., Boulanger, F., Gérard, S.: Extending the standard execution model of UML for real-time systems. In: Hinchey, M., Kleinjohann, B., Kleinjohann, L., Lindsay, P.A., Rammig, F.J., Timmis, J., Wolf, M. (eds.) DIPES 2010. IFIP AICT, vol. 329, pp. 43–54. Springer, Heidelberg (2010)
17. Abdelhalim, I., Schneider, S., Treharne, H.: An integrated framework for checking the behaviour of fUML models using CSP. Int'l Journal on Software Tools for Technology Transfer, 1–22 (2012)
18. Doddapaneni, K., Ever, E., Gemikonakli, O., Malavolta, I., Mostarda, L., Muccini, H.: A model-driven engineering framework for architecting and analysing wireless sensor networks. In: Int'l Workshop on Soft. Eng. Sensor Network App. (SESENA), pp. 1–7 (2012)

19. Anastasi, G., Conti, M., Di Francesco, M., Passarella, A.: Energy conservation in wireless sensor networks: A survey. Ad Hoc Networks **7**(3), 537–568 (2009)
20. Ye, W., Heidemann, J., Estrin, D.: An energy-efficient mac protocol for wireless sensor networks. In: Proceedings of the Twenty-First Annual Joint Conference of the IEEE Computer and Communications Societies, INFOCOM 2002, vol. 3, pp. 1567–1576. IEEE (2002)
21. Duarte-Melo, E.J., Liu, M.: Analysis of energy consumption and lifetime of heterogeneous wireless sensor networks. In: Global Telecommunications Conference, GLOBECOM 2002, vol. 1, pp. 21–25. IEEE (2002)
22. France, R.B., Rumpe, B.: Model-driven development of complex software: a research roadmap. In: Future of Software Engineering, pp. 37–54 (2007)
23. Malavolta, I., Lago, P., Muccini, H., Pelliccione, P., Tang, A.: What industry needs from architectural languages: A survey. IEEE Trans. Softw. Eng. **39**(6) (2013)

A Comparison of Two-Level and Multi-level Modelling for Cloud-Based Applications

Alessandro Rossini[1]([envelope]), Juan de Lara[2], Esther Guerra[2], and Nikolay Nikolov[1]

[1] SINTEF, Oslo, Norway
{alessandro.rossini,nikolay.nikolov}@sintef.no
[2] Universidad Autónoma de Madrid, Madrid, Spain
{Juan.deLara,Esther.Guerra}@uam.es

Abstract. The Cloud Modelling Framework (CLOUDMF) is an approach to apply model-driven engineering principles to the specification and execution of cloud-based applications. It comprises a domain-specific language to model the deployment topology of multi-cloud applications, along with a *models@run-time* environment to facilitate reasoning and adaptation of these applications at run-time. This paper reports on some challenges encountered during the design of CLOUDMF, related to the adoption of the two-level modelling approach and especially the *type-instance* pattern. Moreover, it proposes the adoption of an alternative, multi-level modelling approach to tackle these challenges, and provides a set of criteria to compare both approaches.

Keywords: Domain-specific languages · Metamodelling · Multi-level modelling · Multi-level reasoning · Cloud computing · CLOUDMF · CLOUDML · METADEPTH

1 Introduction

Model-driven engineering (MDE) aims at improving the productivity, quality, and cost-effectiveness of software development by shifting the paradigm from code to model-centric, whereby models and modelling languages are the main artefacts of the development process. In MDE, the abstract syntax of a modelling language is defined by its metamodel, which describes the set of concepts, properties and relations of a domain, as well as the rules for combining them. Based on this paradigm, a software system is represented by a model that conforms to a metamodel. This approach, hereafter called *two-level modelling*, may have limitations [5,15,21] when the metamodel includes the *type-instance* pattern [5,10], which requires an explicit modelling of types and their instances at the same metalevel. In this case, an alternative approach that employs more than two levels, hereafter called *multi-level modelling*, yields simpler models [5,10,21]. However, while some recent studies show the potential applicability of multi-level modelling [10], there are still scarce works showing its benefits for real-life projects.

G. Taentzer and F. Bordeleau (Eds.): ECMFA 2015, LNCS 9153, pp. 18–32, 2015.
DOI: 10.1007/978-3-319-21151-0_2

Cloud computing provides a ubiquitous networked access to a shared and virtualised pool of computing capabilities (*e.g.*, network, storage, processing, and memory) that can be provisioned with minimal management effort. MDE has been applied in the field of cloud computing, where models and modelling languages enable developers and reasoning engines to work at a high level of abstraction and focus on cloud concerns rather than implementation details. One notable example in this area is the Cloud Modelling Framework (CLOUD-MF) [12–14], which consists of: *(i)* the Cloud Modelling Language (CLOUDML), a domain-specific language (DSL) to model the deployment of multi-cloud applications (*i.e.*, applications that can be deployed across multiple private, public, or hybrid cloud infrastructures and platforms); and *(ii)* a *models@run-time* environment to enact the deployment and adaptation of these applications. The run-time environment provides a model-based representation of the underlying running system, which facilitates reasoning and adaptation of multi-cloud applications.

This paper reports on some challenges encountered during the design of CLOUDMF, related to the adoption of the two-level approach and especially the type-instance pattern. Moreover, it proposes an alternative, multi-level approach, and provides a detailed comparison of both approaches along six criteria, which aims to serve as a guideline for prospective adopters of the multi-level solution.

Paper Organisation. Sec. 2 outlines the current design of CLOUDML and its models@run-time environment. Sec. 3 presents a case study used throughout the paper. Secs. 4 and 5 compare how to model the case study using two-level and multi-level approaches. Sec. 6 discusses the pro and contra of the two approaches. Finally, Sec. 7 compares with related work and Sec. 8 ends with conclusions and future work.

2 CloudMF

CLOUDMF is being developed in the context of the EU projects MODAClouds and PaaSage[1], where several industrial partners are adopting it to specify and execute the multi-cloud applications of their use cases. In this section, we outline its two main ingredients: CLOUDML and its models@run-time environment.

2.1 CloudML

CLOUDML has been designed based on the following requirements, among others:

Separation of concerns (R_1): CLOUDML should support a modular, loosely-coupled specification of the deployment. This will facilitate the maintenance as well as the dynamic adaptation of the deployment model.

---

[1] http://www.modaclouds.eu/, http://www.paasage.eu/

Reusability (R_2): CLOUDML should support the specification of types that can be seamlessly reused to model the deployment. This will ease the evolution as well as the rapid development of different variants of the deployment model.

Abstraction (R_3): CLOUDML should provide an up-to-date, abstract representation of the running system. This will facilitate the reasoning, simulation, and validation of the adaptation actions before their actual enactments.

CLOUDML implements a component-based approach [14], which facilitates separation of concerns (R_1) and reusability (R_2). Hence, deployment models can be regarded as assemblies of components and relations between them.

2.2 Models@run-time

Models@run-time [6] is an architectural pattern for dynamically adaptive systems that leverages upon models at both design-time and run-time. In particular, models@run-time provides an abstract representation of the underlying running system, whereby a modification to the model is enacted on-demand in the system, and a change in the system is automatically reflected in its model.

In CLOUDMF, the models@run-time environment provides a model causally connected to the running cloud-based application (addressing requirement R_3). On the one hand, any modification to a CLOUDML model is enacted on-demand in the running application. On the other hand, any change in the running application is automatically reflected in its CLOUDML model.

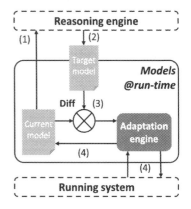

Fig. 1 depicts the architecture of CLOUD-MF. A reasoning engine reads the current model (step 1) and produces a target model (step 2). Then, the run-time environment computes the difference between the current model and the target one (step 3). Finally,

Fig. 1. CLOUDMF architecture

the adaptation engine enacts the adaptation by modifying only the parts of the cloud-based application necessary to account for the difference and the target model becomes the current model (step 4).

3   Case Study

The adoption of CLOUDML as the DSL for specifying models in the models@run-time environment of CLOUDMF introduces some challenges in its design and implementation. In this section, we present these challenges through a case study.

SENSAPP[2] is an open-source, service-oriented application for storing and exploiting large data sets collected from sensors and devices. Suppose that, at

---

[2] http://sensapp.org

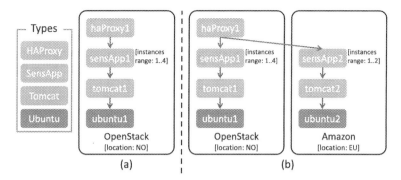

Fig. 2. Deployment model at design-time: (a) with single cloud, (b) with multiple clouds

design-time, we would like to model the deployment of SENSAPP on a single cloud, whereby a SENSAPP cluster should be hosted on a Tomcat container cluster, which in turn should be hosted on a Ubuntu virtual machine cluster, which in turn should be provisioned on a private OpenStack cloud in Norway. Moreover, the SENSAPP cluster should be load balanced by an HAProxy load balancer and should have from one to four instances.

Fig. 2(a) shows the deployment model specified using a graphical syntax for CLOUDML. The left part depicts the available reusable types, while the right part depicts instances of these. The range in instances range represents that a minimum of one and a maximum of four instances of SensApp can be executed at run-time. We assume the range attached to sensApp1 also applies to its (indirect) hosts, *i.e.*, tomcat1 and ubuntu1.

We could have considered the deployment of SENSAPP on multiple clouds, whereby a second SENSAPP cluster is deployed and provisioned on a public Amazon cloud in Europe. Fig. 2(b) shows the deployment model with multiple clouds. In the remainder of the paper, we only consider the single-cloud scenario to keep the models simple and retain only the details that are relevant for the discussion.

Then, suppose that, at run-time, we would like to dynamically adapt the deployment of the application in order to meet service-level objectives (*e.g.*, response time < 50ms) and goals (*e.g.*, minimise cost). A reasoning engine would first read the number of current instances, and then enact adaptations based on these service-level objectives and goals. Therefore, the deployment model above is insufficient, and an additional property is needed to represent the number of current instances. Fig. 3(a) shows the deployment model before and after the adaptation.

Finally, suppose that, also at run-time, we would like to dynamically adapt the deployment of the application in order to prevent impending failures and recover from occurred ones. A reasoning engine would first read, *e.g.*, the CPU load of each individual Ubuntu virtual machine, and then enact adaptations based on scalability rules. Therefore, the deployment in Fig. 3(a) is too high-level

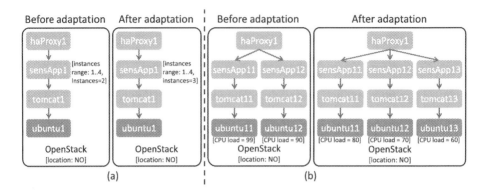

Fig. 3. Deployment model at run-time: (a) with number of current instances, (b) with explicit instances and CPU loads

(or coarse-grained), and a low-level (or fine-grained) deployment model is needed to represent each individual instance of SENSAPP along with the underlying Tomcat container and Ubuntu virtual machine. Fig. 3(b) shows the deployment with explicit instances before and after the adaptation.

The current version of CLOUDML is based on two-level modelling. It supports the specification of single components within a deployment model, but it does not support the specification of clusters of components with ranges.

In the following section, we present a proof of concept of how the current version of CLOUDML could be extended to support the case study.

4   Two-Level Approach

CLOUDML implements the type-instance pattern [4]. To declare and instantiate types (*e.g.*, the type Ubuntu and its instance ubuntu1 in Fig. 2(a)), this pattern requires both types and instances to be represented by classes in the metamodel. This pattern also exploits two flavours of typing: *ontological* and *linguistic* [17]. The latter is the relation between a model and its metamodel, while the former is the relation between elements within a model.

Fig. 4 shows a simplified version of the CLOUDML metamodel along with the model in abstract syntax corresponding to the one in graphical syntax in Fig. 3(a), where several concepts such as the life-cycle scripts attached to the components, the ports provided and required by components, the communications between ports, and the cloud providers are omitted for brevity (see [14] for a detailed description of the CLOUDML metamodel). SensApp represents a reusable type of SENSAPP. It is linguistically typed by the class CompType (short for component type). sensApp1 represents an instance of SENSAPP. It is ontologically typed by SensApp and linguistically typed by CompInst (short for component instance). Similarly, Fig. 5 shows the model in abstract syntax corresponding to the one in graphical syntax in Fig. 3(b), before adaptation.

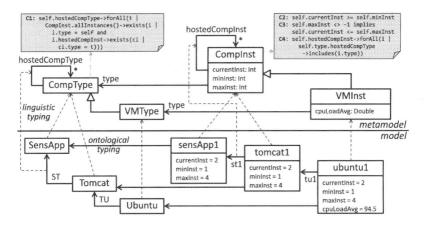

Fig. 4. Deployment model in abstract syntax at run-time, with number of current instances and average CPU load

Figs. 4 and 5 depict one possible approach for allowing CLOUDML to support the specification of clusters of components with ranges. However, it implies the use of two syntactically and semantically disjoint models: one representing the aggregated view of each cluster (Fig. 4) and one representing each individual instance in each cluster (Fig. 5). In order to avoid this, a naive solution could be to merge the two models by applying the type-instance pattern twice, which would lead to a new *type-template-instance* pattern. Fig. 6 shows this merged model. Unfortunately, this solution is both ineffective and insufficient.

First, it is ineffective since applying the type-instance pattern twice leads to six classes to represent components and their instances, and even more references between them in both the metamodel and the model (*e.g.*, CompType, CompTemp, and CompInst in the metamodel and their instances in the model). Please note that the metamodel in Fig. 6 only contains the classes and references necessary to represent components and virtual machines, while the model only contains the elements needed to represent a SENSAPP application cluster, a Tomcat container cluster, and a Ubuntu virtual machine cluster. The figure omits the classes and references needed to represent the life-cycle scripts attached to the components, the ports provided and required by components, the communication between ports, and the cloud providers. Applying the type-instance pattern twice would lead to an explosion of elements for each of these concepts in both the metamodel and the model. Moreover, this solution is ineffective since checking the type-instance conformance within the model requires complex OCL constraints in the metamodel, while applying the type-instance pattern twice requires replicating these constraints (*e.g.*, C1/C5 and C4/C6).

Second, this solution is insufficient, as we are not modelling the allowed number of component instances within a host, but the restriction on instances is checked globally. Please note that this could be naturally expressed if we were able to put cardinalities on the references st1 and tu1.

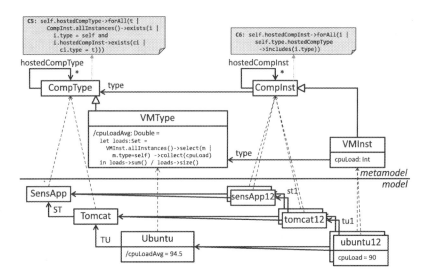

Fig. 5. Deployment model at run-time, with two explicit instances and CPU loads

Altogether, we need to apply the type-instance pattern twice and add complex OCL constraints to the metamodel in order to emulate three ontological levels within a single linguistic level. This makes the two-level approach convoluted and less usable [5].

As an alternative design strategy, we could merge the three classes CompType, CompTemp, and CompInst into one class Component (and similar for VMType, VMTemp, and VMInst). The resulting class Component would have a reference type to itself with optional cardinality as well as a property level to distinguish whether an instance of Component belongs to the type, template, or instance level. In addition, we could add OCL constraints to ensure the correctness of the onto-

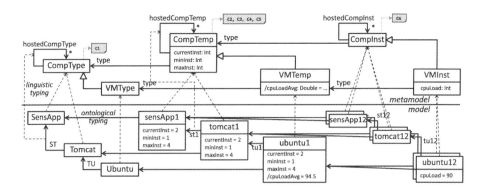

Fig. 6. Proof-of-concept deployment model at run-time, with both number of current instances as well as explicit instances and CPU loads

logical typing. While this solution would make the metamodel more compact, it would lead to a higher complexity of OCL constraints. Moreover, it would also lead to the misuse of model elements, as the properties currentInst, minInst, and maxInst would be present in instances of Component, independently of their level, while they are only necessary at the template level.

In the following section, we present a proof of concept of how CLOUDML could be defined and used adopting a multi-level approach.

5 Multi-level Approach

Multi-level modelling extends traditional two-level modelling by enabling the use of an arbitrary number of levels (rather than just two) in a modelling stack. In scenarios where the type-instance pattern or one of its variants arise [10], this solution yields simpler models, since the additional classes to specify instances become unnecessary.

Fig. 7 shows CLOUDML organised in four levels. The top level contains an excerpt of the refactored CLOUDML metamodel, while the subsequent levels contain the definition of types (e.g., Tomcat, Ubuntu), a high-level deployment model, and a low-level deployment model with explicit instances and CPU loads at run-time. In this solution, it is not necessary to have classes CompType, Comp-Temp, and CompInst at the top level, but a single class Component is sufficient (and similar for VirtualMachine).

In this approach, elements are called *clabjects* (by the contraction of *class*+*object*), as they have both a type and an instance facet. For example,

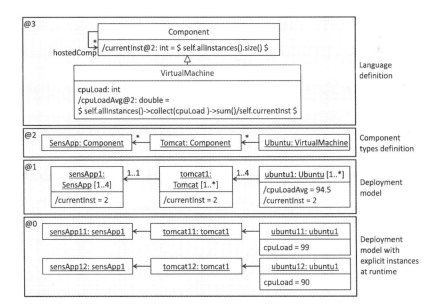

Fig. 7. Simplified multi-level model for CloudML

Ubuntu is an instance of VirtualMachine and the type of ubuntu1. Furthermore, clabjects can specify the features of their instances beyond the next level. For example, VirtualMachine specifies that three levels below, its indirect instances have a cpuLoad, while two levels below, their instances have a cpuLoadAvg. The mechanism used for this deep characterisation of instances beyond the next level is *potency* [4]. A potency is a natural number (or zero) indicating at how many levels an element can be instantiated (*cf.* [21] for a formal discussion of different types of potency). In Fig. 7, the potency is denoted by the @ symbol. At every lower level, the potency decreases, and when it reaches zero, the element cannot be instantiated further. If an element does not declare a potency, it inherits it from its container, and eventually from the enclosing model. Hence, potency is a generalisation of the standard instantiation mechanism in the two-level approach, where types in the metamodel have potency 1, and instances in the model have potency 0.

For the case study, we use multi-level modelling as realised in our META-DEPTH tool [9]. The tool offers textual modelling and integrates the Epsilon languages[3] for model manipulation. METADEPTH also supports derived properties, whose calculation expression can be specified using the Epsilon Object Language (EOL, a variant of OCL). The top model in Fig. 7 contains two derived properties: currentInst on Component, and cpuLoadAvg on VirtualMachine. Both are calculated at level 1: the first counts the number of instances of each deployed component at level 1, and the second computes the average of the cpuLoad of all the instances at the bottom level. We adapted EOL for its use in a multi-level setting [11]. For example, we allow *indirect type referencing*. Because the type names at intermediate levels are unknown when specifying the top level, we can refer to instances of instances of a type by using the type name. Hence, at level 0, an expression like Component.allInstances() returns the set {sensApp11, sensApp12, tomcat11, tomcat12, ubuntu11, ubuntu12}. Since clabjects with potency 1 or more retain a type facet, it is possible to apply the operation allInstances on them.

Similar to clabjects, properties and references also have type and instance facets. Thus, references at intermediate levels can specify cardinalities, as is the case at levels 1 and 2 in the figure. In addition, METADEPTH supports clabject cardinalities. We have used this feature at level 1 to specify the allowed scaling for ubuntu1, tomcat1 and sensApp1.

Finally, multi-level modelling permits linguistic extensions, *i.e.*, elements which are typed linguistically but not ontologically [4]. The typing relation between the elements of consecutive levels in Fig. 7 is ontological, while all the elements are typed by a linguistic metamodel (not shown, but it contains classes like Clabject and Property). In the case study, this feature would allow adding new clabjects and properties with no ontological typing at levels 1 and 2.

---

[3] http://eclipse.org/epsilon/

6   Comparison

In this section, we discuss the advantages and disadvantages of each approach. We base our comparison on a set of criteria that demonstrate the expressiveness and usability of the examined modelling solutions.

Size of Language Definition. A prominent aspect that affects the choice of a modelling approach is the size of the language definition. We claim that a large and verbose language definition is generally undesirable because it is harder to comprehend. This negative effect also projects into the resulting models, since more elements need to be used in order to represent an intended expression. As evidenced by the models in Sec.s 4 and 5, the language definition is three times larger in the two-level approach. For example, the clabject Component in the multi-level approach needs to be unfolded into CompType, CompTemp, and CompInst in the two-level approach. The situation is similar with references (*e.g.*, hostedComp gets tripled). This is so because the two-level approach requires emulating the ontological typing by adding the references type between classes at the type, template, and instance levels, as well as the corresponding OCL constraints. Instead, the ontological typing in the multi-level approach is native.

Complexity of OCL Constraints. Both multi-level and two-level modelling take advantage of OCL constraints to ensure the well-formedness of the produced models. However, there are significant differences related to the complexity and count of the constraints needed to achieve the targeted outcomes. Constraints in the two-level approach tend to be more complex because they can only use the linguistic types (CompType, CompTemp, CompInst), but not the reusable types at the model level (SensApp, Tomcat, Ubuntu). Nevertheless, there are a number of other factors contribute to this additional complexity:

- *Type-conformance constraints.* The two-level approach requires defining OCL constraints to check, *e.g.*, type conformance between the instances of Comp-Temp and the instances of CompType, and between the instances of CompInst and CompTemp. In the case study, these constraints check the correctness of the references hostedCompType and hostedCompInst (see constraints C1 and C4 in Fig. 4, and constraints C5 and C6 in Fig. 5). The multi-level approach does not need to include such constraints, because the type conformance check is embedded into the paradigm.
- *Access to lower levels.* In the two-level approach, to obtain the instances of a class representing a type (*e.g.*, the instances of SensApp), we need to navigate the reference type (*e.g.*, CompInst.allInstances()->select(ci — ci.type = SensApp)). This access is simpler in the multi-level approach, as it is possible to obtain the direct or indirect instances of a clabject using the operation allInstances on the clabject (*e.g.*, sensApp.allInstances()). In the case study, cpuLoadAvg needs to access all instances at the bottom level to obtain the cpuLoad, and currentInst counts the number of instances at the bottom level.

- *Transparent navigation to upper levels.* In the multi-level approach, the expression o.feature looks up the value of feature in the direct type of o, or in some indirect type in upper levels. In the two-level approach, this needs to be done explicitly by using o.type.feature or o.type.type.feature.
- *Constraints on reusable types.* Suppose we need to specify a constraint on some reusable type (*e.g.*Ubuntu). In the multi-level approach, the constraint would be directly specified on the context of the clabject. For example, defining self.cpuLoad < 80 with potency 2 on the clabject Ubuntu ensures that all its instances at level 0 have a cpuLoad lower than 80. In contrast, in the two-level approach, we should add the following constraint to the class VMInst: self.type.type.name = 'Ubuntu' implies self.cpuLoad < 80. In addition, we should add a property name to VMType to be able to identify the instance of Ubuntu. This is necessary because Ubuntu lacks a type facet in the two-level approach, and hence, it cannot specify constraints. Moreover, the constraint should be added to the metamodel, which may not be allowed as metamodel changes are frequently restricted to language developers.
- *Instantiability of classes.* To restrict the number of instances of a certain class (*e.g.*, CompInst), the two-level approach requires adding properties to the class to specify the minimum and maximum number of allowed instances, as well as OCL constraints checking their fulfilment (*e.g.*, properties minInst and maxInst, and constraints C2 and C3, in Fig. 4). Instead, the three-level approach does not require to specify any OCL constraint, but only the clabject cardinality.

Precision. We define precision as a measure that reflects how accurately, in semantic terms, a model can represent an intended expression. Thus, we compare how reference cardinalities are specified. The multi-level approach supports reference cardinalities at level 1, to gain a fine-grained control of the allowed scaling at level 0. The presented two-level approach uses ranges for this purpose. However, it does not constrain *e.g.*, how many instances of SensApp are allowed in a Tomcat, but only that a global maximum of four are allowed, either residing in a single Tomcat or in several ones. To enable this feature, the two-level approach would require to emulate reference cardinalities by adding extra classes to the metamodel (the *Relation Configurator* pattern in [10]).

Extensibility. We define extensibility as the ability to extend a language while minimising changes to its metamodel. This is because languages, like any other software artefact, need to evolve in response to changing requirements. In this respect, the multi-level approach allows adding new properties at levels 1 and 2, due to its support for linguistic extensions (*i.e.*, elements without ontological type). Thus, we could add a property maxSensors to SensApp to configure the maximum number of sensors in SENSAPP applications. Defining this property on Component at level 3 is less appropriate, as some component instances at level 2 may lack the property. In the two-level approach, being able to specify new properties in models would require emulating the infrastructure for property specification/instantiation at the metamodel level.

Flexibility. We define flexibility as the degree of expressiveness of the chosen abstraction in terms of the model element relationships and level of encapsulation. In the multi-level approach, clabjects at level 1 or above can specify operations. Thus, the engineer designing the deployment model could add the following EOL operation to Ubuntu, with a condition for scaling out:

operation Ubuntu scaleOut(): **Boolean** { **return self**.cpuLoadAvg >= 90 }

A reasoner could use this operation as a trigger for scaling out. This flexibility is not possible in the two-level approach, because elements at model level cannot specify operations. Instead, a workaround would be to design a dedicated DSL to express such conditions.

Also concerning flexibility, the multi-level approach supports inheritance at any level. For example, in Fig. 7, the model at level 2 could specify a hierarchy of application servers. In the two-level approach, the semantics of inheritance at the model level would need to be emulated. Nonetheless, the two-level approach allows customising the semantics of the conformance relation (*e.g.*, to permit two ontological types for an element) and the inheritance relation (*e.g.*, to (dis)allow multiple inheritance), while the semantics of these relationships is fixed in the multi-level approach.

Tooling. Lastly, we examine the tool support for each of the methodologies. The de-facto standard in modelling frameworks in the state-of-the-art is the Eclipse Modelling Framework (EMF)[4]. Whereas EMF provides a large ecosystem of tools and languages for two-level modelling, the support for multi-level modelling is limited. METADEPTH is compatible with the Epsilon languages but does not rely on EMF. Similarly, other multi-level tools, like XModeler [7] or Nivel [1] do not rely on EMF. A notable exception is Melanee [2], which is built upon EMF. However, in this case model manipulation languages would need to be adapted to work with it. Alternatively, at the implementation level one could use programming languages enhanced with multi-level concepts, like DeepJava [18], or with strong reflection capabilities [8,16].

Table 1 summarises the studied aspects. Altogether, a multi-level approach for the case study leads to a smaller language definition, with less OCL constraints, and less complex. To achieve the same degree of precision, extensibility and flexibility, the two-level approach would need to include in the metamodel many features that are native in a multi-level framework, like reference cardinalities, properties, operations, or inheritance. Nonetheless, as metamodelling features (like ontological typing or inheritance) are explicitly specified, they can be customised. The case study needed no customisation though. Finally, a richer set of tools is currently available for a two-level approach.

---

[4] https://www.eclipse.org/modeling/emf/

Table 1. Comparison criteria

Dimension	Two-Level	Multi-Level
Size	× 3-fold replication of classes and references	✓ Compact language definition: clabjects and potencies
	× Explicit modelling of type relations	✓ Type relations are native
OCL complexity	× Explicit type-conformance constraints	✓ Constraints can use ontological types
	× Constraints cannot use ontological types	✓ Transparent navigation across ontological levels
	× Explicit navigation through type relations	
Precision	× Lack of cardinality constraints at model level	✓ Fine-grained control by cardinality constraints at level 1
Extensibility	× Dynamic properties need to be emulated	✓ New properties can be added at intermediate levels
Flexibility	✓ Customisable conformance/inheritance rel.s	✓ Operations can be added at intermediate levels
	× Lack of inheritance at model level	✓ Inheritance at the model level is native
Tooling	✓ Large ecosystems of tools and languages	× Limited tool choice, increased integration effort

7   Related Work

In the cloud community, frameworks such as Cloudify, Puppet or Chef[5] provide
DSLs that facilitate the specification and enactment of provisioning, deployment, monitoring, and adaptation of cloud-based applications, without being
language-dependent. Moreover, the Topology and Orchestration Specification
for Cloud Applications (TOSCA) [20] is a specification developed by the OASIS
consortium, which provides a language for specifying the components comprising the topology of cloud-based applications along with the processes for their
orchestration. Similar to CLOUDMF, the aforementioned solutions are based on
a two-level modelling approach, so an alternative, multi-level modelling approach
could also be considered for these solutions.

There are scarce works comparing two-level and multi-level solutions for given
problems. In [3], some comparison criteria for multi-level approaches (*e.g.*, powertypes and deep modelling) are proposed. The criteria include language size
and intended audience. Instead, our criteria are directed to evaluate solutions
to a modelling problem. In our previous work [10], we identified patterns that
signal the need for a multi-level solution, and analysed their occurrence on a
set of metamodels, including an early version of CLOUDML. In [5], the authors
use a simple example to discuss the benefits (regarding size) of a potency-based
multi-level approach compared to powertypes [15] and a two-level approach. In
contrast, we use a real-life example, and discuss other dimensions beyond size.
In [19], the authors detect the multi-level nature of the MARTE profile, and
use an embedding of a potency based multi-level approach using stereotypes
to refactor its definition. Instead, we use a native multi-level framework like
METADEPTH and compare with a two-level solution.

---

[5] http://www.cloudifysource.org/, https://puppetlabs.com/, http://www.opscode. com/chef/

8   Conclusions and Future Work

In this paper, we have compared two metamodelling techniques for the purpose of providing CLOUDML with features that facilitate reasoning and adaptation of multi-cloud applications at multiple levels of abstraction. The results show a smaller language definition in the multi-level case, with some other benefits regarding extensibility, flexibility, and precision.

In the future, we intend to conduct a user-based empirical study on differences between the two-level and multi-level modelling approaches discussed in this paper. The goal is to collect quantitative and qualitative measurements on the two alternatives with respect to the criteria described in Sec. 6, which will allow us to verify if there is any statistically significant difference and evaluate the viability of each. Moreover, we plan to take advantages of the best features from the two-level and multi-level approaches. In this respect, we are building a compiler from METADEPTH to EMF, which, given the top model in Fig. 7, would produce the metamodel in Fig. 6, including the OCL constraints. Hence, designers would deal with a reduced language definition, and the resulting framework would be easy to integrate with the EMF tooling.

Acknowledgments. The research leading to these results has received funding from the European Commission's Seventh Framework Programme (FP7/2007-2013) under grant agreement numbers 317715 (PaaSage), 318392 (Broker@Cloud), and 611125 (MONDO), the Spanish Ministry under project Go Lite (TIN2011-24139), and the Madrid Region under project SICOMORO (S2013/ICE-3006).

References

1. Asikainen, T., Männistö, T.: Nivel: a metamodelling language with a formal semantics. Software and System Modeling **8**(4), 521–549 (2009)
2. Atkinson, C., Gerbig, R., Kennel, B.: Symbiotic general-purpose and domain-specific languages. In: Glinz, M., Murphy, G.C., Pezzè, M. (eds.) ICSE 2012: 34th International Conference on Software Engineering, pp. 1269–1272. IEEE (2012)
3. Atkinson, C., Gerbig, R., Kühne, T.: Comparing multi-level modeling approaches. In: CEUR Workshop Proceedings MULTI 2014: 1st International Workshop on Multi-Level Modelling, co-located with MODELS 2014: 17th ACM/IEEE International Conference on Model Driven Engineering Languages and Systems, vol. 1286, pp. 53–61. CEUR (2014)
4. Atkinson, C., Kühne, T.: Rearchitecting the UML infrastructure. ACM Transactions on Modeling and Computer Simulation **12**(4), 290–321 (2002)
5. Atkinson, C., Kühne, T.: Reducing accidental complexity in domain models. Software and Systems Modeling **7**(3), 345–359 (2008)
6. Blair, G., Bencomo, N., France, R.: Models@run.time. IEEE Computer **42**(10), 22–27 (2009)
7. Clark, T., Gonzalez-Perez, C., Henderson-Sellers, B.: A foundation for multi-level modelling. In: CEUR Workshop Proceedings MULTI 2014: 1st International Workshop on Multi-Level Modelling, Co-located with MODELS 2014: 17th ACM/IEEE International Conference on Model Driven Engineering Languages and Systems, vol. 1286, pp. 43–52. CEUR (2014)

8. Cointe, P.: Metaclasses are first class: the ObjVlisp model. In: Meyrowitz, N.K. (ed.) OOPSLA 1987: Conference on Object-Oriented Programming Systems, Languages, and Applications, pp. 156–167. ACM (1987)

9. de Lara, J., Guerra, E.: Deep meta-modelling with METADEPTH. In: Vitek, J. (ed.) TOOLS 2010. LNCS, vol. 6141, pp. 1–20. Springer, Heidelberg (2010)

10. de Lara, J., Guerra, E., Cuadrado, J.S.: When and How to Use Multi-Level Modelling. ACM Trans. on Software Eng. and Methodology **24**(2), 1–46 (2014)

11. de Lara, J., Guerra, E., Cuadrado, J.S.: Model-driven engineering with domain-specific meta-modelling languages. Software and System Modeling **14**(1), 429–459 (2015)

12. Ferry, N., Chauvel, F., Rossini, A., Morin, B., Solberg, A.: Managing multi-cloud systems with CloudMF. In: Solberg, A., Babar, M.A., Dumas, M., Cuesta, C.E. (eds.) NordiCloud 2013: 2nd Nordic Symposium on Cloud Computing and Internet Technologies, pp. 38–45. ACM (2013)

13. Ferry, N., Rossini, A., Chauvel, F., Morin, B., Solberg, A.: Towards model-driven provisioning, deployment, monitoring, and adaptation of multi-cloud systems. In: O'Conner, L. (ed.) CLOUD 2013: 6th IEEE International Conference on Cloud Computing, pp. 887–894. IEEE Computer Society (2013)

14. Ferry, N., Song, H., Rossini, A., Chauvel, F., Solberg, A.: CloudMF: applying MDE to tame the complexity of managing multi-cloud applications. In: Bilof, R. (ed.) UCC 2014: 7th IEEE/ACM International Conference on Utility and Cloud Computing, pp. 269–277. IEEE Computer Society (2014)

15. Gonzalez-Perez, C., Henderson-Sellers, B.: A powertype-based metamodelling framework. Software and Systems Modeling **5**(1), 72–90 (2006)

16. Kiczales, G., des Rivieres, J., Bobrow, D.G.: The Art of the Metaobject Protocol. MIT Press (1991)

17. Kühne, T.: Matters of (meta-)modeling. Software and Systems Modeling **5**(4), 369–385 (2006)

18. Kühne, T., Schreiber, D.: Can programming be liberated from the two-level style: multi-level programming with deepjava. In: Gabriel, R.P., Bacon, D.F., Lopes, C.V., Jr., G.L.S. (eds.) OOPSLA 2007: 22nd Annual ACM SIGPLAN Conference on Object-Oriented Programming, Systems, Languages, and Applications, pp. 229–244. ACM (2007)

19. Mallet, F., Lagarde, F., André, C., Gérard, S., Terrier, F.: An automated process for implementing multilevel domain models. In: van den Brand, M., Gašević, D., Gray, J. (eds.) SLE 2009. LNCS, vol. 5969, pp. 314–333. Springer, Heidelberg (2010)

20. Palma, D., Spatzier, T.: Topology and Orchestration Specification for Cloud Applications (TOSCA). Tech. rep., Organization for the Advancement of Structured Information Standards (OASIS), June 2013. http://docs.oasis-open.org/tosca/TOSCA/v1.0/cos01/TOSCA-v1.0-cos01.pdf

21. Rossini, A., de Lara, J., Guerra, E., Rutle, A., Wolter, U.: A formalisation of deep metamodelling. Formal Aspects of Computing **26**(6), 1115–1152 (2014)

Empirical Evaluation of UML Modeling Tools–A Controlled Experiment

Safdar Aqeel Safdar[1(✉)], Muhammad Zohaib Iqbal[1,2], and Muhammad Uzair Khan[1]

[1] Software Quality Engineering and Testing Lab (QUEST),
National University of Computer and Emerging Science, Islamabad, Pakistan
safdar.aqeel@questlab.pk, {zohaib.iqbal,uzair.khan}@nu.edu.pk
[2] Interdisciplinary Centre for Security, Reliability and Trust, Luxembourg, Luxembourg

Abstract. Model driven software engineering (MDSE) has shown to provide mark improvement in productivity and quality of software products. UML is a standard modeling language that is widely used in the industry to support MDSE. To provide tool support for MDSE, a large number of UML modeling tools are available, ranging from open-source tools to commercial tools with high price tag. A common decision faced while applying UML in practice is the selection of an appropriate tool for modeling. In this paper we conduct a study to compare three of the well-known modeling tools: IBM Rational Software Architect (RSA), MagicDraw, and Papyrus. In this study we conducted an experiment with undergraduate and graduate students. The goal is to compare the productivity of the software engineers while modeling with the tools. We measure the productivity in terms of modeling effort required to correctly complete a task, learnability, time and number of clicks required, and memory load required for the software engineer to complete a task. Our results show that MagicDraw performed significantly better in terms of learnability, memory load, and completeness of tasks. In terms of time and number of clicks, IBM RSA was significantly better while modeling class diagrams and state machines when compared to Papyrus. However no single tool outperformed others in all the modeling tasks with respect to time and number of clicks.

Keywords: Model driven software engineering · UML · Modeling tools · Controlled experiment · Empirical software engineering

1 Introduction

A large number of commercial and open-source tools are available to support UML modeling, including IBM Rational Software Architect (RSA), MagicDraw, Papyrus, Enterprise Architect, Visual Paradigm, Rational Rose, and Argo UML. The choice of selecting a modeling tool has a great impact on the overall success of MDSE [1, 2, 3, 4]. The available tools not only vary greatly in their price tag, but also vary in terms of their features, and can greatly impact the productivity of an engineer. Feature list and price tag can easily be compared directly, but the other aspects that impact productivity need thorough empirical evaluations. Such evaluations are not easy to conduct for end users due to limited resources and restricted access to full version of the available tools, in particular when evaluating commercial tools.

© Springer International Publishing Switzerland 2015
G. Taentzer and F. Bordeleau (Eds.): ECMFA 2015, LNCS 9153, pp. 33–44, 2015.
DOI: 10.1007/978-3-319-21151-0_3

To evaluate productivity, we compared the tools in terms of modeling effort required to correctly complete a task, learnability, and memory load required for the engineer to complete a task. We consider these factors to be important as they directly or indirectly affect the productivity of software engineer.

Controlled experiments are widely used in the domain of software engineering for the comparison and empirical evaluation of different techniques and tools [5, 6]. We have used controlled experiment for comparison of UML modeling tools. For our controlled experiment we selected one open source and two commercial tools for comparison, which include: IBM Rational Software Architecture, Papyrus, and MagicDraw, whereas Enterprise Architect is used to train the participants. These are three of the widely used modeling tools that are based on eclipse and fully support UML 2.0 and EMF compatible XMI export [1, 3].

In this paper we conducted a controlled experiment with multiple participants to compare the productivity of selected UML modeling tools. The experiment is conducted with 30 students at National University of Computer and Emerging Sciences, Islamabad, Pakistan. In the experiment, we gave three of the most widely used UML diagrams [7], i.e., class diagram, sequence diagram, and state machine to model in an assigned tool and a questionnaire form to fill at the end of the activity. The questionnaire form contains the details related to starting time and completion time corresponding to each diagram, learnability measure, memory load measure, and guidelines for completing the activity. Our results show that MagicDraw performed significantly better in terms of learnability, memory load, and completeness of tasks.

The rest of the paper is organized as follows: Section 2 summarizes the literature review. Section 3 presents the details related to planning of the experiment. Section 4 provides the results and analysis of our experiment corresponding to each research question. In Section 5 we provide overall discussion. Section 6 highlights the threats to validity and finally in Section 7 we conclude our work.

2   Related Work

This section discusses the existing literature related to MDSE modeling tools evaluation in software engineering.

After a thorough search, we found a total of seven studies in literature that compare and evaluate modeling tools. Eichelberger *et al.* [3] conducted a comparative survey in which around 75 modeling tools were evaluated. They derived a hierarchal set of features from UML superstructure document. The purpose of the survey was to assess the compliance with standard UML and classify the tools into different compliance levels. Khaled [2] described a set of desired features of UML modeling tools and compared four modeling tools (i.e., Rational Rose, ArgoUML, MagicDraw, and Enterprise Architect) based on these features. Sengoz *et al.* [8] compared two design modeling tools (UML-SPT-Rhapsody and UML-RT-Rose RT) for the real time software modeling based on their features. Rani and Garg [9] compared four UML modeling tools, i.e., ArgoUML, StarUML, Umbrello UML Modeller, and Rational Rose based on their features. Heena and Ranjna [4] compared five modeling tools, i.e., Rational Rose, MagicDraw, ArgoUML, UMLet and Visual paradigm based on their features.

In [10], the authors compare the UML modeling tools in terms of time required for modeling and subjective opinion of participants regarding tools' features. They also applied goals, operator method, and selection (GOMS) technique to measure the modeling effort required. This study was conducted in 2005.

Almost all of the above discussed studies either compare the tools merely based on their features [2, 4, 8, 9] or are surveys with an intent to classify the tools [3, 11]. There is only one reported experiment to compare UML modeling tools [10]. We believe that such an empirical study is crucial to help the software engineers select a particular tool. In our experience [1, 12], selection of a modeling tool has a great impact on the successful implementation of MDSE in industry. The experiment in [10] was conducted in 2005. Since then the UML as a standard has grown enormously and similarly the corresponding tool support has evolved. The study in [10] cannot be used today to help software engineers in selection of a modeling tool.

In our experiment, we not only measure the time required for modeling (as in [10]), but we also evaluate the tool in terms of how much of the diagrams developed by the participants are complete and correct. Moreover, we also compared the tools in terms of learnability and the memory load required for the engineer to complete a task.

3   Experiment's Planning

In this section, we discuss the details related to the experiment's planning phase. These details are in accordance with the guidelines for reporting experiments provided by Wohlin *et al.* [13]. Section 3.1 provides goals, research questions, and hypotheses, Section 3.2 presents the details related to participants' selection for the experiment whereas in Section 3.3 we provide the details related to experiment material, i.e., case study and questionnaire form. Section 3.4 defines the dependent and independent variables of the experiment. Section 3.5 discusses the experiment design, whereas Section 1.1 provides the details related to training of participants. Finally in Section 3.7 we discuss the details related to statistical tests that we apply to analyze the experiment's data.

3.1   Goals, Research Questions, and Hypotheses

The objective of our experiment is to compare the productivity of three of the widely referred UML modeling tools: IBM RSA, MagicDraw, and Papyrus. We compare the productivity when working with these tools in terms of modeling effort, learnability, and memory load. To evaluate the modeling effort we consider two factors: 1) the time required for completing a given task, 2) the number of clicks required for completing a given task. We also consider completeness of the diagrams developed as part of the modeling effort. Following are the research questions for the experiment conducted in order to evaluate modeling effort, learnability, and memory load:

RQ1: *Which tool among IBM RSA, MagicDraw, and Papyrus is better with respect to modeling effort?*

To answer RQ1 we compare the UML tools in terms of effort required to complete the given modeling tasks correctly. We further divide RQ1 into two sub research questions as follows:

RQ1.1: *In which modeling tool, among IBM RSA, MagicDraw, and Papyrus, the users were able to correctly model more complete diagrams?*

We measure completeness as the percentage of modeling elements modeled correctly by the user for a particular task compared to the total number of modeling elements in the reference model for that task. Measuring completeness will allow us to determine the modeling tool in which the participants were able to correctly model more modeling elements in the given time. By correctness we mean that modeler used the correct meta-elements for modeling a given diagram. For example to add a constraint on a class, modeler should use the UML *Constraint* meta-element. If the modeler used a *Comment* or a *Note* to model the constraint it will be incorrect.

RQ1.2: *Which tool among IBM RSA, MagicDraw, and Papyrus is better with respect to time and number of clicks required for modeling?*

We are interested in comparing the tools in terms of time and number of clicks required to complete the given modeling tasks.

RQ2: *Which tool among IBM RSA, MagicDraw, and Papyrus is better with respect to learnability?*

Learnability, i.e., how easy is it to learn, is an important characteristic of a modeling tool. RQ2 aims to compare the learnability of the three modeling tools.

RQ3: *Which tool among IBM RSA, MagicDraw, and Papyrus is better with respect to memory load?*

Memory load refers to the amount of information a user needs to keep in mind while completing a specific modeling task.

Before the execution of experiment, we assume that there is no difference in terms of any factor, which leads to two-tailed null hypotheses of our research questions as provided in Table 1.

Table 1. Null hypotheses

Research question	Hypotheses
RQ1.1	H1.1.1: There is no difference between IBM RSA and MagicDraw in terms of completeness.
	H1.1.2: There is no difference between IBM RSA and Papyrus in terms of completeness.
	H1.1.3: There is no difference between MagicDraw and Papyrus in terms of completeness.
RQ1.2	H1.2.1: There is no difference between IBM RSA and MagicDraw in terms of effort required for modeling.
	H1.2.2: There is no difference between IBM RSA and Papyrus in terms of effort required for modeling.
	H1.2.3: There is no difference between MagicDraw and Papyrus in terms of effort required for modeling.
RQ2	H21: There is no difference between IBM RSA and MagicDraw in terms of learnability.
	H22: There is no difference between IBM RSA and Papyrus in terms of learnability.
	H33: There is no difference between MagicDraw and Papyrus in terms of learnability.
RQ3	H31: There is no difference between IBM RSA and MagicDraw in terms of memory load.
	H32: There is no difference between IBM RSA and Papyrus in terms of memory load.
	H33: There is no difference between MagicDraw and Papyrus in terms of memory load.

3.2   Participants

The experiment was conducted in two sessions with two different groups of participants having different skill sets. The first group comprises of undergraduate students who have taken just one modeling course and have a working experience with only one modeling tool, i.e., Enterprise Architect. The second group includes graduate students who have working experience with more than one modeling tools.

In the first session, the experiment was conducted with 18 undergraduate students of final year in computer science at National University of Computer and Emerging Sciences, Islamabad, Pakistan. The university has a well-defined unbiased grading policy and we have used students' grades in the undergraduate course on software modeling to form three different blocks: 1) students with A grade, 2) students with B grade, 3) students with C grade. We have selected the grades of this course for blocking because this is the only course related to UML modeling that they have studies. In this course, students study UML language and complete their semester project using Enterprise Architect for modeling. We organized the students in three balanced groups where each group contains an equal number of students from each block.

In the second session, the experiment was conducted with 12 students, who are currently enrolled in "Advance Software Engineering" course of their MS in software engineering at the same university. All students have experience with different modeling tools. We divided them into three groups on the basis of their experience with the modeling tools.

3.3   Experiment Material

Case Study: The case study used for the experiment contains three diagrams, i.e., class diagram, sequence diagram, and state machine diagram. Since it is not feasible to include all UML diagrams in the case study due to limited resources, therefore we have only selected three of the most commonly used UML diagrams [7]. These diagrams have been used for industrial case studies ranging from automated code generation from models [14], to model based testing [15] and model driven refactoring [16]. We could not find a case study, which contains all UML class diagram elements, so we extended the existing diagrams and combined them in one case study. The sequence diagram, we use is taken from "UML 2 Toolkit" [17] and altered by adding missing sequence diagram elements, e.g., constructor, destructor, and asynchronous call. The state machine is taken from "Testing Object-Oriented Systems, Models, Patterns, and Tools" [18] and altered to add missing state machine diagram elements, e.g., OCL constraints and *do* activity. The complete set of diagrams can be found in [19].

Questionnaire Form: The questionnaire form is carefully designed to measure the learnability and memory load of UML modeling tools. To measure the time required for modeling we asked the participant to note down the starting time and completion time for each diagram. We also run an automated script to capture the number of clicks for each diagram. To measure the completeness, we checked the modeled diagrams against their reference diagrams. The questionnaire form contains personal data of individuals, information about their experience with modeling, information about starting time and completion time of each task (diagram), general guidelines, guidelines for each task, and information about the learnability and memory load of UML modeling tool.

3.4   Independent/Dependent Variables

This section presents the independent and dependent variables involved in our experiment. The independent variables include tools and diagrams whereas dependent variables include completeness, time and number of clicks required for modeling, learnability, and memory load.

Tools: We selected three UML modeling tools, i.e., IBM RSA, MagicDraw, and Papyrus as discussed above.

Diagrams: We selected three most commonly used diagrams class diagram (CD), sequence diagram (SD), and state machine (SM) diagram in the domain of MDSE [7].

Completeness: To measure the overall completeness of modeling tasks we measure the completeness of each diagram. The formula for measuring the completeness of each diagram is given below:

$$Completeness_{CD,SE,SM} = \sum_{i=1}^{n}(Completeness\ of\ each\ type\ of\ Construct_i) \quad (1)$$

Here n shows the maximum types of constructs included in a particular diagram. For example in case of class diagram constructs included are classes, enumeration and interface, constraints, cardinality, and relationships. In the same fashion we measured the completeness for sequence diagram and state machine diagram using the above mentioned formula. To compute the completeness of each type of construct we measure the fraction of total instances of a particular type, which are modeled.

Time required for modeling: To measure the time required for modeling we computed the time taken for the participants to model each diagram. The formula for computing the time is given in equation (2).

$$Time = Completion\ Time - Starting\ Time \quad (2)$$

Number of clicks required for modeling: First we captured the number of clicks using an automated script and then used a simple Java program to count the total number of clicks corresponding to each diagram.

Learnability: Learnability refers to the ease with which a novice user can utilize a particular tool to complete a specific task. To measure the learnability of a tool we asked participants to rate it on a scale of five after completing the given modeling tasks.

Memory load: By memory load we mean to keep least information in mind to complete a specific task in the given modeling tool. To measure the memory load of a tool we asked participants to rate it on a scale of five after completing the given tasks.

3.5   Experiment Design

The experiment design summarized in Table 2. We divided the students into three groups and labeled them as group 1, group 2 and group 3. Since these groups are already balanced and have overall same skills set (Section 3.2), therefore, we assigned group 1, group 2 and group 3 to IBM RSA, MagicDraw, and Papyrus respectively. Each group was asked to draw the three given diagrams (class diagram, state machine, and sequence diagram) in the assigned tool.

Table 2. Experiment design

Diagrams to draw	UML modeling tools		
-	IBM RSA	MagicDraw	Papyrus
Class diagram	Group 1	Group 2	Group 3
State machine	Group 1	Group 2	Group 3
Sequence diagram	Group 1	Group 2	Group 3

3.6 Training

All the undergraduate students have studied a course on software modeling in which they were required to complete a semester project that involved creation of a number of UML diagrams using Enterprise Architect. Therefore, they did not need any particular training in using Enterprise Architect. The graduate students have experience of using a variety of modeling tools. Thus to make sure that all the participants have similar expertise of using Enterprise Architect, we gave a 45 minutes training to the graduate students on Enterprise Architect. After the training, we gave them a home assignment to practice class diagram, sequence diagram, and state machine diagram using Enterprise Architect.

3.7 Selection of Statistical Tests

We apply statistical tests in order to assess whether there is a significant difference among the tools being compared (Section 3.1). For this purpose, we used non-parametric Mann Whitney U-test for skewed and parametric T-test for normal data distribution of experimental results [20]. For all statistical tests reported in this paper we have used the recommended significance level of $\alpha = 0.05$. Since our data sample (i.e., the data obtained from results) is small, we used Shapiro-Wilk test to check the distribution of data samples. These tests are commonly applied in literature for analyzing results of such controlled experiments [20].

4 Results and Analysis

This section presents the results and discussion related to each research question defined in Section 3.1. In Table 3 we provide the descriptive statistics for all productivity measures, i.e., completeness, number of clicks and time required for modeling, learnability, and memory load. The raw results of the experiment can be found in [19].

Table 3. Descriptive statistics for all productivity measures

Measures	Diagrams	RSA-MD*		RSA-P*		MD-P*	
		P-value	A12	P-value	A12	P-value	A12
Completeness	CD*	0.191	0.5	0.020	0.62	0.378	0.5
	SM*	2.5e-5	0.34	0.278	0.5	0.006	0.62
	SD*	0.020	0.37	0.326	0.5	0.001	0.68
	Overall	0.025	0.43	0.252	0.5	0.001	0.60
Number of Clicks	CD	0.093	0.5	0.008	0.16	1.00	0.5
	SM	0.177	0.5	0.025	0.3	0.266	0.5
	SD	0.755	0.5	0.730	0.5	0.648	0.5
	Overall	0.962	0.5	0.756	0.5	0.775	0.5
Time	CD	0.968	0.5	0.022	0.27	0.105	0.5
	SM	0.385	0.5	0.003	0.4	0.324	0.5
	SD	0.076	0.5	0.114	0.5	0.604	0.5
	Overall	0.231	0.5	0.656	0.5	0.299	0.5
Learnability	-	0.043	0.31	0.014	0.72	3.89e-5	0.85
Memory load	-	0.123	0.5	0.165	0.5	0.007	0.85

* CD: Class diagram, SM: State machine, SD: Sequence diagrams, MD: MagicDraw, P: Papyrus, RSA: Rational Software Architect, in comparison of A-B where P-value < 0.05, if A12 < 0.5 then B is better than A whereas if A12 > 0.5 then A is better than B.

4.1   Completeness

The data sample for completeness is not normally distributed; therefore we apply the non- parametric Mann-Whitney U-test to check the truthfulness of our hypotheses and Vargha and Delaney's A12 statistic to find the direction and magnitude of difference between the tools. We compared the tools in pairs. The statistical results of the tests for the completeness measure are provided in Table 3. Fig. 1 shows the average percentage of completed tasks in the three tools corresponding to each diagram.

According to the results of statistical tests corresponding to completeness (Table 3), there is no significant difference between RSA-MagicDraw and Magic-Draw-Papyrus in terms of completeness for modeling class diagrams, though

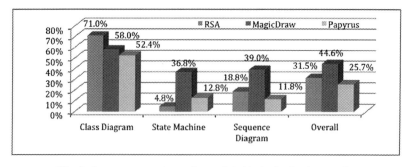

Fig. 1. Average percentage of completed tasks in the three tools

RSA is significantly better than Papyrus in this regard. In terms of completeness for modeling state machines and sequence diagrams, there is no significant difference between RSA-Papyrus. However, MagicDraw is significantly better than RSA and Papyrus for modeling state machines and sequence diagram. We can also observe from Fig. 1 that overall MagicDraw achieved 13% and 20% higher scores for completeness as compared to RSA and Papyrus respectively. Papyrus scored least among all the selected tools. Therefore, among the null hypotheses corresponding to RQ1.1, H1.1.2 holds true whereas H1.1.1 and H1.1.3 are false.

4.2   Effort Required for Modeling

To evaluate the effort required for modeling we measured the time and number of clicks required for modeling. To measure the time we compared the time to draw for each diagram in different modeling tools. Similarly for measuring the number of clicks we compared the number of clicks required for modeling each diagram in different modeling tools. The statistical results of the tests for the time and number of clicks required for modeling are provided in Table 3. We apply the non-parametric Mann-Whitney U-test for all cases while comparing the tools with reference to time and number of clicks required for modeling except in case of state machine. The data sample for state machine has normal distribution; therefore, we apply parametric T-test to compare the time and clicks required for modeling the state machine.

The results of statistical tests corresponding to time required for modeling (Table 3) show that there is no significant different between RSA-MagicDraw and MagicDraw-Papyrus in terms of time required for modeling class diagram, state machine diagram, and sequence diagram. However, in case of RSA-Papyrus results show a significant difference in terms of time required for modeling class diagram and state machine diagram. Participants took significantly more time for modeling class diagram and state machine diagram in Papyrus as compared to RSA. Similarly the results of statistical tests corresponding to number of clicks required for modeling (Table 3) bring us to the same conclusion that participants required significantly more modeling effort for modeling class diagram and state machine diagram in Papyrus as compared to RSA. Among the null hypotheses corresponding to RQ1.2, H1.2.1 and H1.2.3 hold true whereas H1.2.2 is false in case of modeling class diagram and state machine diagram. For all other cases our hypotheses corresponding to RQ1.2 are true.

4.3   Learnability

The data sample for learnability has skewed distribution; therefore, we apply non-parametric Mann-Whitney U-test to compare the selected tools in reference to learnability. The results of statistical tests corresponding to learnability (Table 3) show that there is a significant difference between RSA-MagicDraw, RSA-Papyrus, and MagicDraw-Papyrus in terms of learnability. MagicDraw is significantly better than RSA and Papyrus whereas RSA is significantly better than Papyrus. All the null hypotheses corresponding to RQ2, i.e., H2.1, H2.2, and H2.3 are false. The average values of learnability for each tool on a scale of five are shown in Fig. 2. As one can see from Fig. 2 learnability of MagicDraw was 31% and 14% higher than Papyrus and RSA respectively.

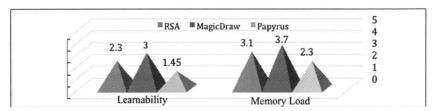

Fig. 2. Average values of learnability and memory load for the three tools

4.4   Memory Load

Our data sample for memory load is skewed, therefore; we apply Mann-Whitney U-test to check the truthfulness of hypotheses and Vargha and Delaney's A12 to find direction and magnitude of difference between two tools. The results of statistical tests for the memory load measure are provided in Table 3. The results of statistical tests suggest that there is no significant difference between RSA-MagicDraw and RSA–Papyrus in terms of memory load measure. However, in comparison of Magic-Draw-Papyrus there is significant difference, MagicDraw is significantly better than RSA in terms of memory load. Among the null hypotheses corresponding to RQ3, H31 and H32 are true whereas H33 is false. The average scores of memory load for each tool on a scale of five is provided in Fig. 2. It can be observed from Fig. 2 that MagicDraw scored 28% higher than Papyrus and 12% higher than RSA Papyrus is the least scoring tool again just like in case of other factors.

5   Discussion

Based on the results provided in Section 4, MagicDraw performed significantly better than the other tools in terms of completeness, learnability, and memory load. Papyrus has the least score in terms of these factors among the three tools. In addition to this we also observed that class diagram has highest score against completeness (i.e., 71%), state machine has a score of 37%, and sequence diagram has only 39% completeness. This can be explained because class diagrams have the least complex modeling elements (e.g., when compared to orthogonal regions in a state machine or combined fragments in a sequence diagram) and is the most widely used of the UML diagrams [7].

Results show that MagicDraw has better learnability as compared to other two tools, which justify why overall MagicDraw is the leading scorer with respect to completeness. We also observed that the models of state machines were the least completed by participants. During the data collection we observed that majority of the participants committed some common mistakes, e.g., they added constraints either using a UML note or in a comment. Similarly a number of students added the *do activity* as a note in state machine. Most likely it is because of the fact that the process of adding such modeling elements, e.g., modeling *do activity* is complex in the modeling tools and require the underlying knowledge of UML meta model.

6   Threats to Validity

In this section we discuss the threats to validity of our experiment in accordance with the guidelines in [13]. The internal threats to validity exist when experiment results are affected by external factors that are not controlled by the researchers. In our case we used different participants for different treatments of independent variable tools to avoid learning and fatigue effect in case of multiple runs of the experiment. Another internal threat can be poorly designed questionnaire form. To address this we asked authors of the paper, other than the author who developed the questionnaire form, to review the questionnaire form. To avoid the biasness in selection of participants, we formed groups using principles of blocking and balancing. We formed groups using university grading policy and experience with variety of modeling tools. The lack of motivation of participants can be another threat to internal validity. To keep them motivated we assured them that this activity would be treated as a credited course assignment. Another threat is due to the fact that we have not selected all UML diagrams. In practice it is very difficult to cover all the thirteen UML diagrams in a single experiment due to limited resources and fatigue of the participants. Therefore, we have selected the most commonly used UML diagrams (according to [7]): UML Class diagram, UML State Machine, and UML Sequence Diagram.

The external threats to validity are due to settings that hinder the generalization of our results of experiment to industrial practices. The participants of our experiment are students who are not professional software engineers. It is a common practice in empirical software engineering to use students in experiments. This is primarily due to the unavailability of industry professionals for long duration that is required by the experiments. In our experiment, we selected the students with suitable educational background (Section 3.2), and gave them a training session so that they can be treated as representatives of professional designers.

7   Conclusion

MDSE has improved the productivity and quality of software products. UML is a standard modeling language and is widely used in industry to apply MDSE. There are a large number of modeling tools available in the market supporting UML, ranging from open-source tools to commercial tools. To apply UML in practice we need to make a critical decision about the selection of an appropriate tool for modeling. Not all end users are in a position to make such a decision. This paper presented an empirical study to evaluate the productivity of three of the well-known modeling tools: IBM Rational Software Architect (RSA), MagicDraw, and Papyrus. For this purpose we compared these tools in terms of modeling effort required for correctly completing a task, learnability, and memory load required for the engineer to complete a task. The results of our experiment suggest that MagicDraw performed significantly better in terms of learnability, memory load, and completeness of state machine and sequence diagram. MagicDraw outperformed IBM RSA and Papyrus in terms of completeness of state machines and sequence diagram, learnability, and memory load. In terms of time and number of clicks, IBM RSA was significantly better while modeling class diagrams and state machines when compared to Papyrus, however no single tool outperformed others in all the modeling tasks.

Acknowledgement. This work was supported by ICT R&D Fund, Pakistan under the project ICTRDF/MBTToolset/2013. Muhammad Zohaib Iqbal was partly supported by National Research Fund, Luxembourg (FNR/P10/03).

References

1. Iqbal, M.Z., Ali, S., Yue, T., Briand, L.: Applying UML/MARTE on industrial projects: challenges, experiences, and guidelines. Software & Systems Modeling, 1–19 (2014)
2. Khaled, L.: A comparison between UML tools. In: Second International Conference on Environmental and Computer Science, pp. 111–114. IEEE (2009)
3. Eichelberger, H., Eldogan, Y., Schmid, K.: A Comprehensive Survey of UML Compliance in Current Modelling Tools. Software Engineering **143**, 39–50 (2009)
4. Heena, R.: A comparative study of UML tools. In: Proceedings of 11th International Conference on Advances in Computing and Artificial Intelligence, pp. 1–4 (2011)
5. Bellon, S., Koschke, R., Antoniol, G., Krinke, J., Merlo, E.: Comparison and evaluation of clone detection tools. IEEE Transactions on Software Engineering **33**, 577–591 (2007)
6. Ali, S., Yue, T., Briand, L.: Assessing quality and effort of applying aspect state machines for robustness testing: a controlled experiment. In: IEEE 6th International Conference on Software Testing, Verification and Validation, pp. 212–221. IEEE (2013)
7. Dias Neto, A.C., Subramanyan, R., Vieira, M., Travassos, G.H.: A survey on model-based testing approaches: a systematic review. In: Proceedings of the 1st ACM International Workshop on Empirical Assessment of Software Engineering Languages and Technologies: Held in Conjunction with ASE Conference, pp. 31–36. ACM (2007)
8. Sengoz, Y.S., Jawawi, A., Deris, S.B.: A Comparison UML Tools for Real-time Software Modeling (2009)
9. Rani, T., Garg, S.: Comparison of different UML tool: Tool approach. International Journal Of Engineering And Computer Science **2**, 1900–1908 (2013)
10. Bobkowska, A.E., Reszke, K.: Usability of UML modeling tools. In: Proceedings of the Conference on Software Engineering: Evolution and Emerging Technologies, pp. 75–86 (2005)
11. Smith, H.H.: On tool selection for illustrating the use of UML in system development. Journal of Computing Sciences in Colleges **19**, 53–63 (2004)
12. Ali, S., Iqbal, M.Z., Arcuri, A., Briand, L.: A search-based OCL constraint solver for model-based test data generation. In: 11th International Conference on Quality Software (QSIC), pp. 41–50. IEEE (2011)
13. Wohlin, C., Runeson, P., Höst, M., Ohlsson, M.C., Regnell, B., Wesslén, A.: Experimentation in software engineering. Springer (2012)
14. Usman, M., Iqbal, M.Z., Khan, M.U.: A model-driven approach to generate mobile applications for multiple platforms. In: Asia-Pacific Software Engineering Conference (2014)
15. Jilani, A.A., Iqbal, M.Z., Khan, M.U.: A search based test data generation approach for model transformations. In: Di Ruscio, D., Varró, D. (eds.) ICMT 2014. LNCS, vol. 8568, pp. 17–24. Springer, Heidelberg (2014)
16. Khan, M.U., Iqbal, M.Z., Ali, S.: A Heuristic-based approach to refactor crosscutting behaviors in UML state machines. In: International Conference on Software Maintenance and Evolution. IEEE (2014)
17. Eriksson, H.-E., Penker, M., Lyons, B., Fado, D.: UML 2 toolkit. John Wiley & Sons (2003)
18. Binder, R.V.: Testing object-oriented systems: models, patterns, and tools. Addison-Wesley Professional (2000)
19. Safdar, S.A., Iqbal, M.Z., Khan, M.U.: Empirical Evaluation of Productivity of Software Engineer in UML Modeling Tools- A Controlled Experiment. Technical report# 3515. Software Quality Engineering & Testing (QUEST) Lab (2015)
20. Sheskin, D.J.: Handbook of parametric and nonparametric statistical procedures. Chapman & Hall/CRC (2007)

A Generative Approach to Define Rich Domain-Specific Trace Metamodels

Erwan Bousse[1]([✉]), Tanja Mayerhofer[2], Benoit Combemale[3],
and Benoit Baudry[3]

[1] University of Rennes 1, Rennes, France
erwan.bousse@irisa.fr
[2] Vienna University of Technology, Vienna, Austria
mayerhofer@big.tuwien.ac.at
[3] Inria, Rennes Cedex, France
{benoit.combemale,benoit.baudry}@inria.fr

Abstract. Executable Domain-Specific Modeling Languages (xDSMLs) open many possibilities for performing early verification and validation (V&V) of systems. Dynamic V&V approaches rely on execution traces, which represent the evolution of models during their execution. In order to construct traces, *generic trace metamodels* can be used. Yet, regarding trace manipulations, they lack both *efficiency* because of their sequential structure, and *usability* because of their gap to the xDSML. Our contribution is a generative approach that defines a *rich* and *domain-specific* trace metamodel enabling the construction of execution traces for models conforming to a given xDSML. Efficiency is increased by providing a variety of navigation paths within traces, while usability is improved by narrowing the concepts of the trace metamodel to fit the considered xDSML. We evaluated our approach by generating a trace metamodel for fUML and using it for semantic differencing, which is an important V&V activity in the realm of model evolution. Results show a significant performance improvement and simplification of the semantic differencing rules as compared to the usage of a generic trace metamodel.

1 Introduction

In recent years, a lot of efforts have been made to provide facilities to design executable Domain-Specific Modeling Languages (xDSMLs) [5,19,22]. Executability of models opens many possibilities in terms of early dynamic verification and validation (V&V) of models, such as debugging [6], runtime verification [16], model checking [4], and semantic differencing [15].

A central concept in dynamic V&V approaches is the *execution trace*, which is the representation of the evolution of a model's state during an execution. While a trace can take numerous forms, we focus in this work on traces containing a sequence of *states* of the model being executed and *event occurrences* related to state changes. All previously mentioned V&V approaches rely on traces: model checking consists in verifying a property of a model by analyzing all its possible

© Springer International Publishing Switzerland 2015
G. Taentzer and F. Bordeleau (Eds.): ECMFA 2015, LNCS 9153, pp. 45–61, 2015.
DOI: 10.1007/978-3-319-21151-0_4

traces and providing traces as counter-examples; runtime verification consists in checking whether or not a trace satisfies a property; debuggers require traces to replay faulty scenarios; semantic differencing consists in comparing traces of two models in order to understand the semantic variations between them.

Therefore, there are at least two significant prerequisites for the V&V of executable models: (1) the definition of a *trace metamodel* to represent traces, and (2) facilities to manipulate large traces efficiently, *i.e.* with good scalability in time. The first prerequisite can be fulfilled by using an existing *generic trace metamodel* (e.g. Compact Trace Format defined in [10]), which can be adopted for any executable language. However, such metamodels cannot take the domain-specific concepts of an xDSML explicitly into account, which makes the development of domain-specific analyses of traces more difficult. To cope with that, a *domain-specific* trace metamodel that is specific to an xDSML (e.g. fUML trace metamodel defined in [18]) can be used. Yet, designing such a metamodel is a time consuming and error-prone task. Also, regarding the second prerequisite, existing trace metamodels only offer to explore a trace by enumerating all states and event occurrence one by one, which can only scale linearly at best.

In this paper, we propose a new way to define domain-specific trace metamodels for xDSMLs through two contributions: (1) a generic approach to automatically derive a domain-specific trace metamodel for a given xDSML by analyzing its definitions of execution states and events; (2) facilities to navigate efficiently within a trace conforming to such a generated metamodel by providing a variety of navigation paths. We evaluated this work by generating a rich and domain-specific trace metamodel for a real world xDSML, namely fUML [21], and by using it for *semantic differencing* [15]. The results show a simplification of the semantic differencing rules and better execution times when using the new trace structure, compared to the usage of a generic trace metamodel.

The remaining sections are organized as follows. Section 2 motivates the problem domain and explains our ideas. Section 3 presents what is executable metamodeling. Section 4 presents our contribution. Section 5 discusses the evaluation of our approach in the domain of semantic differencing. Finally, Section 6 discusses related work and Section 7 concludes the paper.

2   Motivation and Problem Statement

In this section, we first introduce two requirements we identified for trace metamodels, and then present our ideas for complying with these requirements.

2.1   Requirements for a Trace Metamodel

We consider a *metamodel* to be an object-oriented model defining a particular domain. Therefore it is composed of classes, which consist of properties. A property is either an attribute (typed by a datatype) or a reference to another class. A *model* is a set of objects that conforms to a metamodel. Conformity means that each object in the model is an instance of one class defined in the metamodel. An *object* is composed of fields, each representing the object's values for one property of the corresponding class.

In our previous work [3], we highlighted a number of issues that must be considered when constructing and manipulating execution traces. In particular, the potentially large size of a trace compromises the capacity to query it in a reasonable time. For instance, if some element of an executable model only changed at the end of an execution, we might still have to iterate through all states stored in the corresponding trace before noticing that change. Another issue is to manage the manipulation complexity of trace models. Trace analyses can either be *generic* (e.g. comparing the number of different states or the amount of event occurrences), or *domain-specific* (e.g. determining how many tokens traversed a Petri net place). In the former case, manipulations are simple and the structure or content of the trace has little influence on the complexity of the analysis task. However, in the latter case, manipulations handle domain-specific data that can be arbitrarily complex depending on the considered xDSML. Hence, in such cases, defining the right analysis can be error-prone and difficult. A good illustration of these issues is *semantic differencing* [15]. First, it is a hard problem because traces tend to be large and therefore expensive to process. But more importantly, semantic differencing consists in doing *domain-specific* analyses of traces, since they are written according to the semantics of a specific xDSML, and may therefore rely on complex domain-specific data. To sum up, we consider the following requirements on a good trace metamodel:

Scalability in Time. It should provide good scalability in time when manipulating large traces, *i.e.* traces with a lot of state changes.

Usability. It should provide good usability both for generic analyses and domain-specific analyses, e.g. by facilitating the manipulation of traces containing complex domain-specific execution data.

Note that scalability in space or handling distributed systems constitute other important issues which we presented in [3]. In this paper, we only focus on the two aforementioned requirements and other issues are out the scope of this work.

2.2   From Generic to Rich Domain-Specific Trace Metamodels

Considerable effort has been made to design generic trace formats to represent traces of programs or models conforming to any possible language [1,7,8,10]. However, while they may have interesting characteristics (modeling of logical time, handling of distributed systems, etc.), and may be compatible with generic trace analysis tools, they do not deal with the requirements previously mentioned. First, they do not provide facilities to browse traces efficiently: the only way to navigate in the trace is by enumerating each captured execution state one by one. Second, genericity implies a gap between the trace concepts defined by a trace format and the domain concepts specific to a particular xDSML. This semantic gap has a significant impact on usability. Moreover, most of these formats only capture events that occurred during an execution, such as the start of an operation execution, and lack a representation of the execution state, such as the values of the variables of a program. This is due to the large size of traces, which leads to limiting the amount of information stored in them. Yet, as stated previously, we focus in this paper on execution traces containing both states and events. Indeed, traces containing only events need to be replayed in order to reconstruct the states, whereas traces containing states allow direct analyses.

To better comply with the requirements (*i.e.* scalability in time and usability), the underlying intuition of the approach we propose is the following: considering that the benefits of narrowing the scope of a language to a domain are well known [12], defining a trace metamodel specific to a language should bring similar advantages. In particular, by providing concepts of the xDSML directly in the trace metamodel, the usability of the trace should be improved. In previous work [18], we followed this idea by defining manually a complete trace metamodel for fUML and recognized the many benefits such a domain-specific trace metamodel brings. Yet, defining this metamodel was tedious and error-prone, and we observed redundancies between the trace metamodel and the concepts defined in fUML. These redundancies are simply explained: the definition of an xDSML specifies what the state of a model is during its execution as part of the xDSML's semantics [5], and a trace metamodel directly requires such a notion of state. Hence, a first difficulty is the definition of a domain-specific trace metamodel, which can possibly be mitigated by analyzing how the execution state is defined in the xDSML. A second difficulty is that while generic trace metamodels can benefit from existing trace analysis and visualization tools, domain-specific ones require specific tooling. Therefore, our first idea is to go from *generic* trace metamodels to a *generic meta-approach* to define domain-specific trace metamodels. More precisely, we propose to automatically derive a complete domain-specific trace metamodel using the definitions of execution state and events of an xDSML. Such a generic generative approach would allow both to avoid the difficulty of defining domain-specific trace metamodels, and to automatically provide suitable tools for manipulating domain-specific traces.

The second intuition is that while a trace is generally only seen as a *sequence* of states and events, there are in fact many imaginable ways to browse a trace. Having more navigation paths at disposal could be a great way to browse traces more efficiently. An example is finding the next value change of a given model element regardless of any other state changes in the model. Such query can be done easily by traversing the complete trace, yet reifing it as a *navigation path* dedicated to the investigated model element would avoid browsing the whole trace. Henceforth, our second idea is to create *rich* trace metamodels, *i.e.* metamodels that provide many navigation paths to explore a trace.

In a nutshell, our proposal is an approach to automatically generate *rich* and *domain-specific* trace metamodels for an existing xDSML. We evaluate the relevance of our contribution with respect to the following research questions:

RQ#1: Can a rich domain-specific trace metamodel provide better execution times for trace manipulations as compared to a generic trace metamodel?

RQ#2: Can a rich domain-specific trace metamodel simplify the definition of domain-specific analyses of traces as compared to a generic trace metamodel?

3   From Executable Metamodeling to Execution Traces

In this section, we first present what constitutes an xDSML, then give an example of an xDSML, and finally provide our definition of execution trace.

3.1   Executable Metamodeling

While the purpose of metamodeling is to define languages, *executable* metamodeling also aims at including execution semantics in the language definition. This is done through executable Domain-Specific Modeling Languages (xDSMLs), which are languages that include the definitions of the *execution state* of a model conforming to the language, and *execution semantics* that change this state.

To define the execution state of a model, we consider that an abstract syntax metamodel can be extended into an *execution metamodel* with new properties and classes. To this end, a mechanism equivalent to the well-known *package merge* operation can be used. Note that in practice, existing tools and approaches use different but similar extension mechanisms—e.g. Kermeta [13] uses aspect weaving, xMOF [19] uses generalization, Hegedüs et al. [11] use separate classes.

There are two general approaches to define execution semantics: *translational* and *operational* semantics. Translational semantics consists in translating a model m into a model m' to be executed. This means that the execution state of m must be constantly synchronized with the execution state of m'. Operational semantics consist in a set of transformation rules that directly work with the execution state of m. In this paper, we only deal with operational semantics.

Furthermore, we consider two additional elements of an xDSML. First, in order to execute a model originally expressed with the abstract syntax metamodel, the *initialization function* translates such a model into a model conforming to the execution metamodel. Second, the *event metamodel* defines the events that may occur between two states during the execution. Each event corresponds to a specific transformation rule of the semantics. Such a metamodel can be directly inferred from the semantics (e.g. an event per transformation rule) or manually defined for a subset of the rules. Note that our approach does not require this metamodel, and that in such a case it won't provide event-based facilities to construct or manipulate event occurrences in a trace.

Definition 1. *An* xDSML *is defined by:*

- *An* abstract syntax, *which is a metamodel. We call* immutable *a property introduced in this metamodel. At the model level, we also call immutable an object's field based on an immutable property.*
- *An* execution metamodel, *which extends the abstract syntax by package merge. We call* mutable *a property introduced in this metamodel. At the model level, we also call mutable an object's field based on a mutable property.*

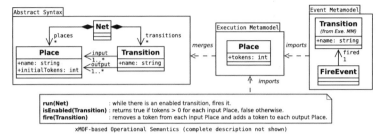

Fig. 1. Petri net xDSML defined using metamodels and xMOF

- Operational semantics, *which are a set of transformation rules that modify a model conforming to the execution metamodel by changing values of mutable fields and by creating/destroying instances of classes introduced in the execution metamodel.*
- An event metamodel, *which is a metamodel containing events that may occur during an execution. Each event is related to a transformation rule. An instance of an event class is called an* event occurrence.
- An initialization function, *which given a model conforming to the abstract syntax, returns a model conforming to the execution metamodel.*

Figure 1 shows an example of a Petri net xDSML. On the top left corner, its abstract syntax is depicted with three classes Net, Place and Transition. Next to the abstract syntax, the execution metamodel is shown. It extends the class Place using *package merge* with a new mutable property `tokens`. The initialization function (not shown) transforms each original object (e.g. a Place object without a `tokens` field) into an executable object (e.g. a Place object with a `tokens` field) as defined in the execution metamodel. It also initializes each `tokens` field with the value of `initialTokens`. At the bottom, the rules defined in the operational semantics with xMOF [19] are depicted. On the right, the event metamodel is shown containing a single class FireEvent corresponding to the *fire* rule.

3.2 Execution Trace

While execution traces can take various forms, we consider in this work that an *execution trace* is a sequence of states and event occurrences. Thereby, an execution state contains all the values of all the mutable fields of a model, *i.e.* the values of the fields defined by properties introduced in the execution metamodel. At each application of a transformation rule defined by the operational semantics, the execution state of the model changes. As rules are responsible for state changes, events associated to these rules occur between states.

Definition 2. *An* execution trace *is a sequence of execution states and event occurrences. While the first state is given by the initialization function, each other state is reached through the application of a transformation rule and contains at least the values of the mutable fields of the executed model. If this transformation* *rule is associated to an event, there is a corresponding event occurrence preceding the state.*

4   Generating Rich Domain-Specific Trace Metamodels

To answer RQ #1 and RQ #2, we propose a generative approach to define rich and domain-specific trace metamodels that provide facilities for efficiently processing traces. In this section, we present this approach by first presenting the challenges we had to overcome, second explaining our generation procedure based on the introduced Petri net xDSML, third discussing the resulting benefits of the approach, and fourth providing details on our implementation.

4.1   Observations and Challenges

There are many possible ways to generate a domain-specific trace metamodel for an xDSML. Regarding the execution states, a simple yet working idea is to reuse the complete execution metamodel of the xDSML in the trace metamodel. As the executed model conforms to the execution metamodel, we can *clone* it at each execution step and store it as a state in the trace. However, this solution has multiple drawbacks. First, by duplicating the whole model to store each execution state, we create redundancies between the states for both immutable fields (as they never change) and mutable fields (as they may not change in each step). Scalable model cloning [2] would mitigate this issue at runtime by sharing immutable data among clones, but would not be of any help when serializing the trace. Second, the mutable fields we are interested in are scattered among the immutable fields, which may require complex queries to access them within a state. These issues compromise RQ #2. Lastly, such a trace metamodel does not provide any efficient way to browse a trace, since the only possibility is to enumerate each state one by one. Thus it would be, for instance, tedious and inefficient to look for the next value of a given mutable field, compromising both RQ #1 and RQ #2. From these observations, we identified three *challenges*:

(1) Narrowing the concepts introduced in a trace metamodel, e.g. by focusing on the mutable properties of the execution metamodel.
(2) Avoiding redundancy in traces, e.g. by not storing the same value twice consecutively for a given mutable field.
(3) Providing alternative navigation paths, e.g. among the sequence of values of a specific mutable field.

4.2   Trace Metamodel Generation

Algorithm 1 shows our trace metamodel generation procedure. Note that the algorithm is simplified for illustration purposes, meaning that some parts are reduced to functions, and that special cases, such as abstract classes, are not considered. The inputs of the procedure are the abstract syntax (mm_{as}), the execution metamodel (mm_{exe}) and the event metamodel (mm_{events}) of an xDSML.

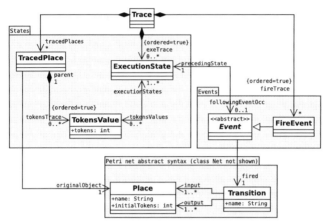

Fig. 2. Trace metamodel generated for the Petri net xDSML

Algorithm 1. Trace metamodel generation (simplified)

Input: mm_{as}, mm_{exe}, mm_{events}
Result: mm_{trace}: the trace metamodel

1 **begin**
2      $c_{trace}, c_{exeState} \leftarrow$ createBaseGenericClasses()
3      $mm_{trace} \leftarrow \{c_{trace}, c_{exeState}\}$
4   **foreach** $c_{exe} \in \{c \mid$ containsMutableProperties$(c)\}$ **do**
5          $c_{traced} \leftarrow$ createClass()
6          $mm_{trace} \leftarrow mm_{trace} \cup \{c_{traced}\}$
7   c_{trace}.createReferenceTo(c_{traced}, [0..*], *unordered*)
8   **if** containsImmutableProperties(c_{exe}) **then**
9              $c_{orig} \leftarrow$ getClassFromAbstractSyntax(c_{exe})
10   c_{traced}.createReferenceTo(c_{orig}, [1..1])
11   **foreach** $p \in$ getMutablePropertiesOf(c_{exe}) **do**
12             $c_{value} \leftarrow$ createClass()
13             $mm_{trace} \leftarrow mm_{trace} \cup \{c_{value}\}$
14   c_{value}.**properties** $\leftarrow \{$ copyProperty(p) $\}$
15   c_{traced}.createReferenceTo(c_{value}, [0..*], *ordered*)
16   c_{value}.createReferenceTo(c_{traced}, [1..1])
17             $c_{exeState}$.createReferenceTo(c_{value}, [0..*], *unordered*)
18   c_{value}.createReferenceTo($c_{exeState}$, [1..1])

19   **if** $mm_{events} \neq \varnothing$ **then**
20          $c_{event} \leftarrow$ createEventClass()
21          $mm_{trace} \leftarrow mm_{trace} \cup \{c_{event}\}$
22          $c_{exeState}$.createReferenceTo(c_{event}, [0..1])
23   c_{event}.createReferenceTo($c_{exeState}$, [1..1])
24   **foreach** $c_{exeevent} \in mm_{events}$ **do**
25             $c_{eventcopy} \leftarrow$ copyClass($c_{exeevent}$)
26             $mm_{trace} \leftarrow mm_{trace} \cup \{c_{eventcopy}\}$
27             $c_{eventcopy}$.**superTypes** $\leftarrow c_{eventcopy}$.**superTypes** $\cup \{c_{event}\}$
28   c_{trace}.createReferenceTo($c_{eventcopy}$, [0..*], *ordered*)

29   replaceReferencesToExecutionMM(mm_{trace}, mm_{as}, mm_{exe})

The procedure is independent from executable models, since the obtained meta-model is valid for any execution trace of any model of the considered xDSML. Note that the classes Trace and ExecutionState are always created (lines 2–3) and that the class Event is created only when the event metamodel is not empty (lines 20–21). In the following paragraphs, we explain the generation procedure based on the Petri net xDSML, starting with trace concepts for capturing the smallest unit of an execution state, *i.e.* an object's field values, up to the concepts for capturing the complete execution state of a model. The trace metamodel generated for the Petri net xDSML is shown in Figure 2.

Capturing the Values of Fields (lines 11–14). At any given point in time, all mutable fields of an object of the executed model have a *value*. To represent such a value in a trace, we create one class per mutable property of the execution metamodel, and we copy this mutable property into this new class (lines 12–14). This enables us to capture each value of a mutable field as an instance of this generated class. For Petri nets this means creating one class called TokensValue for the property tokens. Thereby, we precisely narrow the trace metamodel to the mutable part of the execution metamodel (challenge 1).

Capturing the States of Objects (lines 4–10, 15–16). The state of an object of the executed model at any point in time is defined by the values of all its mutable fields. To represent all states reached by an object, we create one class for each class of the execution metamodel containing at least one mutable property (lines 4–5). In addition, we make all instances of these generated classes accessible through a single instance of the class Trace. For Petri nets this means creating a class TracedPlace for the class Place, and a reference tracedPlaces from the class Trace. An instance of such a generated class shall contain all values reached by all mutable fields of an object of the considered type in chronological order. This is achieved by creating an ordered unbounded reference to each corresponding generated value class discussed previously (line 15). For Petri nets this means generating a reference tokensTrace for the class TracedPlace to the class TokensValue. When creating an execution trace, one TracedPlace object will be created per Place object, each storing a sequence tokensTrace of all the values reached by the tokens field of the respective Place object. A first benefit of this structure is that we avoid redundancy by creating a single object per value change of a mutable field (challenge 2). A second benefit is that such sequences provide additional navigation paths in the trace, making it possible to directly access all changes of one specific mutable field (challenge 3). The last concern for capturing the state of an object is that the object may also contain *immutable* fields, which remain an important piece of information. Since the corresponding immutable properties are all defined in a class introduced in the abstract syntax, our solution is to create a reference to this class (lines 8–10). For Petri nets this means adding a reference originalObject for the traced class TracedPlace to the class Place of the abstract syntax. A TracedPlace object is thus linked to the Place object whose states it captures.

Capturing the State of the Model (lines 17–18). An execution state can be seen as the n-tuple of the values of all mutable fields in an executed model at a given point in time. However, n is not xDSML-specific, but *model*-specific, as the number of mutable fields depends on the number of objects in the executed model. For instance, in our Petri net xDSML, n equals the number of `tokens` fields of one given model, *i.e.* the number of Place objects. In addition, n can change during the execution, as new objects can be created for classes introduced in the execution metamodel. To represent this n-tuple, we create a bidirectional reference between each generated value class and the class ExecutionState, which represents one execution state of a model. By that means, an execution state references an unbounded set of values of mutable fields. For Petri nets this means introducing the references `tokensValue` and `executionState` between the classes ExecutionState and TokensValue.

Capturing Event Occurrences (lines 19–28). An event may occur between two execution states if its corresponding transformation rule was responsible for the respective state change. This is represented by the references `preceding-State` and `followingEventOcc` between the classes ExecutionState and Event (lines 22–23). Since the abstract class Event represents any kind of event, we need to copy all classes from the event metamodel into the trace metamodel and add generalization links to the class Event (lines 25–27). For Petri nets this means copying the class FireEvent and making it a subclass of Event. In the same manner as for values, all event occurrences are stored chronologically within the unique Trace object (line 28). For Petri nets this means having an ordered reference `fireTrace` in the Trace class to the class FireEvent. This gives direct access to all event occurrences of a specific event in chronological order, which is an interesting additional navigation path for a trace (challenge 3).

Replacing References to the Execution Metamodel (line 29). When mutable properties and event classes were copied in the trace metamodel, this included copying references to classes of the execution metamodel. Yet, such classes may contain mutable properties that were already copied in the trace metamodel. To avoid having twice the same concept in the trace metamodel (challenge 1) or twice the same value stored in a trace (challenge 2), our solution is to replace all references to the execution metamodel by references either to the abstract syntax or to classes representing the states of objects (e.g. TracedPlace). This is indicated by the function *replaceReferencesToExeMM* (line 29).

Example Trace. Figure 3 shows a rich domain-specific trace of a Petri net model. Note that to construct such a trace, one must instrument the semantics of an xDSML, which is out the scope of this paper. In the upper part, we use the concrete syntax of Petri nets to show the execution. In the lower part, we use an object diagram to show the content of the executed model and of the trace at the end of the execution. In the example model, the transitions $t1$ and $t2$ are fired, leading to a trace with three states and two event occurrences. To represent the states, three ExecutionState objects are linked to a set of Tokens-Value objects, which represent the marking of the Petri net. Some are linked to

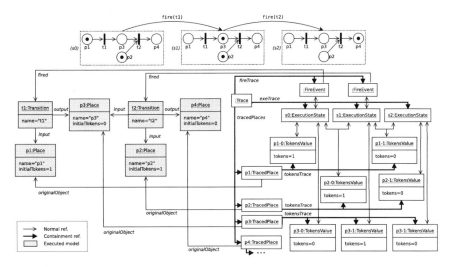

Fig. 3. Example of Petri net model and rich domain specific execution trace

FireEvent objects, which represent the firing of $t1$ and $t2$. There is one `tokens-Trace` sequence per `tokens` field: $(1, 0)$ for $p1$ and $p2$, $(0, 1, 0)$ for $p3$ and $(0, 2)$ for $p4$ (not shown). These sequences constitute alternative navigation paths that facilitate queries, e.g. we can find the maximum number of tokens reached by $p1$ by reading only two values. Moreover, we can go from one such sequence back to the complete trace, e.g. to find all states in which $p4$ had at least two tokens. Regarding events, we have access to the list of the fired transitions by browsing the fireEvent trace, e.g. to find states following directly a firing of $t2$.

Note that this example does not illustrate the creation or deletion of objects within an execution. Such case is handled with the help of the variable number of references from a ExecutionState element to values. Hence, an object created just before a state means that this state and the following ones have references to the values of this object. Likewise, an object deleted just before a state means that this state and the following ones have no references to its values.

4.3 Resulting Benefits

Among all the concepts we create in a trace metamodel, some are generic (e.g. Trace), but the others are specific to the xDSML (e.g. TokensValue). Also, we make sure not to have any redundancy of concepts. In other words, we *precisely define* the structure of execution traces of models conforming to an xDSML. Thereby, domain-specific analyses of traces have direct access to these concepts, and do not have to rely on complex queries or introspection to use domain-specific data. We aim by that means to provide good usability (RQ #2).

In addition, we provide several *navigation paths* for browsing traces. Indeed, we create for each mutable property (e.g. `tokens`) and each event (e.g. FireEvent) of an xDSML a dedicated navigation path (e.g. `tokensTrace` and `fireTrace`).

This allows to enumerate each value of a particular field, or each event occurrence of a particular event, without having to enumerate all the states of the trace. Moreover, all values and event occurrences are connected through execution states, allowing to go from one navigation path to another. These navigation facilities offer better usability and scalability in time (RQ #1 and RQ #2).

4.4   Implementation

We implemented our approach for the Eclipse Modeling Framework (EMF). Our completely generic trace metamodel generator is written using EMF and Xtend. Parts of our prototype are specific to the xMOF framework, including both a transformation that derives an event metamodel from xMOF semantics and a trace builder that can construct a trace from the execution of any xMOF-based model. For more information, the source code (EPL 1.0 licensed) is available at our project web page: https://gforge.inria.fr/projects/lastragen/.

5   Evaluation

In this section, we present the evaluation of our approach, which consists in a case study applying rich and domain-specific traces for semantic differencing. We first introduce our semantic differencing framework, then present our case study, and finally discuss the obtained results regarding RQ #1 and RQ #2.

5.1   Semantic Differencing

Semantic differencing of models is concerned with identifying differences among distinct versions of models. Thereby, not only syntactic differences among models are taken into account, but differences in their semantics are especially considered. In previous work [15], we have proposed a semantic differencing approach for xDSMLs, which is based on the analysis of execution traces. In this approach, execution traces obtained from the execution of two models to be compared are analyzed for identifying semantic differences among these models. This analysis is performed by applying semantic differencing rules on the traces, which are match rules [14] indicating which syntactic differences among the traces constitute semantic differences among the models. The match rules are specific to the used xDSML as well as the relevant semantic equivalence criterion.

Our semantic differencing approach utilizes a *generic trace metamodel* for capturing execution traces. More precisely, a trace conforming to this metamodel is a sequence of clones of the model after each event occurrence causing a state change. The usage of a generic trace metamodel has two key implications on the trace analysis: *(i)* As a state is simply a collection of objects of any type, type checks and type casting are required to analyze the captured execution data. This implies complex rules that are hard to read and comprehend. *(ii)* Analyzing state changes of an executed model requires the traversal of all states captured in a trace. This implies an execution time that scales at best linearly to the number of captured states. To mitigate these issues, we propose the application of rich and domain-specific traces as presented in this work.

5.2   Case Study

As proposed above, we have adapted our semantic differencing framework [15] so that it relies on execution traces conforming to generated rich and domain-specific trace metamodels instead of a generic trace metamodel. Thereby, we conducted a case study with a real world xDSML, namely fUML [21]—a subset of UML comprising class and activity diagrams having well defined execution semantics. In the case study, we have defined the execution semantics of fUML using xMOF and used our proposed approach to generate a rich and domain-specific trace metamodel for fUML. The execution metamodel extends one metaclass and defines 57 new classes. The generated trace metamodel consists of 56 classes for values and 58 classes for object states. The implemented semantic differencing rules determine whether two fUML activity diagrams are trace equivalent, *i.e.* whether all sequences of action executions possible in one activity diagram are also possible in the other. We developed two variants of these rules: one for performing the analysis on trace models conforming to the generic trace metamodel, and one for performing the analysis on trace models conforming to the generated domain-specific trace metamodel.

For evaluating the performance improvement gained by relying on the proposed rich domain-specific trace metamodels, we applied the semantic differencing rules on example fUML models. The example models constitute real world models taken from the case study of Maoz et al. for evaluating their semantic differencing operator *ADDiff* [17]. These models may be found at http://www.se-rwth.de/materials/semdiff/.

5.3   Results

In the following, we present the results of the evaluation and discuss how they give answers to the research questions stated in Section 2.2.

Complexity Reduction of Semantic Differencing Rules (RQ #2). Table 1 compares the complexity of the semantic differencing rules defined for fUML based on the generic trace metamodel and the rich domain-specific trace metamodel. For all elements, we observe a significant reduction of the complexity of the rules reaching from 20% to 100%. This is mainly due to the rich structure of the generated domain-specific trace metamodel. In contrast to the generic trace metamodel, there is no need to traverse the complex data structure of the execution metamodel of fUML, but instead the actions and the evolution of their values can be directly accessed. Other improvements are due to the fact that the trace metamodel is domain-specific, such as type checks that become obsolete. These results allow us to answer RQ #2 as follows: rich domain-specific trace metamodels simplify the definition of domain-specific trace analyses.

Performance Improvement of Semantic Differencing Rules (RQ #1). Figure 4 shows the execution times measured for applying the semantic differencing rules on the traces of the considered example models. This experiment was performed on an Intel Core i7-4600U CPU, 2.10GHz, 2.69GHz, with 12GB

Table 1. Complexity of the semantic differencing rules of fUML defined for the generic (G) and rich domain-specific (DS) trace metamodel

Elements	G	DS	Reduction
Lines of code	136	55	60%
Statements	58	21	64%
Operation calls	32	13	59%
Loops	5	4	20%
Type checks	4	0	100%

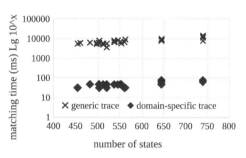

Fig. 4. Execution time of the semantic differencing rules of fUML for generic and rich domain-specific traces

RAM, running Windows 8.1 Pro. The X-axis of Figure 4 shows the number of states contained by the generic and domain-specific traces. The Y-axis shows the measured execution time on a logarithmic scale. Each execution time was measured ten times and the arithmetic mean values are shown in the figure. As can be seen from the measurements, the rules analyzing traces conforming to the domain-specific trace metamodel outperform the match rules analyzing generic traces since they are between 170 and 400 times faster with an average of 250. The main reason for this result is the rich structure of the domain-specific trace metamodel allowing to efficiently explore the trace through dedicated navigation paths related to specific model elements. These results allow us to answer RQ #1 as follows: rich domain-specific trace metamodels enable better execution times for trace manipulations as compared to a generic trace metamodel.

6   Related Work

To our knowledge, little work has been done on the topic of domain-specific traces. Hegedus et al. [11] worked on many aspects of xDSMLs, such as trace replay and back-annotation. However they do not provide an approach to obtain trace metamodels for an xDSML. More recently, Meyers et al. introduced the ProMoBox framework [20], which generates a set of metamodels from an annotated xDSML, including a property metamodel and a trace metamodel. Their trace metamodel generation has multiple differences with our approach. Among others, they consider an abstract syntax whose properties are annotated either as *runtime* or *event* to identify mutable elements and event-related elements, while we consider the abstract syntax and the execution metamodel to be separated. Indeed, such separation makes possible a better separation of concerns and interchangeability of semantics. Also, they use generalization to extend a base trace metamodel, while we generate new classes to avoid having to rely on introspection and casting when manipulating traces. In addition, they do not provide alternative ways to explore a trace, while we provide various navigation paths. Finally, Gogolla et al. [9] generate *filmstrip models* from UML class diagrams. Such filmstrip models match what we call domain-specific trace meta-models, and also provide some navigation paths among objects states. However, they do not tackle redundancy since object states are always recreated at each model change, and they do not consider value states.

Regarding the richness of traces, we will in the future look more thoroughly at the mostly undocumented and transient traces manipulated by V&V tools.

7   Conclusion and Perspectives

Dynamic V&V of models requires the ability to model executions traces. We identified two important requirements regarding the definition of a *trace meta-model* for an xDSML: it must provide good *scalability in time* when manipulating traces, and good *usability* to analyze traces containing domain-specific data and events. Generic trace metamodels are not adequate because of their distance to the domain of an xDSML and because of their lack of alternative trace exploration means. The approach we presented consists in generating a *rich* and *domain-specific* trace metamodel of an xDSML, using its definition of what the execution state of a model is, and which events may occur during an execution. We reify the mutable properties of the execution metamodel into classes, allowing both to reduce redundancy and to narrow the trace metamodel. We also provide navigation paths both to follow the evolution of each mutable field of the model over time, and to follow the event occurrences of each event. This allows an efficient navigation of traces, *i.e.* an exploration without visiting each state of the trace. Our evaluation was done by the generation of a trace metamodel for fUML and its utilization for *semantic differencing* of several models. The results show a simplification of the semantic differencing rules and faster execution times of the rules, when compared to a naïve and generic trace metamodel.

The direct perspectives of this work include defining a common interface for all generated trace metamodels using model subtyping, enabling compression by detecting patterns in sequences of values, or handling *deltas* instead of states for certain types of value changes (e.g. collections, strings).

Acknowledgments. This work is partially supported by the ANR INS Project GEMOC (ANR-12-INSE-0011) and by the European Commission under the ICT Policy Support Programme grant no. 317859.

References

1. Alawneh, L., Hamou-Lhadj, A.: Execution traces: a new domain that requires the creation of a standard metamodel. In: Ślezak, D., Kim, T., Kiumi, A., Jiang, T., Verner, J., Abrahão, S. (eds.) ASEA 2009. CCIS, vol. 59, pp. 253–263. Springer, Heidelberg (2009)
2. Bousse, E., Combemale, B., Baudry, B.: Scalable armies of model clones through data sharing. In: Dingel, J., Schulte, W., Ramos, I., Abrahão, S., Insfran, E. (eds.) MODELS 2014. LNCS, vol. 8767, pp. 286–301. Springer, Heidelberg (2014)

3. Bousse, E., Combemale, B., Baudry, B.: Towards scalable multidimensional execution traces for xDSMLs. In: 11th Workshop on Model Design, Verification and Validation. CEUR-WS, vol. 1235, pp. 13–18. CEUR (2014)
4. Combemale, B., Crégut, X., Garoche, P.L., Thirioux, X.: Essay on Semantics Definition in MDE - An Instrumented Approach for Model Verification. Journal of Software **4**(9), 943–958 (2009)
5. Combemale, B., Crégut, X., Pantel, M.: A design pattern to build executable DSMLs and associated V&V tools. In: 19th Asia-Pacific Software Engineering Conference, pp. 282–287. IEEE (2012)
6. Corley, J., Eddy, B.P., Gray, J.: Towards efficient and scalabale omniscient debugging for model transformations. In: 14th Workshop on Domain-Specific Modeling, pp. 13–18. ACM (2014)
7. DeAntoni, J., Mallet, F.: Timesquare: treat your models with logical time. In: Furia, C.A., Nanz, S. (eds.) TOOLS 2012. LNCS, vol. 7304, pp. 34–41. Springer, Heidelberg (2012)
8. Eschweiler, D., Wagner, M., Geimer, M., Knüpfer, A., Nagel, W.E., Wolf, F.: Open trace format 2: the next generation of scalable trace formats and support libraries. In: 14th Int. Conf. on Parallel Computing. Advances in Parallel Computing, vol. 22, pp. 481–490. IOS Press (2011)
9. Gogolla, M., Hamann, L., Hilken, F., Kuhlmann, M., France, R.B.: From application models to filmstrip models: an approach to automatic validation of model dynamics. In: Modellierung 2014. LNI, vol. 225, pp. 273–288. GI (2014)
10. Hamou-Lhadj, A., Lethbridge, T.C.: A metamodel for the compact but lossless exchange of execution traces. Software & Systems Modeling **11**(1), 77–98 (2010)
11. Hegedüs, A., Ráth, I., Varró, D.: Replaying Execution Trace Models for Dynamic Modeling Languages. Periodica Polytechnica - Electrical Engineering **56**(3), 71–82 (2012)
12. Hutchinson, J., Whittle, J., Rouncefield, M., Kristoffersen, S.: Empirical assessment of MDE in industry. In: 33rd Int. Conf. on Software Engineering (ICSE), pp. 471–480. ACM (2011)
13. Jézéquel, J.M., Combemale, B., Barais, O., Monperrus, M., Fouquet, F.: Mashup of metalanguages and its implementation in the Kermeta language workbench. Software & Systems Modeling, 1–16 (2013)
14. Kolovos, D.S., Di Ruscio, D., Pierantonio, A., Paige, R.F.: Different models for model matching: an analysis of approaches to support model differencing. In: 2009 ICSE Workshop on Comparison and Versioning of Software Models, pp. 1–6. IEEE (2009)
15. Langer, P., Mayerhofer, T., Kappel, G.: Semantic model differencing utilizing behavioral semantics specifications. In: Dingel, J., Schulte, W., Ramos, I., Abrahão, S., Insfran, E. (eds.) MODELS 2014. LNCS, vol. 8767, pp. 116–132. Springer, Heidelberg (2014)
16. Leucker, M., Schallhart, C.: A brief account of runtime verification. The Journal of Logic and Algebraic Programming **78**(5), 293–303 (2009)
17. Maoz, S., Ringert, J.O., Rumpe, B.: ADDiff: semantic differencing for activity diagrams. In: 19th ACM SIGSOFT Symposium and 13th Europ. Conf. on Foundations of Software Engineering, pp. 179–189. ACM (2011)
18. Mayerhofer, T., Langer, P., Kappel, G.: A runtime model for fUML. In: 7th Workshop on Models@run.time, pp. 53–58. ACM (2012)

19. Mayerhofer, T., Langer, P., Wimmer, M., Kappel, G.: xMOF: executable DSMLs based on fUML. In: Erwig, M., Paige, R.F., Van Wyk, E. (eds.) SLE 2013. LNCS, vol. 8225, pp. 56–75. Springer, Heidelberg (2013)
20. Meyers, B., Deshayes, R., Lucio, L., Syriani, E., Vangheluwe, H., Wimmer, M.: ProMoBox: a framework for generating domain-specific property languages. In: Combemale, B., Pearce, D.J., Barais, O., Vinju, J.J. (eds.) SLE 2014. LNCS, vol. 8706, pp. 1–20. Springer, Heidelberg (2014)
21. Object Management Group: Semantics of a Foundational Subset for Executable UML Models (fUML), V 1.1, August 2013. http://www.omg.org/spec/FUML/1.1
22. Tatibouët, J., Cuccuru, A., Gérard, S., Terrier, F.: Formalizing execution semantics of UML profiles with fUML models. In: Dingel, J., Schulte, W., Ramos, I., Abrahão, S., Insfran, E. (eds.) MODELS 2014. LNCS, vol. 8767, pp. 133–148. Springer, Heidelberg (2014)

On Lightweight Metamodel Extension to Support Modeling Tools Agility

Hugo Bruneliere[1]([✉]), Jokin Garcia[1], Philippe Desfray[2],
Djamel Eddine Khelladi[3], Regina Hebig[3], Reda Bendraou[3], and Jordi Cabot[4]

[1] AtlanModTeam (Inria, Mines Nantes & LINA), Nantes, France
{hugo.bruneliere,jokin.garcia-perez}@inria.fr
[2] SOFTEAM Cadextan, Paris, France
philippe.desfray@softeam.fr
[3] UPMC - LIP6, Paris, France
{djamel.khelladi,regina.hebig,reda.bendraou}@lip6.fr
[4] ICREA - UOC, Barcelona, Spain
jordi.cabot@icrea.cat

Abstract. Modeling in real industrial projects implies dealing with different models, metamodels and supporting tools. They continuously have to be adapted to changing requirements, involving (often costly) problems in terms of traceability, coherence or interoperability. To this intent, solutions ensuring a better adaptability and flexibility of modeling tools are needed. As metamodels are cornerstones in such tools, metamodel extension capabilities are fundamental. However, current modeling frameworks are not flexible or dynamic enough. Thus, following the ongoing OMG MOF Extension Facility (MEF) RFP, this paper proposes a generic lightweight metamodel extension mechanism developed as part of the MoNoGe collaborative project. A base list of metamodel extension operators as well as a DSL for easily using them are introduced. Two different implementations of this extension mechanism (including a model-level support when (un)applying metamodel extensions) are also described, respectively based on Eclipse/EMF and the Modelio modeling environment.

Keywords: Modeling tool · Metamodel extension · Adaptability · Flexibility

1 Introduction

Model Driven Engineering (MDE) in general and modeling environments/tools in particular are used within the industry in various contexts and for varied purposes [6]. In many cases, companies (both solution providers and users) have to adapt their model-based infrastructure because of changing requirements or technological constraints. This usually comes with a range of potential issues including traceability, coherence or interoperability ones regarding both the modeling artifacts and data conforming to them. This is particularly true for modeling tools that heavily rely on their core supported metamodel(s). Indeed, such

© Springer International Publishing Switzerland 2015
G. Taentzer and F. Bordeleau (Eds.): ECMFA 2015, LNCS 9153, pp. 62–74, 2015.
DOI: 10.1007/978-3-319-21151-0_5

metamodels may need to evolve over time and new/other ones may have to be additionally supported by these tools (e.g. due to customer or market requirements). Compatibility with already existing models must be preserved, but new models (conforming to completely different metamodels not yet supported or to slightly modified versions of existing ones) have to be considered too. Both cases should be addressed, ideally in such a way that the effort implied by the corresponding modifications to the tools is limited as much as possible. Thus, there is a clear need for adaptability and flexibility in modeling tools/environments. This *agility* requires lightweight metamodel extension capabilities having several interesting properties such as compatibility preservation but also genericity, non-intrusiveness, transparency or some dynamicity (as explained later in the paper).

Intending to face up current limitations and the lack of standard solutions (e.g. the OMG MOF Extension Facility (MEF) is still an ongoing RFP [13]), we propose a dedicated solution in the context of the MoNoGe French collaborative project[1]. A generic lightweight metamodel extension approach is being developed and experimented in an industrial environment where rapid and efficient adaptations of the used modeling tools are required. Of course, these tools have to be modified once to somehow integrate the proposed mechanism. However, among other reasons detailed later, we consider it *lightweight* because it then does not require model migration/transformation processes anymore. It provides metamodel extension operations to cover real scenarios involving addition, updating and filtering changes to existing metamodels. Metamodel extension declarations can be defined and then shared between different modeling tools using a dedicated Domain Specific Language (DSL). Thus, the main contributions of the paper are: i) a base list of metamodel extension operators and corresponding generic DSL, ii) an overall architecture for implementing a metamodel extension mechanism based on Eclipse/EMF, transparent from an end-user point of view and iii) (complementarily) an alternative DSL-compliant solution relying on the Modelio modeling environment as needed in the MoNoGe project.

The remainder of the paper is structured as follows. We start by explaining with more details our motivation in Section 2, setting the goals and scope of our work. In Section 3, we introduce a core list of metamodel extension operators and the related textual DSL we propose. Then, we describe in Section 4 the proposed capabilities and architecture to implement a corresponding metamodel extension mechanism relying on Eclipse/EMF modeling technologies. We also present in Section 5 an alternative DSL-compliant solution based on the Modelio modeling environment. We discuss the related work in Section 6 before we finally conclude in Section 7 with some remaining challenges and future work.

2   Motivation and Industrial Background

As introduced before, the use of MDE-based environments and modeling tools is relatively widespread in the industry. For various reasons (e.g. new customer

---

[1] http://www.images-et-reseaux.com/en/content/monoge

needs, technical constraints or business decisions to cite a few), these solutions have to evolve quite frequently. Related changes can concern several different aspects: UI can be modified, new features can be added or previous ones removed, tool's core can be restructured, etc. In all cases, it is important for software providers to be able to adapt their tools as easily as possible when implementing these modifications. According to the promises of MDE, minimizing the cost/-effort of such evolution is fundamental.

In the particular context of modeling environments, core supported meta-models are key elements since most components are derived from them (parsers, editors, verifiers, generators, etc.). Core modification of such environments generally implies the adaptation of these metamodels and related tooling features. Modelio is a concrete example of a modeling tool implementing popular standards such as UML, BPMN, SysML, etc. Users frequently need to reuse pieces of these standards and create extensions related to domain-specific solutions for System, Enterprise Architecture or Requirement modeling (for instance). Thus, already supported metamodels need to be modified to reflect some changes: new complementary concepts could be added, previously existing ones could be updated or even filtered if not relevant anymore. In addition, brand new metamodels may also have to be supported ensuring quality properties such as traceability of the different versions or coherence between dependent artifacts. While compatibility with existing models must usually also be preserved, new models (that can conform to modified or different metamodels) have to be taken into account too. Both kinds of models need to coexist smoothly within the tool. As a consequence, modeling environments have to be able to adapt to all these situations with as much agility as possible.

Illustrating this situation, the MoNoGe main industrial use case comes from DCNS, a world-leading company in naval defense and energy that notably develops *CMS* (*Combat Management Systems*) for ships. In one of its programs, DCNS is using two separate modeling tools: one (System Architect) for system-level modeling using the *DoDAF* (*U.S. Department of Defense Architecture Framework*) standard, the other (Modelio) supporting software design and development. DCNS needs to manage permanent consistency between the system and software modeling levels (plus related traceability and impact analysis), but cannot customize System Architect.

Thus, part of the work in MoNoGe consists in building a metamodel extension, in Modelio, to trace and enrich software models with DoDAF elements (from a subset of the DoDAF metamodel). The objective is to allow architects and developers to work as before on their current models while, at the same time, both types of models can be exchanged between the two modeling environments and linked together. Only the users who need to see traceability and impact analysis have access to these extended models combining software- and system- levels. Interoperability and consistency management stay straightforward as there is no actual model transformation/migration, just this extended view of the models in Modelio depending on the user profile.

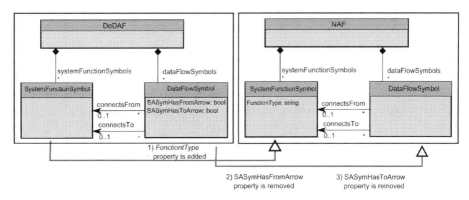

Fig. 1. Defining NAF by extending DoDAF (excerpt)

Another use case, still in the same DCNS domain, is also being conducted using an Eclipse/EMF-based environment to demonstrate the genericity of the proposed extension mechanism and to provide an open source alternative. DCNS wants to evolve their existing DoDAF models and related tooling support to *NAF (NATO Architecture Framework)*, which is another architecture framework deriving its main concepts from *MoDAF (British Ministry of Defense Architecture Framework)*. As NAF is based on Enterprise Architecture concepts relatively close to the ones existing in DoDAF, the more direct way to make this happen is to define an extension of the DoDAF metamodel for supporting NAF. The goal is notably to enable the automatic reuse of existing DoDAF models in a NAF context. Due to space limit, we introduce here only small parts of the concerned metamodels and highlight a few required changes. As examples, the following modifications can be seen in Figure 1:

1. Adding a property *FunctionType* in the concept *SystemFunction.*
2. Deleting a property *SASymHasFromArrow* from the concept *DataFlowSymbol.*
3. Deleting a property *SASymHasToArrow* from the concept *DataFlowSymbol.*

Based on these two case studies we conclude that flexible extensions that do not necessarily require to migrate existing models, and that allow preserving viewpoints/models of current stakeholders, are an efficient mean to smoothly integrate modeling tools and increase their scope. To support this, a lightweight metamodel extension mechanism is needed, like the one we describe in the next sections.

3   Defining Metamodel Extensions

The first key ingredient of our metamodel extension mechanism is to have an easy way to express extensions. For that, we provide in this section a textual DSL that offers an initial list of extension operators (providing base semantics for extension) to be used when specifying metamodel extensions. After a few introductory definitions, we review the list of operators and textual DSL we are proposing based on them.

3.1 Terminology and Definitions

In this paper we consider the following definitions. An **original metamodel** is an already existing metamodel that has a life on its own (e.g. is integrated in various tools/solutions, has models that conform to it, etc.). A **metamodel extension** is the definition of an extension that is, partially or completely, relying on concepts coming from original metamodel(s) or from other previously extended metamodel(s). An **extended metamodel** is the result of the application of one (or several) metamodel extension(s) onto original or already extended metamodel(s). An **existing/legacy model** is an already existing model that conforms to an original metamodel, but not necessarily to the extended metamodel(s) that could have been specified from this metamodel.

3.2 A Base Set of Metamodel Extension Operators

A metamodel extension specification consists in a set of atomic extension operations, usually applied on existing metamodel elements. Notably to simplify the management of extensions (see next section), our goal is to minimize the number of base operators. These operators can be combined later on to express more complex changes. Such combinations could also be offered on modeling infrastructures supporting them, e.g. as a more powerful predefined extension library.

Our definition of these operators is not linked to any particular technical environment and therefore could be adopted by all modeling frameworks. Since metamodels are typically specifying a set of concepts with properties (possibly attributes or references), we follow the same approach for introducing the operators hereafter:

- **ADD** (a new concept to the metamodel)
    - **Create** "from scratch" a completely new concept.
    - **Specialize** (subtype) a concept.
    - **Generalize** (supertype) one or several concept(s).
- **MODIFY** (an existing concept in the metamodel)
    - **Add property** to an existing concept.
    - **Filter property** from an existing concept.
    - **Modify property** of an existing concept (equivalent to Filter + Add).
    - **Add constraint** to an existing concept or one of its properties.
    - **Filter constraint** from an existing concept or one of its properties.
- **FILTER** (an existing concept in the metamodel).

Constraints on metamodels can be expressed using either natural language or more dedicated languages depending on implementations (cf. Section 4 for instance). Note that we are voluntarily using the term FILTER and not DELETE. For coherence and compatibility with the existing/legacy models, we want our extension mechanism to be as little intrusive as possible. Thus, we do not want to actually delete elements but rather hide them when asked for. Filtering is applied on cascade (e.g. in the case of generalizations or derived properties) and related constraints updated accordingly[11].

3.3 A Textual DSL for Metamodel Extension

Extensions should be easily written by modelers/engineers in a comprehensive way, justifying the need for a DSL [19]. A textual DSL has been designed in order to make available the previously introduced extension operators via a textual concrete syntax very close to our metamodel extension terminology. This syntax is intended to be intuitive and easy-to-learn for people already familiar with (meta)modeling, and reflects the full list of base extension operators as presented before. Having genericity and portability in mind, it has been defined independently from any particular metamodel or modeling framework/environment.

The overall structure to declare an extension includes its name, the metamodel(s) it extends and the list of applied operators (as well as the metamodel elements they are applied to). Figure 2 presents the full grammar of our textual DSL, thus highlighting its main concepts and structure.

```
Model:'define' extensionName=ID 'extending' metamodel+=Metamodel ':'
    prefix+=Prefix ("," metamodel+=Metamodel ':'  prefix+=Prefix)*
    '{' extensions += Extension* '}';
Extension: Create | Refine | Generalize | ModifyClass | FilterClass;
Metamodel:  name=ID;
Prefix:  name=ID;
Create: 'add class' class=ID;
Refine: 'add class' classNew=ID 'specializing' prefix=[Prefix] '.'
    classOriginal=ID;
Generalize: 'add class' classNew=ID 'supertyping' prefix+=[Prefix]
    '.' class+=ID ("," prefix+=[Prefix] '.' class+=ID)*;
ModifyClass:
    'modify class' prefix=[Prefix] '.' class=ID '{'
        modifyOperators += ModifyOperator*
    '}';
ModifyOperator: AddProperty | ModifyProperty | FilterProperty |
    AddConstraint | FilterConstraint;
AddProperty:    'add property' property=ID 'type' type=ID;
ModifyProperty: 'modify property' property=ID value+=ValueAssignment
    ("," value+=ValueAssignment)*;
ValueAssignment:    attribute=ID '=' value=EString;
FilterProperty: 'filter property' property=ID;
FilterClass:    'filter class' prefix=[Prefix] '.' class=ID;
AddConstraint:  'add constraint' constraint=ID value=EString;
FilterConstraint:   'filter constraint' constraint=EString;
```

Fig. 2. Grammar of our metamodel extension textual DSL

Based on the same small example than introduced at the end of Section 2, Figure 3 shows a sample metamodel extension illustrating the defined concrete syntax.

```
//Extension to transform DoDAF into NAF
define DoDAFextension extending DoDAF:dodaf{
    modify class dodaf.SystemFunctionSymbol {
        add property FunctionType type String
    }
    modify class dodaf.DataFlowSymbol{
        filter property SASymHasFromArrow
        filter property SASymHasToArrow
    }
}
```

Fig. 3. Example of a metamodel extension definition using our textual DSL

4   Architecture of a Metamodel Extension Mechanism

Once extensions are defined, we need to provide a modeling infrastructure able to understand and deploy them as part of a normal modeling process. This mainly includes (de)activating the use of extensions for specific models, and eventually storing the extension data to be reused in the future. This section presents such an infrastructure for the Eclipse/EMF framework.

4.1   Expected Characteristics

There are different ways to implement a metamodel extension mechanism (cf. Section 6). However, we believe such a mechanism should comply with the following list of characteristics, as determined mainly by the industrial partners in MoNoGe according to their actual needs:

- **Genericity.** The extension approach cannot be linked to a particular metamodel, tool or implementing framework. Relying on the same base mechanism, metamodel extensions can be defined on all metamodels and should be exchangeable between different modeling environments.
- **Non-intrusiveness.** Defined extensions should not directly modify original metamodels but rather complement them in an external manner. Thus, tools relying on these metamodels do not need to be deeply modified when their metamodels are extended.
- **Persistence and Interoperability.** Extensions should be specified, stored and shared in a user-comprehensive format, but also be easily machine-readable for reusability purposes. For separation of concerns (cf. also Non-intrusiveness), they should be persisted separately from metamodels.

– **Compatibility/conformance preserving.** Models should not be altered when extensions are defined on their respective metamodels: prior metamodel conformance should always be preserved. Backward conformance is also interesting: models that conform to a given extension could "forget" elements brought by this extension (e.g. default values could be used).

– **Transparency.** From user and tooling perspectives, an extended metamodel should be presented and manipulated as any regular metamodel. Models can conform to extended metamodels and dedicated tooling can directly rely on them.

– **Dynamicity and synchronization.** Metamodel extensions can be applied and removed. Corresponding models and tooling should be able to react/adapt accordingly in order to preserve consistency and usability (notably concerning compatibility and conformance).

– **Runtime computation.** (Parts of) Models conforming to an extended metamodel could be computed at runtime, i.e. from predefined expressions at extension-level (e.g. queries on the original metamodel). Related models and tooling should reflect the result of such computations.

4.2   An Eclipse/EMF Implementation

The proposed architecture relies on several existing technologies, reused and/or refined when needed, from the lively open source ecosystem around Eclipse and its well-known Eclipse Modeling Framework.

Our Eclipse/EMF implementation first comprises a dedicated parser and editor for the textual DSL (based on Xtext[2]) so that users can create their own metamodel extensions at development time. These extensions are then managed and processed using the architecture shown in Figure 4.

A *Base Operators API* consumes, in addition to the original metamodel, the DSL model generated by Xtext from the user textual definitions of the extension. Thanks to an ATL[3] model transformation, this component produces the appropriate data required by the *Virtualization API* to realize the metamodel extension and corresponding model.

There are different options for linking (meta)models together (cf. Section 6). In our implementation, we rely on model virtualization techniques to interconnect (meta)models together transparently on an on-demand basis. A virtual (meta)model is a (meta)model that do not hold concrete data but rather kind of proxies to original (meta)models, making it relevant in a lightweight metamodel extension context. As already providing virtualization capabilities, we adapted EMF Views[4] (a refinement of Virtual EMF [1]) to implement the required *Virtualization API* supporting the previously introduced extension operators. Thus, "virtual" extended metamodels and models are realized automatically by this API using the original (meta)models and complementary information computed

---

[2] https://eclipse.org/Xtext

[3] https://eclipse.org/atl

[4] http://atlanmod.github.io/emfviews

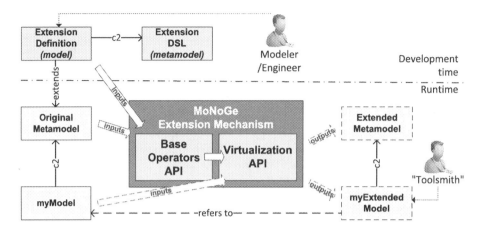

Fig. 4. Overall architecture for the Eclipse-EMF implementation

by the *Base Operators API*. For conformance reasons, and in case deriving from already existing models (i.e. prior to metamodel extension), "virtual" models may need to be completed at runtime (e.g. with some default values) according to the applied extension operators at metamodel-level (e.g. when a new property is added). Some initial support is provided via the use of ECL[5] as an automated matching engine in EMF Views. However, this has not been extensively tested so far in the current version. It can also be noted that constraints on metamodels are expressed using OCL[6].

Interestingly, such extended (meta)models can be manipulated as any EMF (meta)models in Eclipse, by other existing EMF-based technologies relying on the standard EMF model handling API or by both kinds of users (cf. Figure 4). Source code and screencasts of the current implementation are available online[7].

The described architecture and Eclipse/EMF implementation globally satisfy the expected characteristics, as introduced in Section 4.1. It is *generic* as extensions can be defined and then applied on top of any metamodel. Keeping the DSL tooling independent from the other components makes the overall extension mechanism even more generic, as defined extensions can be reused by different modeling environments. The proposed solution is also *interoperable* because extension declarations are *persisted* separately from original metamodels and thus can be shared easily between various modeling tools using the same base extension mechanism (cf. Section 5). The EMF Views *non-intrusive* and *transparent* approach, as well as its extensible architecture, made it a natural good candidate for our extension mechanism and offers concrete support to these important properties. *Synchronization* is ensured because the "virtual" extended (meta)models simply hold proxies to the real data actually contained in different

---

[5] http://eclipse.org/epsilon/doc/ecl

[6] http://wiki.eclipse.org/OCL

[7] https://github.com/atlanmod/monoge

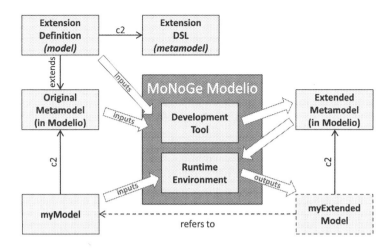

Fig. 5. Overall architecture for the Modelio implementation

(meta)models. Moreover, *compatibility* and *conformance* are also preserved as original metamodels are not actually modified. Finally, partial *runtime* support is also available via the use of an automated matching engine connected to EMF Views.

5   An Alternative Compliant Solution

Our textual DSL for specifying metamodel extensions is independent from any specific modeling tooling, framework or environment. This way, related meta-model extension mechanisms can be implemented on different technological plat-forms while still exchanging extension definitions based on the same proposed DSL. This is an important validation requirement from the MoNoGe industrial project's perspective. Thus, in addition to the Eclipse/EMF architecture and implementation presented before, this section briefly describes an alternative but DSL-compliant solution being integrated within the Modelio environment[8].

In contrast with the Eclipse/EMF solution, the Modelio-based one relies on a more generative approach (thus partially affecting some of the characteristics introduced in Section 4.1). There are two very distinct phases in the Modelio implementation, as summarized in Figure 5.

Firstly, there is a so-called *development phase* where the extension declara-tion is processed and transformed into a UML Class model, that is then trans-formed into a Java implementation model. This later is further processed by a Java code generator to produce a corresponding metamodel extension Jar (using the Modelio internal module mechanism) to be loaded in Modelio. Thus, the Modelio-based solution is able to consume metamodel extensions defined using the previously introduced DSL. Importantly, this solution also relies on

---

[8] http://www.modelio.org

the same base extension operators (excepting the MODIFY operations which will be supported in later developments).

Secondly, there is a *runtime phase* where the packaged metamodel extension is actually deployed within Modelio. This results in the modification of the Modelio original metamodel with content from the deployed extension, thus forming the extended metamodel. Any model that conforms to an extended metamodel can be imported, seen and used in the Modelio environment. The possible dynamic loading/unloading of such metamodel extension modules is currently being evaluated (as impacting more deeply the Modelio application's core).

6   Related Work

We compare here our work with other existing metamodel extension approaches, or solutions that can be applied in this context even if originally designed with a different purpose in mind.

A first group of related work is the one of metamodel evolution approaches. Metamodel evolution consists in supporting metamodel changes and their impact on related models, transformations, etc. An evolution can be perceived as an extension but, in an evolution context, the old (original) metamodel is generally abandoned and all the effort is put on adapting related artifacts to the new metamodel. Several approaches have been proposed to semi-automate the process concerning model migration [17], transformation migration [4] or DSL migration [2]. We aim to avoid these complex migration processes and make the two versions of the metamodel (and related models) coexist.

Metamodel extensions have also been addressed via the the concept of profiles, starting with the case of the well-known UML Profile mechanism [14] or its generalization to an EMF/Ecore context [12]. Following the same underlying principles, (meta)model decoration/annotation approaches [10] have also been used in an extension context, to represent usage-specific information for instance. However, both kinds of approaches have a limited expressivity as they are mainly restricted to adding complementary information or metadata. As presented before, we intend to address a wider range of possible extension operations.

The proposed extension mechanism can be also related to model composition techniques that may present similar operators to manipulate the models to be composed [3,5,7,9,16,18]. Model composition can be defined as the creation of a single model by merging elements coming from several ones [15]. Main problems then concern the synchronization between original and resulting models, as well as scalability issues regarding the needed memory and time to actually perform the merge. In our case, the "new" and "old" models are the same (only the extensions can be kept separated) and therefore our solution does not suffer from these problems.

In addition to these approaches, runtime-oriented solutions have been proposed such as EMF Facet[9] that allows (meta)model extension by runtime

---

[9] http://eclipse.org/facet

instantiation of additional concepts, attributes or references (computed from queries defined at metamodel-level). Nevertheless, EMF Facet can only manage derived information and no new "materialized" data can be part of the extension.

As explained in Section 4, the proposed MoNoGe solution intends to combine the best of different existing approaches. While the extension declaration is actually persisted via a DSL and can include the three main types of extension operations, the extended metamodel and related models are concretely realized by relying on a model virtualization mechanism.

7   Conclusion

We have proposed a lightweight metamodel extension mechanism, based on a textual DSL for specifying metamodel extensions. We have also described two alternative implementations, based on Eclipse/EMF and Modelio respectively, that concretely enable them. Our main objective is to improve the agility of modeling frameworks by allowing them to be more flexible and adaptable to changes on the metamodels they provide support for. The results obtained so far, according to our industrial partners in the MoNoGe project, are quite promising in terms of capabilities such as genericity, compatibility preservation, non-intrusiveness, transparency or dynamicity.

However, the already available DSL and mechanism have to be stressed-out in more contexts. First, we plan to explore with a couple of other concrete syntaxes (including a graphical one) that may be easier to use for some different user profiles. Moreover, some basic validation support for the defined extensions is required, e.g. to make sure that a set of extensions applied on a same metamodel (or extension of metamodel) is coherent. Another interesting aspect would be to build more elaborated metamodel extension algebra(s) by combining the proposed based operators, and to tackle related issues such as complex changes detection [8], consistency management, etc. In addition, the potential use of our extension approach within other already existing EMF-based tools (such as Papyrus for instance) could be explored. We could also provide general feedback to the ongoing OMG MEF standardization process whenever relevant.

Acknowledgments. The presented work is co-funded by the MoNoGe collaborative project (french FUI 15). We would also like to thank Juan David Villa Calle for the important amount of work performed on improving the EMF Views tooling in the past couple of years.

References

1. Clasen, C., Jouault, F., Cabot, J.: VirtualEMF: a model virtualization tool. In: De Troyer, O., Bauzer Medeiros, C., Billen, R., Hallot, P., Simitsis, A., Van Mingroot, H. (eds.) ER Workshops 2011. LNCS, vol. 6999, pp. 332–335. Springer, Heidelberg (2011)
2. Di Ruscio, D., Lämmel, R., Pierantonio, A.: Automated Co-evolution of GMF Editor Models, pp. 143–162 (2010). CoRR,abs/1006.5761

3. Didonet Del Fabro, M., Bézivin, J., Valduriez, P.: Weaving models with the eclipse AMW plugin. In: Eclipse Modeling Symposium, Eclipse Summit Europe (2006)
4. Garcés, K., Vara, J.M., Jouault, F., Marcos, E.: Adapting Transformations to Metamodel Changes via External Transformation Composition. Software & Systems Modeling **13**(2), 789–806 (2014)
5. Heidenreich, F., Henriksson, J., Johannes, J., Zschaler, S.: On language-independent model modularisation. In: Katz, S., Ossher, H., France, R., Jézéquel, J.-M. (eds.) Transactions on Aspect-Oriented Software Development VI. LNCS, vol. 5560, pp. 39–82. Springer, Heidelberg (2009)
6. Hutchinson, J., Rouncefield, M., Whittle, J.: Model-driven engineering practices in industry. In: 33rd ICSE, 2011, pp. 633–642. IEEE, May 2011
7. Jayaraman, P., Whittle, J., Elkhodary, A.M., Gomaa, H.: Model composition in product lines and feature interaction detection using critical pair analysis. In: Engels, G., Opdyke, B., Schmidt, D.C., Weil, F. (eds.) MODELS 2007. LNCS, vol. 4735, pp. 151–165. Springer, Heidelberg (2007)
8. Khelladi, D.E., Hebig, R., Bendraou, R., Robin, J., Gervais, M.-P.: Detecting complex changes during metamodel evolution. In: Zdravkovic, J., Kirikova, M., Johannesson, P. (eds.) CAiSE 2015. LNCS, vol. 9097, pp. 263–278. Springer, Heidelberg (2015)
9. Kolovos, D.S., Paige, R.F., Polack, F.A.C.: Merging models with the epsilon merging language (EML). In: Wang, J., Whittle, J., Harel, D., Reggio, G. (eds.) MoDELS 2006. LNCS, vol. 4199, pp. 215–229. Springer, Heidelberg (2006)
10. Kolovos, D.S., Rose, L.M., Drivalos Matragkas, N., Paige, R.F., Polack, F.A.C., Fernandes, K.J.: Constructing and navigating non-invasive model decorations. In: Tratt, L., Gogolla, M. (eds.) ICMT 2010. LNCS, vol. 6142, pp. 138–152. Springer, Heidelberg (2010)
11. Kusel, A., Etzlstorfer, J., Kapsammer, E., Retschitzegger, W., Schoenboeck, J., Schwinger, W., Wimmer, M.: Systematic Co-evolution of OCL expressions. In: 11th APCCM), vol. 27, p. 30 (2015)
12. Langer, P., Wieland, K., Wimmer, M., Cabot, J.: EMF Profiles: A Lightweight Extension Approach for EMF Models. Journal of Object Technology **11**(1), 1–29 (2012)
13. OMG. Metamodel Extension Facility (MEF) RFP (2011). http://www.omg.org/cgi-bin/doc.cgi?ad/2011-6-22. (Accessed March-2015)
14. OMG. Unified Modeling Language (UML) (2011). http://www.omg.org/spec/UML/2.4.1/. (Accessed March-2015)
15. Pottinger, R.A., Bernstein, P.A.: Merging models based on given correspondences. In: 29th VLDB 2003, pp. 862–873. Morgan Kaufmann, San Fransisco, September 2003
16. Reddy, R., France, R., Ghosh, S., Fleurey, F., Baudry, B.: Model composition - a signature-based approach. In: Aspect Oriented Modeling (AOM) Workshop (2005)
17. Rose, L.M., Herrmannsdoerfer, M., Williams, J.R., Kolovos, D.S., Garcés, K., Paige, R.F., Polack, F.A.C.: A Comparison of model migration tools. In: Petriu, D.C., Rouquette, N., Haugen, Ø. (eds.) MODELS 2010, Part I. LNCS, vol. 6394, pp. 61–75. Springer, Heidelberg (2010)
18. Sabetzadeh, M., Easterbrook, S.: View Merging in the Presence of Incompleteness and Inconsistency. Requirements Engineering **11**(3), 174–193 (2006)
19. Völter, M.: MD*/DSL best practices (version 2.0), April 2011

Type Inference in Flexible Model-Driven Engineering

Athanasios Zolotas[(✉)], Nicholas Matragkas, Sam Devlin,
Dimitrios S. Kolovos, and Richard F. Paige

Department of Computer Science, University of York, York, UK
{amz502,nicholas.matragkas,sam.devlin,dimitris.kolovos,
richard.paige}@york.ac.uk

Abstract. In Model-Driven Engineering (MDE), models conform to metamodels. In *flexible modelling*, engineers construct example models with free-form drawing tools; these examples may later need to conform to a metamodel. Flexible modelling can lead to errors: drawn elements that should represent the same domain concept could instantiate different types; other drawn elements could be left untyped. We propose a novel *type inference* approach to calculating types from example models, based on the Classification and Regression Trees (CART) algorithm. We describe the approach and evaluate it on a number of randomly generated models, considering the accuracy and precision of the resultant classifications. Experimental results suggest that on average 80% of element types are correctly identified. In addition, the results reveal a correlation between the accuracy and the ratio of known-to-unknown types in a model.

1 Introduction

In traditional MDE approaches, engineers build models that conform to (typically pre-defined) metamodels. *Flexible modelling tools* [1,2] seek to combine free-form modelling (e.g., sketching on a whiteboard) and more formal modelling (e.g., modelling with a MDE tool). Flexible modelling tools sacrifice some formality to facilitate exploratory modelling of the domain, but as a result cannot provide the powerful domain-specific editors generated by MDE tools. Flexible modelling is arguably accessible to domain experts, who may sketch elements that represent concepts of a future metamodel; these experts may also assign types to these drawn elements, when they believe it is suitable to do so.

When examples are constructed using flexible modelling tools, there is no guarantee that they will consistently obey syntactic and semantic rules that a rigid metamodel would impose: elements that in traditional MDE would instantiate the same class could have different types assigned by domain experts. This could happen for a variety of reasons:

1. *User input errors:* incorrectly assigning different types to nodes/edges that should have the same type due to typing errors.

© Springer International Publishing Switzerland 2015
G. Taentzer and F. Bordeleau (Eds.): ECMFA 2015, LNCS 9153, pp. 75–91, 2015.
DOI: 10.1007/978-3-319-21151-0_6

2. *Changes:* a domain expert may assign a type to an element, and then later choose to assign a different type to a different instance of the same element.
3. *Inconsistencies:* the participation of multiple experts in building examples could lead to the assignment of different types to elements (nodes/edges) that are conceptually instances of the same type.
4. *Omissions:* for example, if the examples are large, it may be easier to overlook some elements, and not assign them types.

This paper addresses the challenges associated with identifying and managing omissions during type assignment in flexible modelling; such challenges need to be overcome in order to provide support for eventual transition from flexible to more rigorous (metamodel-based) modelling approaches.

There are at least two approaches that can help to address these challenges. The first is to provide a mechanism to validate that all elements drawn on the canvas have exactly one type assigned to them. If not, the domain expert could be prompted to assign missing types and resolve any inconsistencies; a constraint and repair language [3] can be used to support this. However, this approach may force users to make decisions about types when they are not ready to do so. Also, such approaches tend to reveal *all* omissions and inconsistencies at once, and so it can be difficult to find and repair specific problems.

The second alternative is that of *type inference*[4]: missing types could be inferred by computing and analysing matches between untyped and typed elements that share the same characteristics. The benefit of this approach is that users can avoid re-applying the same type to elements that are already defined in the diagram.

This paper contributes a novel approach to type inference for flexible models, allowing types to be calculated from example models using *classification algorithms*, specifically CART [5]. In our approach, the metamodel of the example models is *not* needed to perform the type inference, as it runs on instances only. We present the approach in detail, using an illustrative flexible modelling approach based on GraphML and the flexible modelling technique called *Muddles* [1]. We demonstrate the approach's accuracy, precision and limitations via experiments on a number of randomly generated models. The 80% success rate indicates that fully automated CART-based type derivation shows promise when applied to arbitrary muddles.

2   Related Work

In this section, we present literature from the fields of type or metamodel inference and model matching. Flexible modelling is also briefly summarised. We describe classification algorithms in more detail in Section 4.2.

Type inference has been widely studied in programming languages, particularly for dynamically typed languages. Type inference often relies on the Hindley-Milner [6] [7] algorithm and its extension by Milner and Damas [8]. In these approaches, program statements are reduced to basic constructs for which a type is already known. Such approaches are challenging to apply in flexible modelling where there is no predefined abstract syntax.

Inferring types (or metamodels) from example models boils down to a *matching* problem: elements that are "sufficiently similar" may have similar or identical types. Model matching has been widely studied, particularly to support model differencing and versioning. What is important about much of this work is that different techniques for identifying identical or similar elements have been proposed; a classification was published in [9]. In [10], a model matching technique is used for the generation of traceability links in MDE. Matching is performed by checking the *name similarity* between the data nodes of two attributed graphs (that represent models). Alanen and Porres [11] use each element's unique MOF identifier to calculate the difference and union of models that belong to the same ancestor model; both approaches are of limited flexibility as they depend on names or persistent identifiers for inference. In [12] the authors present a signature-based matching approach that is used for model merging. The signatures are written manually and include the names of the attributes/operations of each element that should be checked when two elements are examined for their similarity in order to be merged.

In the domain of flexible modelling, Cho et al. [13] propose the use of example models to calculate the metamodel in a semi-automatic way. Example drawings, in [14], created by domain experts, are used as the basis for the definition of a metamodel. In [15], a tool for the recovery of the original metamodel that was evolved, using instances models is presented. Finally, in [1], users use a simple drawing tool to define example models which are then amenable to programmatic model management (validation, transformation). To the best of our knowledge, this paper presents the first application of type inference in the domain of flexible modelling; it also is the first application of CART as the predictive mechanism. In addition, in contrast with the methods presented in this section, the matching mechanism is not based on name similarity between the types, the attributes, etc. but on other structural and semantic characteristics, based on the assumption that different domain experts that will express example models to define the same domain may use different names to express the same behaviour.

3   Background: Muddles

In this section, the Muddles [1] flexible modelling approach is presented. We use Muddles to illustrate our approach to inference.

3.1   Overview

In Muddles, drawing editors are used for the construction of example models (in [1] yEd[1] which is based on GraphML is used to prove the concept). Language engineers draw examples and then annotate elements with types and attributes,

---

[1] http://www.yworks.com/en/products_yed_about.html

while also expressing relations (references and containments) between elements using edges and group containers. The annotated diagram is then automatically transformed to an intermediate Muddle (the Muddle metamodel is shown in Figure 1). Using the Epsilon platform [3], muddles can be consumed so that model management programs (e.g. transformations) can be executed against them.

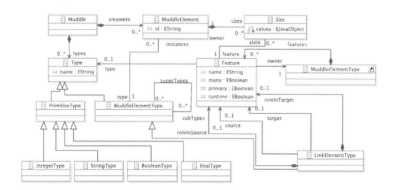

Fig. 1. The Muddle metamodel

3.2 Example

We illustrate "muddling" with an example, creating a language for zoos. The process starts with the creation of an example zoo diagram (see Fig. 2). Next, diagram elements are annotated with basic type information. For instance, one can define the type of the diamond shape as *Doctor* and the type of the directed edges from *Doctor* to *Animal* nodes (circles) as instances of the *cures* relationship. The types are not bound to the shape but to each element, meaning that in another example or even in the same drawing, a diamond can be of type *Doctor* while a different diamond can be of type *Animal*. Types and type-related information like properties (attributes of the type), roles and multiplicity of edges are specified using the appropriate fields in the yEd's custom properties dialog. More details about these properties are presented in [1].

Model management programs use this type-related information to access and manipulate elements of the diagram. For example, if the circle element (typed as *Animal*) has a String attribute named *name* assigned to it, then the following Epsilon Object Language (EOL) [16] script returns the names of all the elements of Type *Animal*. As such, muddles can be programmatically processed like other models, without having to transform them to a more rigorous format (e.g., Ecore).

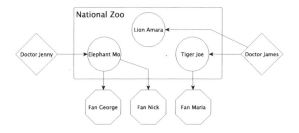

Fig. 2. An example Zoo diagram

4   Type Inference Approach

In this section we describe type inference for flexible models. An overview is shown in Figure 3. The source code for all the algorithms described in Sections 4 and 5 along with detailed instructions can be found at the paper's website[2].

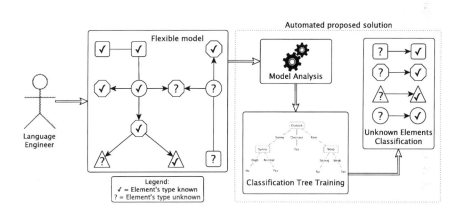

Fig. 3. An overview of the proposed approach

A language engineer constructs a flexible model using a GraphML-compliant drawing tool. The engineer annotates the model with as much type information as they see fit; after this, some elements will have known types, others will have no type. This annotated model is then analysed to extract characteristics of interest, and these characteristics are passed to the CART algorithm, which performs type inference. We now explain this process in more detail.

4.1   Model Analysis and Feature Selection

In order to be able to match untyped element with those that are typed, we first specify a set of characteristics that describe attributes of each element. Each

---

[2] http://www.zolotas.net/type-inference/

characteristic is known as a *feature*; the set of characteristics for each node is a *feature signature*. At the end of the signature, the type of the element (if known) is also attached. In this approach we used a set of five features that are presented in Table 1. These were selected because our intention is to base the similarity measurement and prediction on structural and semantic characteristics of the models; arguably these features measure these characteristics. As mentioned in Section 2, the names that domain experts use to express the same behaviour may vary, and our feature selection was based on this. However, we need to highlight that we do not claim that the names should be totally ignored as they can carry useful information. Methodologies proposed in Section 2 which base their similarity measurement on name matching could be combined with the approach we propose and possibly improve the prediction results. Plans for this combination are described in Section 7.

Table 1. Signature features for nodes

Name of Feature	Description
Number of Attributes	The number of attributes that the node has.
Number of different types of incoming references	The number of all the types of references that target that node. If a node is targeted by more than one references of the same type, only 1 instance of them is taken into account (unique references).
Number of different types of outgoing references	The number of all the types of references that come from that node. As above, multiple outgoing references of the same type are counted once.
Number of different types of children	The number of all the unique types that the node contains. Multiple contained elements of the same type are counted once.
Number of different types of parents	The number of all the types that the node is contained in.

The example muddle shown in Figure 4(b)) is conceptual instance of the example metamodel shown in Figure 4(a)). The feature signature of the node "aZoo" is [2,0,0,1,0,Zoo], as it has 2 attributes, no incoming or outgoing references, 2 children which are of the same type (so 1 unique child) and 0 parents. The 6th position of the signature declares the type of the element, which is useful for training the classification algorithm that will be used. Similarly, the feature signature of the node "anAnimal1" is [3,2,1,0,1,Animal] as it has 3 attributes, 2 unique outgoing references (partner and fans), 1 unique incoming reference (partner), 0 children and 1 parent. Its class is Animal. Note here that although the Animal class in the metamodel has a reference named "cures" of * multiplicity, it is not added to the signature of the "anAnimal1" element as it is not instantiated in the model. This means that two entities of the same type may have different signatures. For instance, the signature of the element "anAnimal2" is [3,1,2,0,1,Animal]. This justifies the choice of using a classification algorithm to perform the matching. Classification algorithms do not look for perfect matches but are trained to classify elements by using each time those features that are

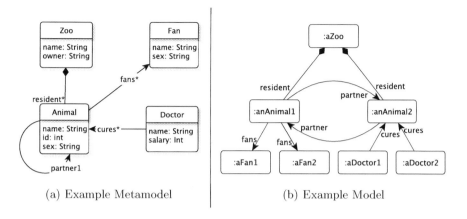

(a) Example Metamodel   (b) Example Model

Fig. 4. Signature Example

most important in the specific set they are trained on, increasing the possibilities of identifying true positives even if two elements are not identical.

A simple querying algorithm was implemented as part of this approach. The algorithm parses each of the nodes in the drawing and constructs its feature signature. All the feature signatures for the elements in which the type is known are stored in a text file that will be used to train the classification algorithm.

4.2   Training and Classification

Classification algorithms are a form of supervised machine learning for finding hypotheses that approximate functions mapping input features to a discrete output class from a finite set of possible values. They require a training dataset with labelled examples of the output class to process, after which they can generalise from the previous examples to new unseen instances.

Many classification algorithms exist, some of the most established being decision trees, random forests, support vector machines and neural networks [17]. For this work we chose to use decision trees due to the interpretable output representing the hypothesis learnt. In practice other classification algorithms can often have higher accuracy, but will produce a hypothesis in a form that is not human readable. Given the high accuracy of classification achieved using decision trees in this application, these other algorithms were not deployed in favour of the aid to debugging provided by being able to interpret how the learnt hypothesis would classify future instances. Specifically, we used the rpart package (version 4.1-9)[3] that implements the functionality of Classification and Regression Trees (CART) [5] in R[4].

---

[3] http://cran.r-project.org/web/packages/rpart/index.html
[4] http://www.r-project.org/

An example decision tree is illustrated in Figure 5. Internal nodes represent features (e.g. Number of Attributes, Parents, etc.), branches are labelled with values of the parent node and leaf nodes represent the final classification given. To classify a new instance, start at the root of the tree and consider the feature specified and take the branch that represents the value of that feature in the new instance. Continue to process each internal node reached in the same manner until a leaf node is reached where the predicted classification of the new instance is the value of that leaf node. For example, given the tree in Fig. 5, a new instance with less than 3 attributes and 1 unique children would be classified as Zoo (path is highlighted in Fig. 5).

The success of a classification algorithm can be evaluated by the accuracy of the resultant model (e.g. the decision tree learnt by CART) on test data not used when training. The accuracy of a model is the sum of true positives and negatives (i.e. all correctly classified instances) divided by the total number of instances in the test set. A single measure of accuracy can be artificially inflated due to the learnt model overfitting bias in the dataset used for training. To overcome this k-fold classification can be implemented [18]. This approach repeats the process of training the model and testing the accuracy k times each time with a different split of the data into training and test data sets. The final accuracy using this method is then the mean value generated from the k repeats.

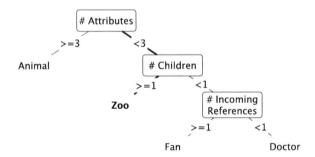

Fig. 5. Example Decision Tree

In our approach, the feature signatures list that contains the signatures of the known elements of the model are the input features to the CART algorithm. A trained decision tree is produced. This tree can be used to classify (identify the type of) the untyped nodes using their feature signatures.

5   Experiment

In this section, we present the experimentation process that was used to evaluate the proposed approach. An overview of the experiment is shown in Figure 6. Details about each step follow.

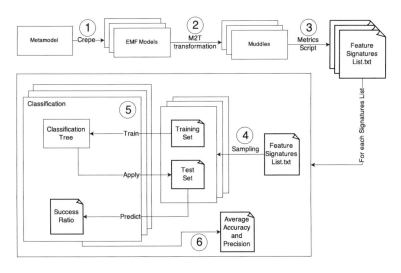

Fig. 6. The experimentation process

In order to carry out an evaluation we applied our approach to a number of publicly available metamodels that were collected as part of the work presented in [19]. For each of these metamodels we produced 10 random instances using the Crepe model generator tool [20] (step ① in Figure 6). Crepe generates random models that conform to the provided metamodel, using a genetic algorithm. For our approach, the values that were assigned to the attributes of the instance models were randomly selected, as the content of the attributes does not affect the final feature signature of the element. We address any threats to validity of using randomly generated models in Section 6.3.

Having the experimentation models generated, we had to transform them into muddles and then randomly erase the types of some of them in order to simulate a real scenario where some node types are known while others are not. For that purpose, a Model-to-Text (M2T) transformation was implemented that transforms instances of Ecore metamodels to GraphML files that conform to the Muddles metamodel (step ②).

Steps ① and ② could be avoided either by directly using available muddles or by drawing muddles on our own. The first solution was rejected because flexible modelling approaches are quite new and there is not a repository/zoo available that hosts such flexible models. The second was also rejected because it would be a time consuming process but more importantly it could introduce bias to the process. We decided to follow the 2-step process instead firstly because we would be able to have a bigger number of test muddles and secondly because these muddles are randomly generated and are not biased to fit our approach.

After generating the muddles we are now able to extract the feature signature of each node. As mentioned in Section 3, each muddle conforms to the metamodel shown in Figure 1. Building atop the Epsilon EMC driver (see Section 3) we developed a script that iterates through all the nodes of the graph stored in the GraphML file and collects the information needed for each node: the number of attributes, unique outgoing and incoming references, children and parents. This information is encoded in the comma-separated format presented in Section 4.1 producing one list for each model that contains the feature signatures of the nodes of this model (step ③).

At this point the types of all the nodes are known to us and saved in the features signatures list. In order to test the performance of the approach, we need to simulate the scenario where some nodes in a model are left without a type. To simulate this we perform the k-fold cross-validation described in Section 4.2. Each feature signature list is split into two parts, the training and the test set (step ④). The first set contains the feature signatures of the nodes that will be used to train the CART algorithm. This set can be thought as the set that contains all the nodes of which the type is known in the hypothetical scenario where not all the nodes have types assigned to them. The second set contains the elements that will perform the role of the nodes of which the type is not known and will be used to evaluate the accuracy of the trained CART tree. In reality the types are known, but are ignored during the prediction process and are only used at the end, to identify if the predictions were correct. The standard 10-Fold cross-validation will be used in our study: each feature signatures list will be split 10 times to produce 10 different couples of training and test sets. Each time, one training set will be used to train the algorithm and its coupling test set will evaluate its success (step ⑤). The success ratio (also referred as accuracy) is defined as the total number of correct predictions to the total number of nodes with missing type. The precision of the algorithm incorrectly predicting each type is also calculated. The precision is defined as the number of true positives divided by the sum of the true and false positive predictions for this class. [21] The algorithm is then reset and is trained and evaluated with the next couple of training and test sets, respectively. At the end the average accuracy and precision are calculated (step ⑥).

The size of the training and the test set may be important in the algorithm success. We perform the same process for 7 different sampling rates: 30%, 40%, 50%, 60%, 70%, 80% and 90%. For example, in the 80% sampling experiment, 80% of the nodes are placed in the training set and the rest 20% in the test set. The sampling, the training and the prediction are carried out in R using the RPart library for the classification. Custom-made scripts were implemented to automate the calculations of the accuracy, its average values and the precision for each type.

6   Results and Discussion

Before discussing the results, we present data on the random generated models that were used in the experimentation process (see Table 2). The smallest metamodel, a toy example, comprises only 2 types. The largest metamodel is

Table 2. Data summary table

Model Name	#Types	Min	Max	Average #Elements in instances
Chess	2	17	26	21.3
Professor	4	25	36	29.2
Conference	4	30	61	42.5
Zoo	5	47	73	57
Ant	6	53	78	65.3
Use Case	6	35	71	54.2
Bugzilla	7	21	56	39.9
BibTeX	8	56	106	78.8
Cobol	11	33	92	63.7
Wordpress	19	42	71	58.6
Muddle	20	105	105	105

the one that is used to describe Wordpress Content Management System websites (taken from [19]) with 19 different types of classes. On average the test metamodels had 7.2 types with a median of 6. These numbers do not include abstract classes but only those that could be instantiated in the random models. For each metamodel, 10 models were instantiated each of which was of a different size. The size of the smallest (Min) and the largest (Max) instance model for each metamodel is shown in Table 2. The average number of elements for the instances of each metamodel are also given. We also provide the values for a muddle drawing we examined. This muddle was part of a side project and was created before commencing this work. It was used to describe requirements of a hotel booking system. We only provide this muddle as an indication that the performance of the algorithm on the random generated muddles from Ecore metamodels does not differ from the that of applying it to real muddles. All raw data, results and charts can be found at the paper's website[5].

6.1 Quantitative Analysis

As discussed in the previous section, 10 random models were instantiated from each of the 10 metamodels. Seven different sampling rates were applied to each of these models and the CART was run 10 times (10-fold) for each sampling rate of each model. That sums up to 700 experiments for each of the 10 metamodels (7,000 runs in total). A summary of the results is presented in Table 3. In the table, we also include the calculated values for the muddle drawing. However, we do not include it in the results' analysis as we have only one instance available in contrast with the 10 random instances of the other metamodels and thus not the variability needed to extract safe conclusions from it.

In Table 3, one can see the average accuracy for all the models of each metamodel split into columns based on the sampling rate that was used each

---

[5] http://www.zolotas.net/type-inference/

Table 3. Results summary table

Model Name	#Types	Average Success Ratio (Accuracy) for Different Sampling Rates							Avg.	Corel. 1
		30%	40%	50%	60%	70%	80%	90%		
Chess	2	1.00	1.00	1.00	1.00	1.00	1.00	1.00	1.000	-
Professor	4	0.96	0.97	0.98	0.98	0.98	1.00	0.99	0.980	0.90
Conference	4	0.87	0.92	0.95	0.97	0.98	0.99	0.98	0.951	0.90
Zoo	5	0.95	0.98	0.99	1.00	1.00	1.00	1.00	0.989	0.83
Ant Scripts	6	0.69	0.72	0.74	0.74	0.76	0.75	0.77	0.739	0.92
Use Case	6	0.75	0.78	0.79	0.8	**0.81**	0.79	0.81	0.790	0.82
Bugzilla	7	0.47	0.52	0.54	0.56	0.56	0.58	0.54	0.539	0.75
BibTeX	8	0.66	0.67	0.68	0.67	0.66	0.68	0.69	0.673	0.62
Cobol	11	0.53	0.59	0.62	0.65	0.66	0.67	0.67	0.627	0.92
Wordpress	19	0.44	0.51	0.61	0.66	0.72	0.74	0.77	0.636	0.98
Muddle	*20*	*0.55*	*0.56*	*0.59*	*0.65*	*0.59*	*0.67*	*0.64*	*0.607*	*0.82*
Avg.		0.732	0.766	0.790	0.803	0.813	0.82	0.822		0.94
Corel. 2		-0.80	-0.78	-0.70	-0.65	-0.57	-0.55	-0.49	-0.67	
Corel. 3		0.77	0.72	0.64	0.58	0.53	0.49	0.45		

time. For instance, the highlighted value **0.81** indicates that on average, 81% of the missing types were successfully predicted for the 10 instance models of the Use Case motamodel, using 70% sampling rate.

Considering the raw values, there are some cases where even with small sampling rates (30%, 40%) all of the missing elements' types were successfully identified. More specifically, for smaller models (that were produced from metamodels with fewer than 5 types) the average success ratio was above 98.9% (between all the 7 different sampling rates). For metamodels with more types (> 6), that average dropped to between 53.9% and 79%. However, these values are affected by the fact that in the relatively large metamodels, the prediction scores are lower in small sampling rates, but they keep increasing as the sampling rate (which equals to the amount of knowledge that the CART algorithm is trained with) is increased.

This observation leads us to two interesting questions, shown under the column labeled *Corel. 1* and the row labeled *Corel. 2*. Below are the definition of these correlations.

Corel. 1: How strong is the dependency between the sampling rate and the success score?

Corel. 2: How strong is the dependency between the number of types in a metamodel (size of metamodel) and the success score?

As expected, the correlation coefficient values for Corel. 1 indicate a strong or perfect dependency for all the metamodels, except one (BibTeX). The correlation coefficient value on the averages of the accuracy for the different sampling rates is also strong (0.94). This means that prediction scores increase as training sets become larger. Regarding the second correlation (Corel. 2) we observe a strong (negative) correlation between the number of types in a metamodel and the success score when the sampling rate is lower than 50%. The correlation becomes moderate or weak when the sampling rate is larger than 60%. The outcome from this observation is that when a drawing is left heavily untyped (less than half of the elements are having a type assigned to them) the success score is affected by the number of the different types in the drawing: fewer types lead to better results. In contrast, if the drawing has more information (more than 60% of the nodes have a type assigned to them) then the number of the types of the envisioned metamodel doesn't affect the prediction performance.

The above metrics take only into account the sampling rate. However, it is of interest to check if the frequency that each type appears to a drawing, increases the prediction performance of the algorithm. We define frequency as the ratio of the total number of different types to the total number of elements in the drawn model. The results are shown in Table 3 (row labelled as *Corel. 3*) while the definition of this correlation is the following.

Corel. 3: How strong is the dependency between the frequency with which a type appears in a drawing and the success score?

Analysing the results, we are led to the same conclusions as with Corel. 2: For low sampling rates ($< 50\%$), the frequency with which a type appears in a drawing strongly affects its correct prediction chances. If the sampling rate increases, this relation no longer exists (or is moderate).

Finally, we analysed the precision of the classifications. Precision is interpreted as the certainty in predicting each specific class. Its values vary from 0 (the algorithm never predicted correctly this specific type) to 1 (the algorithm always predicted correctly this type). The calculation of the precision scores could be of value in our prediction mechanism because one could initially perform a simulation of the prediction in the set that contains all the known types by splitting it into a new training set and a new test set, running the CART algorithm and calculating the precision value for each type based on this simulated training. Then proceed by re-training the CART on the whole original training set and predict the types of the nodes originally left untyped. If a node is predicted to be of a type that in the previously described simulation had a high precision, then assign the type automatically. If the predicted type scores a very low precision value, then suggest the type for the node but mark this as an assignment that needs manual reviewing by the domain expert (semi-automatic assignment).

6.2   Qualitative Analysis

In order to better understand the quantitative results and expose useful information on how to improve the performance of the approach we examined the results from a qualitative perspective, too. Our goal was to identify common patterns and characteristics, if any, in metamodels, where the performance of the approach was lower. Taking a closer look at all the experimental results of the Bugzilla metamodel we identified that all incorrect predictions occurred between types that extend the same abstract class. More specifically, the 4 types (Keywords, DependsOn, Cc, Blocks) that extend the same class named "StringElt" were all identified as being of the same type: the one with the greatest presence in the training data. Looking at the metamodel, these 4 classes had no attributes, references or containment relations assigned to them which is a type of structure, modelling inheritance [22] with no concrete differentiating characteristics.

The same behaviour was also discovered in the BibTeX metamodel. More specifically, wrong predictions occurred between types that were extending the same class but their differentiating point was that they both had an extra attribute than the parent class. The same issue occurred between classes that had the same grandparent, where their parents had no differentiating characteristics.

Such a behaviour is expected as the elements that belong to the category described above, share the same characteristics that inherit from their ancestors. In addition, they do not have any of their own specific characteristics (Bugzilla scenario) or they have the same feature which differs (e.g. both have an extra attribute as in the Bibtex scenario). This means that these elements share exactly the same features signature. A way to tackle such a behaviour could be the introduction of other features which are not calculated based on semantic characteristics that are always the same in such situations. Ideas on the introduction of new features that could solve this problem are discussed in Section 7. However, having such a behaviour might be of interest if the goal is not restricted to type inference but is extended to metamodel inference. CART supports the functionality of collecting such entities that share enough common characteristics but are of different type in the same "bucket". This could also serve in tackling problems 1-3 identified in Section 1.

6.3   Threats to Validity

In the experimentation process the data for testing the performance of the proposed approach was generated using a random model generator. There are two issues with this. The first is that we are using models (that conform to a metamodel) and not *muddles*, to run the experiments. This was done for largely pragmatic reasons: we have an efficient model generator available; no muddle generator currently exists; and we wanted to evaluate the feasibility of using the CART-based approach for type inference first, before carrying out more detailed experiments on user-created flexible models. We do not believe that the use of models instead of muddles will have significant impact on the experimental results, because the accuracy of our classification algorithm depends only on the features identified in Table 1; randomly generated models and muddles will not be observably different in terms of these features. To support this argument, we ran the prediction on a real muddle and the results suggest that the performance of the predictions is not affected by this fact. However, other user-defined models and muddles *may* differ - and as such our future work will involve conducting experiments with more user-created muddles.

A second issue in using this generator is that although it generates random models, the number of attributes that each node has is always the same for nodes of the same type. However, this does not work in favour of our approach, because in cases where two different types have the same number of attributes, all instances will have the same value in the attributes feature in their signature. A work-around for this would be the implementation of a post-generation script that would randomly delete attributes from the elements to make sure that different instances will not always have the same number of attributes.

Ten metamodels were used in total to generate testing models. These ten metamodels were picked randomly from a set of 500 metamodels and the number of different concrete types in each of them varied from 2 up to 19. It would be of interest to apply the approach to even larger metamodels, although our experience (extracted from experimenting with the real muddle provided in this paper) suggests that having a flexible model with more than 20 different types is marginal and is not a terribly realistic scenario – generally, language engineers switch to more formal metamodelling infrastructure for larger languages. The number of instances for each metamodel and the number of repeats (700 runs for each metamodel) that the experiment was run on each of them is sufficient as it complies with the standard 10-fold methodology used in the domain of classification algorithms.

7 Conclusions and Future Work

We have proposed and evaluated an approach to support type inference for flexible modelling, thus contributing towards making it easier to transition from (untyped) example models to MDE models. More specifically, we have presented a type inference approach to flexible modelling based on CART. The CART algorithm is trained with elements that have been typed (e.g., by domain experts), in order to predict the types of the elements that have been left untyped. Experiments suggest that the average prediction success ratio was 80% of the elements between all the generated models. A positive correlation between the ratio of known to unknown elements with the success score was also identified, along with a threshold in sampling after which the success score is not affected by the number of total types in the tested model.

The approach is intended to be used to support flexible modelling, where examples can be created in ways that are not restricted by metamodels. However, it could be applied directly to traditional MDE: the CART algorithm could be used, for example, to infer types from an already-typed model, which may potentially reveal poor or incorrect type assignments or misuses of the metamodel.

In the future, we plan to introduce and test additional features that could be used to characterise the nodes other than the five that we used in this paper. These new features are inspired by the fact that in flexible modelling there may be spatial and graphical characteristics that could be useful – for example, the shape of the nodes, their size or their color, or the semantics that these characteristics denote [23]. In essence, we will experiment with the extent to which concrete syntax information can be used to further enrich the CART classification. In addition, the names that the domain experts choose to assign to the semantic characteristics could also be assessed to improve the predictions (e.g.

the name of the attributes of each class). As mentioned, we base this work on the assumption that domain experts may use different naming conventions to express the same behaviour however we could overcome this by assigning custom weight to the importance of name-matching feature: if the examples are generated by a lot of different people then decrease the impact of the name matching in the prediction; if they are generated by a few then increase it. Of interest is the calculation of the level of importance of each feature (those used in this approach and those proposed in this last paragraph) in the classification decision. This will help us identify a set of features that maximises the classification performance and thus discard those that do not offer any valuable information to the algorithm or even reduce its performance.

Acknowledgments. This work was carried out in cooperation with Digital Lightspeed Solutions Ltd, and was supported by the EPSRC through the LSCITS initiative and part supported by the EU, through the MONDO FP7 STREP project (#611125).

References

1. Kolovos, D.S., Matragkas, N., Rodríguez, H.H., Paige, R.F.: Programmatic muddle management. In: XM 2013-Extreme Modeling Workshop, p. 2 (2013)
2. Gabrysiak, G., Giese, H., Lüders, A., Seibel, A.: How can metamodels be used flexibly. In: Proceedings of ICSE 2011 Workshop on Flexible Modeling Tools, Waikiki/Honolulu, vol. 22. (2011)
3. Paige, R.F., Kolovos, D.S., Rose, L.M., Drivalos, N., Polack, F.A.: The design of a conceptual framework and technical infrastructure for model management language engineering. In: 2009 14th IEEE International Conference on Engineering of Complex Computer Systems, pp. 162–171. IEEE (2009)
4. Mitchell, J.C.: Concepts in programming languages. Cambridge University Press (2003)
5. Breiman, L., Friedman, J., Stone, C.J., Olshen, R.A.: Classification and regression trees. CRC Press (1984)
6. Hindley, R.: The principal type-scheme of an object in combinatory logic. Transactions of the american mathematical society, 29–60 (1969)
7. Milner, R.: A theory of type polymorphism in programming. Journal of computer and system sciences **17**(3), 348–375 (1978)
8. Damas, L., Milner, R.: Principal type-schemes for functional programs. In: Proceedings of the 9th ACM SIGPLAN-SIGACT Symposium on Principles of Programming Languages, pp. 207–212. ACM (1982)
9. Kolovos, D.S., Di Ruscio, D., Pierantonio, A., Paige, R.F.: Different models for model matching: an analysis of approaches to support model differencing. In: Proceedings of the 2009 ICSE Workshop on Comparison and Versioning of Software Models, CVSM 2009, pp. 1–6. IEEE Computer Society, Washington, DC (2009)
10. Grammel, B., Kastenholz, S., Voigt, K.: Model matching for trace link generation in model-driven software development. In: France, R.B., Kazmeier, J., Breu, R., Atkinson, C. (eds.) MODELS 2012. LNCS, vol. 7590, pp. 609–625. Springer, Heidelberg (2012)
11. Alanen, M., Porres, I.: Difference and union of models. In: Stevens, P., Whittle, J., Booch, G. (eds.) UML 2003. LNCS, vol. 2863, pp. 2–17. Springer, Heidelberg (2003)

12. Reddy, R., France, R., Ghosh, S., Fleurey, F., Baudry, B.: Model composition-a signature-based approach. In: Aspect Oriented Modeling (AOM) Workshop (2005)
13. Cho, H., Gray, J., Syriani, E.: Creating visual domain-specific modeling languages from end-user demonstration. In: 2012 ICSE Workshop on Modeling in Software Engineering (MISE), pp. 22–28. IEEE (2012)
14. Sánchez-Cuadrado, J., de Lara, J., Guerra, E.: Bottom-up meta-modelling: an interactive approach. In: France, R.B., Kazmeier, J., Breu, R., Atkinson, C. (eds.) MODELS 2012. LNCS, vol. 7590, pp. 3–19. Springer, Heidelberg (2012)
15. Javed, F., Mernik, M., Gray, J., Bryant, B.R.: Mars: A metamodel recovery system using grammar inference. Information and Software Technology **50**(9), 948–968 (2008)
16. Kolovos, D.S., Paige, R.F., Polack, F.A.C.: The epsilon object language (EOL). In: Rensink, A., Warmer, J. (eds.) ECMDA-FA 2006. LNCS, vol. 4066, pp. 128–142. Springer, Heidelberg (2006)
17. Jiawei, H., Kamber, M.: Data mining: concepts and techniques. Morgan Kaufmann, San Francisco (2001)
18. Mitchell, T.M.: Machine learning, vol. 45. McGraw Hill, Burr Ridge (1997)
19. Williams, J.R., Zolotas, A., Matragkas, N.D., Rose, L.M., Kolovos, D.S., Paige, R.F., Polack, F.A.: What do metamodels really look like? Eessmod@ Models **1078**, 55–60 (2013)
20. Williams, J.R., Paige, R.F., Kolovos, D.S., Polack, F.A.: Search-based model driven engineering. Technical report, Technical Report YCS-2012-475, Department of Computer Science, University of York (2012)
21. Powers, D.: Evaluation: From precision, recall and f-factor to roc, informedness, markedness & correlation (tech. rep.). Adelaide, Australia (2007)
22. Meyer, B.: Object-oriented software construction, vol. 2. Prentice hall, New York (1988)
23. Zolotas, A., Kolovos, D.S., Matragkas, N., Paige, R.F.: Assigning semantics to graphical concrete syntaxes. In: XM 2014-Extreme Modeling Workshop, p. 12

AspectOCL: Extending OCL
for Crosscutting Constraints

Muhammad Uzair Khan[1(✉)], Numra Arshad[1], Muhammad Zohaib Iqbal[1,2],
and Hafsa Umar[1]

[1] Software Quality Engineering and Testing Lab (QUEST),
National University of Computer and Emerging Science, Islamabad, Pakistan
{uzair.khan,zohaib.iqbal,hafsa.umar}@nu.edu.pk,
numra.arshad@questlab.pk
[2] Software Verification and Validation Lab, Interdisciplinary
Centre for Security, Reliability and Trust, Luxembourg, Luxembourg

Abstract. Constraints play an important role in Model Driven Software Engineering. Industrial systems commonly exhibit crosscutting behaviors in design artifacts. While modeling of crosscutting behaviors has been addressed in literature, the modeling of crosscutting constraints remains a problem. Presence of crosscutting constraints makes it difficult to maintain constraints defined on the models of large-scale industrial systems. Multiple elements in a model may share common crosscutting constraints with minor variation. Aspect orientation is well-established approach to model crosscutting behavior. Current OCL specification does not support writing crosscutting constraints separately as aspects. In this paper, we propose an extension of OCL language that brings benefits of aspect orientation to OCL constraints. In our language, crosscutting constraints are specified as aspects, which can be woven in OCL constraints. We demonstrate our proposed language through application on a published open source case study. Results show that specifying crosscutting constraints as aspects can reduce the number of constraints to be specified.

Keywords: Model driven software engineering · Crosscutting constraints · Object constraint language · Aspect orientation · Unified modeling language

1   Introduction

Constraints play an important role in Model Driven Software Engineering (MDSE) [1, 2]. When used with UML models, they enable the models to be complete, consistent and precise by providing information about models that cannot otherwise be incorporated [3]. Object Constraint Language (OCL) [3, 4] is the OMG standard language for specifying constraints on models. OCL is being gradually adopted in industry and is used in an increasing number of large-scale industrial projects [5-7]. Constraints modeled in OCL are applied across a range of design artifacts and models for representing the system. Similar to crosscutting behaviors we can have crosscutting

© Springer International Publishing Switzerland 2015
G. Taentzer and F. Bordeleau (Eds.): ECMFA 2015, LNCS 9153, pp. 92–107, 2015.
DOI: 10.1007/978-3-319-21151-0_7

constraints [7, 8]. It is entirely possible for different modeling elements to share common constraints. This results in the same constraint to be specified multiple times in the constraints part of design artifacts often with minor variations. The problem of crosscutting behaviors has been extensively explored in literature. Crosscutting behaviors make the design artifacts difficult to understand and hard to maintain [9, 10]. Aspect orientation [11-13] is considered a well-established solution to modeling and implementing crosscutting behaviors in design models and the underlying implementation. Research has shown that while aspect-orientation adds overhead in terms of identifying crosscutting behaviors and weaving them in the underlying artifacts, it makes the artifacts significantly easier to understand and maintain [10, 14].

This work is motivated in part from our experience of working with large-scale industrial systems [15, 16] featuring crosscutting behaviors. In our previous work, we addressed the problem of crosscutting behaviors in design models, in particular the UML state machines. However, in addition to crosscutting behavior, we also encountered crosscutting constraints in these systems. A number of research efforts have targeted the modeling of crosscutting behaviors [16, 17] but modeling of crosscutting constraints is not sufficiently explored. The few existing approaches either introduce new constraint languages that have little to no industrial acceptance or are incompatible with OCL. Our work focuses on modeling of crosscutting constraints.

In this paper, we propose an extension to OCL through AspectOCL language that allows modeling of crosscutting constraints as aspects. Our approach is a forward engineering approach and the crosscutting constraints can be identified and written as aspects at design time. The rest of the constraints are specified as per normal practice in OCL. A weaver is used to weave the crosscutting constraints (written as aspects) in the OCL constraints. OCL is supported by a number of tools and APIs [18] and maintaining compatibility with the existing toolset is an important consideration [15]. Unlike some other approaches to handling crosscutting constraints [7], our approach maintains compatibility with existing tools and APIs by requiring the weaver to produce standard OCL as output of the weaving process. Therefore existing tools and APIs that support OCL can be used with weaved constraints.

Our main contributions in this paper are: (i) an extension of OCL to support modeling of crosscutting constraints. We present the proposed language constructs and demonstrate their application; (ii) we use the proposed language to model crosscutting constraints identified from a publicly available case study EU-Rental [19]. The case study has been widely used as a benchmark for model-driven software engineering and OCL [20-22]. We demonstrate that the proposed language shows a lot of promise and can potentially reduce the constraint modeling effort by requiring fewer constraints to be written. We also provide an editor built on eclipse Xtext [23] open source framework for our language. This allows our editor to be easily integrated to modeling tools built on eclipse platform such as IBM RSA and Papyrus.

The rest of the paper is organized as follows: Section 2 presents related work and positions our work in relation of existing literature. Section 3 presents our proposed language extension of OCL for modeling crosscutting constraints. Section 4 demonstrates our language by modeling cross cutting constraints from a published case study and presents the limitations of our approach. Section 5 concludes the paper.

2   Related Work

Constraints specification languages are an active area of research. In this section we discuss the works reported in literature that provide support for modeling crosscutting constraints or that extend OCL to add new features.

Application of aspect orientation on various design and code artifacts to address crosscutting behavior is well established [15, 16, 24]. Authors in [25] have used aspect oriented techniques for monitoring level of abstraction in software by developing a UML based specification environment for validating software against the design constraints specified in OCL. A number of OCL extensions have been suggested over the years (e.g.,[26, 27]). OCLR [26] is an extension of OCL that augments the standard OCL by adding support for temporal constraints. MOF Query Language (MQL) [27] extends OCL to support queries on MOF (Meta Object Facility) based models. All the mentioned works have extended OCL to support features that cannot be easily supported using OCL. However, such additions make the language non-compatible with existing tools and APIs. In contrast, we provide an extension to OCL language to reduce the effort required for specifying and maintaining OCL constraints by reducing the number of constraint to be written.

The Model Constraint and Query Language (MOCQL) [28]   is developed to model constraints and to define queries on underlying UML models. Empirical evaluation is presented to show that MOCQL is easier to understand than OCL. Similar efforts to improve the OCL syntax have been made in OCL/P [29]. One limitation of the presented works is lack of empirical evidence regarding adoption of these languages in industry. Neither work addresses crosscutting constraints. The work by Laszlo *et al* [8], presents a somewhat similar concept of modeling crosscutting concerns using aspects. However the work is focused on handling crosscutting constraints in meta-model based transformations. The representation of constraint as aspect contains both the constraints written in OCL and the meta-model elements on which the constraints are to be applied. On the other hand, we propose a generic aspect oriented extension to OCL where the aspects have textual representation similar to OCL constraints. Authors in [30] presents a UML profile for modeling crosscutting behavior and constraints. However, the presented work does not support separating crosscutting constraints from base OCL constraint and writing them separately as aspects. Embedded Constraint Language (ECL) [7] supports writing crosscutting constraints as aspects. The proposed language however uses underlying model elements as joinpoints and therefore cannot support complex crosscutting constraints, e.g., constraints that must be weaved in other OCL constraints. Also, constraints specification languages not based on OCL have little acceptance by the industry.

To summarize, large-scale systems contain crosscutting behaviors as well as crosscutting constraints. There is a lack of approaches in literature for modeling crosscutting constraints. In this paper, we propose a new modeling language that extends OCL to support writing of crosscutting constraints. We present the language constructs and demonstrate its applicability by using it to model crosscutting constraints identified from a published open source case study. Results indicate that our language shows a lot of promise and can reduce the number of constraints to be written by separating out crosscutting constraints as aspects. However, the overall reduction in effort depends on the nature and the number of crosscutting constraints.

3   AspectOCL

MDSE has been successfully applied to solve a number of industry problems ranging from automated code generation [31], automated test data generation [32] to model driven refactoring [16]. Constraints play an important role in MDSE. In this section, we present the AspectOCL language that extends OCL to support crosscutting constraints. We present the language constructs, its syntax and a number of examples to show how the various constructs are utilized to model crosscutting constraints.

3.1   Language Constructs

Defining an aspect-oriented language requires definition of some basic aspect oriented concepts such as *joinpoint(s), pointcut, advice* and *introduction* [12]. In the following we describe these basic constructs along with other important elements of the language and show their usage. The language constructs identified for AspectOCL are partly inspired from other aspect-oriented languages such as AspectJ [12]. Therefore we define common aspect oriented constructs such as joinpoints, pointcuts, advice, introduction, etc. The grammar for defining an aspect (an important part of the language) is given in Appendix.

Joinpoint. In aspect oriented programming, joinpoint(s) are locations in a program where an *advice* is to be inserted [11, 12]. In order to write aspects and weave them on OCL constraints, we must first identify well-defined locations in OCL constraints where we can insert (weave) the crosscutting constraint(s). We identify language constructs that can be uniquely identified in a given OCL constraint, and use them as joinpoints. Table 1 describes our identified joinpoints in OCL constraints. Together, these joinpoints act as weaving points in OCL constraint where we may add (or append) a new constraint. A *pointcut* selects one or more of these joinpoints.

Pointcut. In an aspect-oriented language, a pointcut selects one or more joinpoints where an *advice* (also a constraint in our case) is to be applied. In simple terms, a pointcut works as a selection query, selecting one or more joinpoints. For AspectOCL, we define the following (simplified) outline for a pointcut in Fig. 1.

Table 1. Joinpoints in AspectOCL

Joinpoint	Description
<Classname>	Using class name as a joinpoint allows specifying aspect constraints on instances of class, for example, restricting number of instances for a particular class
select	*select* is used to pick a specific subset of data from a collection
reject	*reject* is used to select the elements from a collection for which the expression evaluates to false
collect	*collect* is used to hold the values generated as a result of performing computation on every element of a collection
forall	*forall* is used to specify a condition that must be hold true for all the elements of a collection. This construct allows us to traverse collections in OCL
orderby	*orderby* is used to arrange the elements of a collection in an ascending or descending order
isUnique	*isUnique* specifies that each element in a collection should have a different value for an expression
exists	*exists* specify that at least one element of collection must meet the specified condition
if-else statements	All conditional OCL expressions of type *if*, *if- else*, and *if- then* are also joinpoints in AspectOCL

```
pointcut <name>:
context <name of class or method>
<Pointcut Expression>
<introduction | advice>
```

Fig. 1. Syntax of a Pointcut

We define a syntax that closely resembles the OCL syntax to gain maximum benefit of designer's familiarity with OCL. The context keyword selects a class or a method from which joinpoints are selected through the pointcut expression.

Advice. Advice determines how the cross cutting constraint is weaved at the join-point(s) selected by the pointcut. In AspectOCL we can either use *advice* or *introduction* to insert a crosscutting constraint. We use an advice when some constraint is already specified at the joinpoint. The common aspect oriented advices such as *before*, *after* and *around* found in languages like AspectJ [12] do not apply in case of AspectOCL. In case of constraints the entire constraint must hold true, i.e., the order in a given constraint is not important in this case. Therefore rather than the position of the advice (before or after the joinpoint) the importance is given to how the constraint is added/inserted. For example, we can use *and* advice to add a constraint. Table 2 presents the four advice types.

Table 2. List of possible advice type

Advice	Description
or	*or* is a type of AspectOCL advice in which a new constraint is attached to already written constraint using *or* operator. This Boolean operator can work with all of the AspectOCL pointcuts
and	*and* is a type of AspectOCL advice in which a new constraint is attached to already written constraint using *and* operator. This Boolean operator can work with all of the AspectOCL pointcuts
xor	*xor* is a type of AspectOCL advice in which a new constraint is attached to already written constraint using *xor* operator. This Boolean operator can work with all of the AspectOCL pointcuts
implies	*implies* is a logical operator in OCL. In AspectOCL it can be used to append a cross cutting constraint at a specified joinpoint selected by pointcut. When first part of a constraint is true then second part of it must also be true otherwise the entire constraint evaluates to false

Introduction. An introduction is a way to add a new constraint on a model element where there are no previously defined constraints. For example, adding an invariant to a class that does not have an invariant defined. Introduction adds a constraint at the joinpoint(s) selected by the pointcut. Introduction can be used to add a constraint to pre-condition of a method, post-condition of a method, or to add a new class invariant (or a state invariant in case of state machines). The possible types of introduction are listed in Table 3. When a constraint is already specified, we use one of the available advices instead of introduction to add a constraint.

Context. An OCL expression or constraint is applied in a limited scope. This scope is specified by a *context*. Context in AspectOCL is used in a manner similar to context in OCL and can be a class, an interface, a method and an attribute. For example, in Fig. 2 the first context declaration selects the class on which the crosscutting constraint is to be applied. The second context declaration selects an operation.

Table 3. Types of Introduction

Type	Description
pre	*pre* is used to define the conditions that must hold true before the execution of an operation
post	*post* is used to define the conditions that must hold true after the execution of an operation
inv	*inv* (invariant) is a type of advice that must remain true for all the instances of a class declared in context

```
1. context ClassName
2. context ClassName:: MethodName (Arguments) : ReturnType
```

Fig. 2. Context example

allMethods(). *allmethods()* is a helper function which returns all the methods of a class. The method can be used in two different variations: pre.allmethods() and post.allmethods(). When *pre* is used with allmethods(), it returns all the pre-conditions of all the methods of a class declared as context. When *post* is used with allmethods(), it returns the post-conditions of all the methods of class declared as context.

Result. *result* is used in a post condition of an operation for holding its result.

```
1. let  Var: ClassContext / OperationContext / AttributeContext
2. let {VarX}->{VarY}:(ClassContext/OperationContext/AttributeNames)
            -> (ClassContext/ OperationContext/ AttributeNames)
```

Fig. 3. Usage of let in AspectOCL

Let: Use of *let* is similar to its usage in OCL for defining a local variable. However, we also use let for defining a mapping between a class, methods and attributes. A mapping allows us to define sequence wise replacements and defines a relationship between elements of two sets. Whenever an element of first set occurs, the sequentially corresponding entry from second set is selected. In case of let, these sets contain classes, operations or attributes. The use of *let* is illustrated in Fig. 3. The first let expression is used for defining classes that include the cross cutting constraint. The second expression demonstrates the use of let for defining the mappings. The second expression specifies the mapping among multiple variables. *VarX* represents a composite statement that contains members from a set of classes, operations or attributes. *VarY* represents the statement that contains members from a similar set. Whenever particular variable from a set of *VarX* or *VarY* is used in the aspectual constraint, corresponding *ClassContext* or *OperationContext* or *AttributeNames* will replace it. If the context contains the let variable name, then it can only be *ClassContext* or *OperationContext*, as OCL does not allow context to be an attribute.

3.2   Defining a Crosscutting Constraint as an Aspect in AspectOCL

We define aspects in AspectOCL using the above-defined constructs. Each crosscutting constraint is specified as a separate aspect and contains a mapping, context declaration, a pointcut that selects one or more joinpoints, an advice type followed by the crosscutting constraint. The grammar of an aspect is shown in Appendix.

To better understand how we write aspects consider an example scenario where we have four classes, Course, Student, Teacher and Seminar. Each class has some existing constraints as shown in Fig. 4. We consider a case where a constraint ensuring uniqueness of identifiers is to be applied to all above classes. Using OCL the current practice is to add this constraint in each of the classes shown in Fig. 4.

Repeatedly writing a crosscutting constraint multiple times (once in each affected class) is a valid approach. However, it results in redundant constraints. Any modifications to such constraints must be applied at all locations individually and in a consistent manner. Using AspectOCL we can model this constraint as a crosscutting constraint and define an aspect for it. The aspect modeling the crosscutting constraint is shown in Fig. 5. Separating this crosscutting constraint from the other constraints as an aspect results in fewer constraints. The constraint specification without the crosscutting constraints is shown in Fig. 6. The first part of the aspect definition, defines the mapping as previously discussed. The mapping can be a part of the aspect or can be provided in a separate file. Any required mappings can be included through the import keyword. The let expression inside the mapping section of the *Uniqueness-Constraint* aspect defines a mapping between the classes and the attributes from those classes that should be used during weaving. The *context* selects the classes that appear in the mapping thus iteratively applying the crosscutting constraint using an advice of type *and* to Course, Student, and Teacher and Seminar classes. When weaving the constraint, *var1, var2* is replaced by variables of the current class selected by the *context*.

```
-- Course name should be unique and should be 10 to 20
characters long
context Course inv:
    courseName.size() >= 10 and courseName.size() <=20
    and Course.allInstances()->isUnique(courseCode)

-- Student must pay fee to get registered and student
roll no should be unique
context Student inv:
    feespaid= false implies registersFor ->isEmpty()
    and Student.allInstances() ->isUnique(rollNo)

-- Teacher age should be greater than 50 and teacher Id
should be unique
context Teacher inv:
    Teacher.allInstances() ->select (
    t:Teacher | t.age> 50) ->isEmpty()
    and Teacher.allInstances()->isUnique(teacherId)

-- No of attendees in seminar should be greater than 30
and seminar Id should be unique.
context Seminar inv:
    Seminar.allInstances() ->forall (
    s1 | s1.noOfAttendees > 30)
    and Seminar.allInstances() ->isUnique(SeminarId)
```

Fig. 4. Constraints on example classes

3.3   Writing and Weaving Crosscutting Constraints in OCL

We provide an editor to support writing crosscutting constraints as aspects. The editor is built using Xtext open source framework that provides support for developing tools for domain specific language. This allows our language editor to work as a plugin of EMF modeling tools that can be easily integrated with existing modeling tools such as IBM RSA and Papyrus. Once the aspects are written, they can be weaved in OCL constraints using the aspect weaver. The output of the weaving process is standard OCL constraints. For our language, we rely mostly on text matching for weaving. Fig. 7, Fig. 9 and Fig. 10 show three significant aspects for the EU-Rental case study written in the developed AspectOCL editor. Text matching is used to match each location. String operations are used to insert or add new constraints. The let expression requires a more refined approach. The let expression is expanded to obtain each individual mapping. A new instance of aspect is produced for each mapping (intermediate, not visible outside the weaver). Each instance of aspect is then weaved like a separate aspect with the exception

```
mapping mapUniquenessConstraint
{
    let T -> A: {Course  -> Course  :: courseCode,
                Student -> Student :: rollNo,
                Teacher -> Teacher :: teacherId,
                Seminar -> Seminar :: seminarID}
}
aspect UniqunessConstraint
{
    import_mapping mapUniquenessConstraint
    pointcut selectUniquenessTarget
    context T
    advice inv:
            and selectUniquenessTarget
            T.allInstances() ->isUnique(A)
}
```

Fig. 5. Aspect UniquenessConstraint

```
context Course inv:
    courseName.size() >= 10
            and courseName.size() <=20
context Student inv:
    feespaid= false implies registersFor ->isEmpty()
context Teacher inv:
    Teacher.allInstances() ->select (
            t | t.age> 30) ->isEmpty()
context Seminar inv:
    Seminar.allInstances() ->forall (
            s1 | s1.noOfAttendees > 30)
```

Fig. 6. Constraint specification without crosscutting constraints

that now the context in each instance selects only one class or method. While this is not the most efficient approach, it serves the purpose for this initial case study. For mappings defined separately, a pre-processor fetches the mappings and inserts them in the aspect file. A more optimized weaver may be developed in future.

4   Case Study

4.1   Description of Case Study

In this section we discuss modeling crosscutting constraints identified from an existing open source case study the EU-Rent a Car Rental specifications [33]. The case study is a publicly available case study that models a Car Rental System with over 1000 branches in different countries. The EU-Rent specifications was initially developed by Model Systems, Ltd [19] and then extended by Frias *et al.* [33]. EU-Rent Specifications is considered as a modeling benchmark and has been used in multiple studies for evaluation and demonstration [20-22]. Specifications of the case study are developed using various UML 2.0 diagrams and OCL 2.0 constraints. The case study comprises of four class diagrams and 246 OCL constraints are defined on them.

4.2   Application of AspectOCL

We apply the proposed approach to a case study to demonstrate that there are crosscutting constraints in existing systems that can be modeled using our approach instead. For this reason, we identified the possible crosscutting concerns from the EU Rent case study. The OCL constraints from the case study were manually analyzed to identify crosscutting constraints. Our manual analysis of 246 constraints revealed 44 constraints that are crosscutting constraints. Against these 44 crosscutting constraints, we write 16 aspects that fully specify these 44 constraints, completely capturing the intent of the designers. Essentially this means that if the modeler used AspectOCL approach, she will need to write 26 fewer constraints out of a total of 246 constraints. Given the amount of effort required to manage the constraints, minimizing the redundancy in these constraints can significantly reduce the maintenance effort. The extent to which we can reduce the number of constraints in a given system using our proposed language is something that depends on the nature of the system being modeled and the nature of constraints it must adhere to. However, from the EU Rent case study it can be inferred that when a number of crosscutting constraints are present, a significant reduction can be achieved in using aspects. Following we discuss three significant aspects that correspond to highest number of crosscutting concerns from the case study. The first aspect is the *NameUniqueness* aspect shown in Fig. 7.

The aspect defines a name uniqueness constraint on the method *nameIsKey()*. In the case study this method has a post condition indicating that no two names can be same. The constraint appears with slight variation (name of the containing class is different) in different classes and can be modeled as a cross cutting constraint. We use

```
EuroRentalNameUniquenessConstraint.aodsl ⌦

mapping mapNameUniqueness {
    let T:{ Branch,BranchType, PerformanceIndicator, Country,
            CarModel, CarGroup, RentalDuration, ServiceDepot, Discount }
}
aspect NameUniqueness{
import mapping mapNameUniqueness
pointcut uniqueNames:
context T::nameIsKey() : Boolean
intro :
post uniqueNames
result="T.allInstances()->select(t|t.name=self.name)->size()=1"
}
```

Fig. 7. Constraint-AspectNameUniqueness

```
     -- Name uniqueness constraints

     context Branch:: nameIsKey() : Boolean
     post:
        result=Branch.allInstances()->select(
                     b|b.name=self.name)->size()=1
     contextBranchType:: nameIsKey() : Boolean
     post:
        result=BranchType.allInstances()->select(
                     b|b.name=self.name)->size()=1
     context Country:: nameIsKey() : Boolean
     post:
        result=Country.allInstances->select(
                     b|b.name=self.name)->size()=1
     contextPerformanceIndicator::nameIsKey() : Boolean
     post:
        result=PerformanceIndicator.allInstances()->select(
                     b|b.name=self.name)->size()=1
     contextServiceDepot::nameIsKey() : Boolean
     post:
        result=ServiceDepot.allInstances()->select(
                     s|s.name=self.name)->size()=1
     contextCarModel::nameIsKey() : Boolean
     post:
        result=CarModel.allInstances()->    select(
                     b|b.name=self.name)->size()=1
     contextCarGroup::nameIsKey() : Boolean
     post:
        result=CarGroup.allInstances()->    select(
                     b|b.name=self.name)->size()=1
```

Fig. 8. Uniqueness crosscutting constraint

the let expression to map multiple classes as context, i.e., when weaving the constraint is inserted in post condition of *nameIsKey()* method of each class in the set defined by *let*. As the method does not have any other post condition, we use *intro* to introduce a new post condition.

Fig. 8 shows the crosscutting uniqueness constraint in the original specification. The constraint appears on *nameIsKey()* method across seven different classes.

Fig. 9 presents the second aspect that we discuss from the case study. The *bestPrice-Limit* aspect captures a crosscutting constraint that specifies a time related constraint on *bestprice()* method of *RerservationWithSpecialDiscount* and *RentalAgreement* classes. For this constraint we use *and* advice to append a new constraint to previously existing post conditions of the selected method.

Finally Fig. 10 presents the third and last aspect that we discuss in this paper. The aspect *ExistingGroup* fully demonstrates the power of the language's *let* construct that allows us to define complex mappings.

The constraint captures six post conditions defined on the methods *car()*, *carG()*, *carM()*, *discount()*, *duration()* and *perfInd()* of classes *ExistingCar*, *ExistingCarGroup*, *ExistingCarModel*, *ExistingDiscount*, *ExistingRentalDuration* and *ExistingPerformance Indicator*. Let expression in the constraint defines a mapping between classes, operations and attributes. Variable S in let statement defines class context in a similarly way as in OCL, variable A defines the attribute *registrationNumber* of class Car, variable B defines the attribute *regNumber* of class *ExistingCar* and variable TT defines a class only. When weaving the aspect, the context in the constraint will be replaced by value of possible mappings of variable S defined in let expression;   variable A will be replaced by the car attribute, variable 'B' will be replaced by *ExistingCar* attribute and variable 'TT' will be replaced by the class Car.

4.3   Limitations

We have presented our proposed extension to OCL for handling crosscutting constraints. This paper focuses mostly on presenting the language constructs and showcasing its applicability on large-scale systems. In this paper we mainly discuss the reduction in number of constraints. While this is important, this is not the sole factor that determines the effort required to model constraints using our language. The language shows itself to be promising but we do not have empirical evaluation of its readability and understandability. Aspect orientation has shown to improve the understandability and readability of models [10]. Though the definition of context is

```
EuroRentalMapBestPriceTLimitAspect.aodsl ⊠
mapping mapBestPriceTimeLimit {
     let T:{ RentalAgreement, ReseservationWithSpecialDiscount}
}
aspect bestPriceLimit{
import mapping mapbestPriceTimeLimit
  pointcut IntroduceNewConstraint:
  context T::bestprice() : Money
post()-> select ("exp:OCLExpression | exp.oclIsTypeOf(ifExp)"
                    and
                    "exp.condition.referredVariable = T::accInterval")
advice post :
  and IntroduceNewConstraint
  "tup.accInterval >=timeMax"
   }
```

Fig. 9. Constraint-aspect bestPriceTimeLimit

detailed, we believe that the effort is still less than repeating and maintaining the same constraints scattered throughout the models.

Another limitation can be that the constraint specifications are decoupled from the modeling elements on which they are applied on. To address this limitation, AspectOCL editor is built as a plugin of the EMF modeling tools and the 'weaved constraints' are also visible with the modeling elements that they are applied on.

Our proposed language currently does not support writing composite aspects. Also, we only support weaving aspects at the identified joinpoints only. In case the designer wants to add a predicate inside a constraint that is not a joinpoint, the designer has to rewrite the crosscutting constraint. Finally, our proposed language lacks formal semantics. While not directly applicable, in a way, lack of formalism of AspectOCL can be side stepped as the woven constraints are in standard OCL. These can still benefit from the formalisms proposed for OCL even though our intermediate representation (aspects) is not formalized.

```
EuroRentalExistingGroupAspect.aodsl ⊠

mapping mapExisintGroups {
    let S->{A,B,TT}:
  ExistingCar::car() : Car   ->
    { Car::registrationNumber, ExistingCar::regNumber, Car}
  ExistingCarGroup::carG() : CarGroup   ->
    { CarGroup::name,ExistingCarGroup::carGroup,CarGroup}
  ExistingCarModel::carM() : CarModel ->
    { CarModel::name, ExistingCarModel::carModel,CarModel}
  ExistingDiscount::discount(): Discount ->
    { Discount::name,ExistingDiscount::discountName,Discount}
  ExistingRentalDuration::duration() : RentalDuration ->
    { RentalDuration::name, ExisitngRentalDuration::
      durationName, RentalDuration}
  ExistingPerformanceIndicator::perfInd():PerformIndicator->
    { PerformanceIndicator::name, ExistingPerformanceIndicartor::name,
      PerformanceIndicator }
  }
aspect existingGroup{
import mapping mapExisintGroups
pointcut existGroup:
context S
intro :
post existGroup
"let CarVal: Set(TT)=TT.allInstances()-> select(c|c.A = self.B)
  in CarVal ->notEmpty() implies result = CarVal ->any()"
}
```

Fig. 10. Constraint-aspect ExisitingGroup

5   Conclusion

Constraints play a vital part of modeling and engineering of large-scale industrial systems. In our experience of working with such systems and from the literature, such systems are often seen exhibiting crosscutting behaviors in various design artifacts. Crosscutting behaviors in various design artifacts such as UML class diagrams, state machines and the underlying implementations have all received a lot of attention from the researchers. However, few approaches exist to deal with crosscutting constraints. All problems identified as a result of crosscutting behavior in models or code also exist in case of crosscutting constraints. None of the existing approaches offer support for generic modeling of crosscutting constraints while keeping compatibility with OCL. Such compatibility is important as designers often utilize OCL due to wide range of tools and APIs available. Aspect orientation is a well-established technique to handle crosscutting features. In this paper, we proposed an extension of OCL language to support writing of crosscutting constraints in the form of aspects. Cross cutting constraints are specified as aspects, which can be woven in OCL constraints. Our language keeps compatibility with OCL by requiring the weaver to produce standard OCL output. We demonstrate our proposed language through application on a published open source case study. Results show that specifying crosscutting constraints as aspects can reduce the number of constraints to be specified. While our proposed language shows a lot of promise, we currently do not have empirical evaluation on diverse set of industrial systems. Such an evaluation is considered an important future consideration.

Acknowledgement. This work was supported by ICT R&D Fund, Pakistan under the project ICTRDF/MBTToolset/2013. Muhammad Zohaib Iqbal was partly supported by National Research Fund, Luxembourg (FNR/P10/03).

Appendix

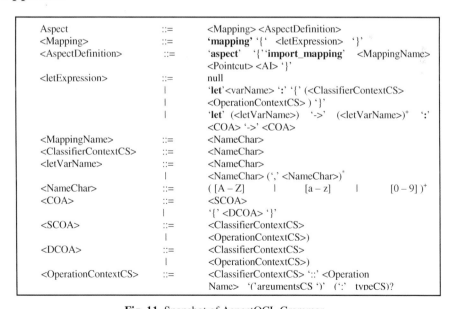

Fig. 11. Snapshot of AspectOCL Grammar

References

1. Völter, M., Stahl, T., Bettin, J., Haase, A., Helsen, S.: Model-driven software development: technology, engineering, management. John Wiley & Sons (2013)
2. Brambilla, M., Cabot, J., Wimmer, M.: Model-driven software engineering in practice. Synthesis Lectures on Software Engineering **1**, 1–182 (2012)
3. Warmer, J.B., Kleppe, A.G.: The Object Constraint Language: Precise Modeling With Uml (Addison-Wesley Object Technology Series) (1998)
4. Specification, O.M.G.A.: Object Constraint Language (May 2006)
5. Ali, S., Yue, T., Zohaib Iqbal, M., Panesar-Walawege, R.K.: Insights on the use of OCL in diverse industrial applications. In: Amyot, D., Fonseca i Casas, P., Mussbacher, G. (eds.) SAM 2014. LNCS, vol. 8769, pp. 223–238. Springer, Heidelberg (2014)
6. Ali, S., Iqbal, M.Z., Arcuri, A., Briand, L.: Generating Test Data from OCL Constraints with Search Techniques. IEEE Trans. Softw. Eng. **39**(10), 1376–1402 (2013)
7. Gray, J., Bapty, T., Neema, S., Tuck, J.: Handling crosscutting constraints in domain-specific modeling. Communications of the ACM **44**, 87–93 (2001)
8. Lengyel, L., Levendovszky, T., Mezei, G., Forstner, B., Charaf, H.: Metamodel-based model transformation with aspect-oriented constraints. Electronic Notes in Theoretical Computer Science **152**, 111–123 (2006)
9. Murphy, G.C., Walker, R.J., Baniassad, E.L.A., Robillard, M.P., Lai, A., Kersten, M.A.: Does aspect-oriented programming work? Communications of the ACM **44**, 75–77 (2001)
10. Ali, S., Yue, T., Briand, L.C.: Does Aspect-Oriented Modeling Help Improve the Readability of UML State Machines? Software & Systems Modeling, Springer **13**(3), 1189–1221 (2014)
11. Clarke, S., Baniassad, E.: Aspect-oriented analysis and design. Addison-Wesley Professional (2005)
12. Laddad, R.: AspectJ in Action: Practical Aspect-Oriented Programming. Manning Publications (2003)
13. Elrad, T., Filman, R.E., Bader, A.: Aspect-oriented programming: Introduction. Communications of the ACM **44**, 29–32 (2001)
14. Mguni, K., Ayalew, Y.: An Assessment of Maintainability of an Aspect-Oriented System. International Scholarly Research Notices (2013)
15. Ali, S., Briand, L.C., Hemmati, H.: Modeling Robustness Behavior Using Aspect-Oriented Modeling to Support Robustness Testing of Industrial Systems. Software and Systems Modeling **11**(4), 633–670 (2012)
16. Khan, M.U., Iqbal, M.Z., Ali, S.: A Heuristic-Based Approach to Refactor Crosscutting Behaviors in UML State Machines. In: 2014 IEEE International Conference on Software Maintenance and Evolution (ICSME), pp. 557–560. IEEE (2014)
17. France, R., Ray, I., Georg, G., Ghosh, S.: Aspect-oriented approach to early design modelling. IEE Proceedings-Software **151**, 173–185 (2004)
18. Steinberg, D., Budinsky, F., Merks, E., Paternostro, M.: EMF: eclipse modeling framework. Pearson Education (2008)
19. Wilson, B.: EU-Rent Car Rentals Case Study. Model Systems & Brian Wilson Associates (1994)
20. Tairas, R., Cabot, J.: Cloning in DSLs: experiments with OCL. In: Sloane, A., Aßmann, U. (eds.) SLE 2011. LNCS, vol. 6940, pp. 60–76. Springer, Heidelberg (2012)
21. Cabot, J., Gogolla, M.: Object constraint language (OCL): a definitive guide. In: Bernardo, M., Cortellessa, V., Pierantonio, A. (eds.) SFM 2012. LNCS, vol. 7320, pp. 58–90. Springer, Heidelberg (2012)

22. Costal, D., Gómez, C., Queralt, A., Raventós, R., Teniente, E.: Improving the definition of general constraints in UML. Softw Syst Model **7**, 469–486 (2008)
23. http://eclipse.org/Xtext/
24. Wimmer, M., Schauerhuber, A., Kappel, G., Retschitzegger, W., Schwinger, W., Kapsammer, E.: A survey on UML-based aspect-oriented design modeling. ACM Computing Surveys (CSUR) **43**, 28 (2011)
25. Richters, M., Gogolla, M.: Aspect-oriented monitoring of UML and OCL constraints. In: AOSD Modeling With UML Workshop, 6th International Conference on the Unified Modeling Language (UML), San Francisco, USA. Citeseer (2003)
26. Dou, W., Bianculli, D., Briand, L.: OCLR: a more expressive, pattern-based temporal extension of OCL. In: Van Cabot, J., Rubin, J. (eds.) ECMFA 2014. LNCS, vol. 8569, pp. 51–166. Springer, Heidelberg (2014)
27. Hearnden, D., Raymond, K., Steel, J.: MQL: a powerful extension to OCL for MOF queries. In: Proceedings Seventh IEEE International Enterprise Distributed Object Computing Conference, 2003. pp. 264–276. IEEE (2003)
28. Störrle, H.: MOCQL: a declarative language for ad-hoc model querying. In: Van Gorp, P., Ritter, T., Rose, L.M. (eds.) ECMFA 2013. LNCS, vol. 7949, pp. 3–19. Springer, Heidelberg (2013)
29. Rumpe, B.: ≪ Java≫ OCL Based on New Presentation of the OCL-Syntax. In: Clark, T., Warmer, J. (eds.) ECMFA 2013. LNCS, vol. 2263, pp. 189–212. Springer, Heidelberg (2002)
30. Aldawud, O., Elrad, T., Bader, A.: UML profile for aspect-oriented software development. In: Proceedings of Third International Workshop on Aspect-Oriented Modeling. Citeseer (2003)
31. Usman, M., Iqbal, M.Z., Khan, M.U.: A model-driven approach to generate mobile applications for multiple platforms. In: 21st Asia-Pacific Software Engineering Conference (APSEC), pp. 111–118 (2014)
32. Jilani, A.A., Iqbal, M.Z., Khan, M.U.: A search based test data generation approach for model transformations. In: Di Ruscio, D., Varró, D. (eds.) ICMT 2014. LNCS, vol. 8568, pp. 17–24. Springer, Heidelberg (2014)
33. Frias, L., Queralt, A., Ramon, A.O.: EU-Rent car rentals specification (2003)

Reusable Model Interfaces with Instantiation Cardinalities

Sunit Bhalotia and Jörg Kienzle[✉]

School of Computer Science, McGill University, Montreal, Canada
Sunit.Bhalotia@mail.mcgill.ca, Joerg.Kienzle@mcgill.ca

Abstract. The power of aspect-oriented modelling is that structural and behavioural properties of a crosscutting concern can be modularized within an aspect model. With proper care, such an aspect model can also be made reusable. If the functionality provided by such a modularized concern is needed repeatedly within a system, the reusable aspect model can be applied multiple times within the same target model. This paper reviews the pending issues related to multiple aspect model instantiations identified in past research, and then proposes to extend the customization interface of aspect models with instantiation cardinalities. This removes potential customization ambiguities for the model user, and gives the model designer fine-grained control about how many instances of each structural and behavioural element contained in an aspect model are to be created in the target model. The approach is illustrated by presenting the aspect-oriented design of a behavioural, a structural and a creational design pattern.

1 Introduction

In the context of model reuse, the *artifact designer*, i.e., the developer creating the reusable artifact, and the *artifact user*, i.e., the developer applying the artifact to a specific application, are usually different people. The designer has in-depth domain knowledge about the concern that the reusable artifact addresses, and knows about the specific details of the functionality / properties / solutions encapsulated by the artifact that he created. The user on the other hand has in-depth domain knowledge about the application he is building, knows that the application he is building could benefit from reusing the reusable artifact, but is unaware of the artifacts inner working and limitations.

Aspect-orientation is a development paradigm that adds a new dimension to modularization. In aspect-oriented modelling (AOM), aspect models encapsulate structural and behavioural elements related to a particular concern. With proper care, aspect models can also be made reusable. However, the potentially crosscutting nature of the concern requires that the structure and functionality provided by the model can be applied several times within the same application. Different aspect-oriented modelling approaches provide different means to apply a reusable aspect within a target model. Some approaches require the specification of explicit mappings [6,14,19], whereas others allow the use of wildcards in so-called pointcut expressions [8,10,20].

© Springer International Publishing Switzerland 2015
G. Taentzer and F. Bordeleau (Eds.): ECMFA 2015, LNCS 9153, pp. 108–124, 2015.
DOI: 10.1007/978-3-319-21151-0_8

To the best of our knowledge, none of the current AOM approaches specifies precisely how a *model user* should go about applying a reusable aspect model multiple times. Since *the model user does not know about the inner workings and limitations* of the reusable aspect model, he is faced with multiple possibilities: instantiating an aspect model multiple times, specifying multi-mappings or multiple individual mappings, or specifying a single complex pointcut expression vs. using several pointcut expressions. Furthermore, it has been shown in [16] that in practice, *the model designer* of a reusable aspect model *needs fine-grained control over how many instances of each reusable model element are created in the target model* when an aspect is applied.

This paper presents *instantiation cardinalities*, a novel concept that solves the aforementioned ambiguity while giving the designer explicit control over the number of instances of each model element that is created in the target model. Our proposed approach is illustrated in this paper using the *Reusable Aspect Models* notation (RAM)) [14], an aspect-oriented multi-view modelling approach for software design modelling.

The remainder of the paper is structured as follows. Section 2 introduces model interfaces, aspect-oriented modelling and the problem with multiple applications of the same aspect within a target model. Section 3 presents instantiation cardinalities, and illustrates them by means of the *Observer* design pattern. Section 4 introduces automated call forwarding, an extension to aspect-oriented weaving that integrates polymorphism and separation of concerns in the presence of multi-mappings. Section 5 illustrates the elegance of instantiation cardinalities by showing the aspect-oriented design of two additional design patterns. Section 6 presents related work, and the last section draws some conclusions.

2 Background

To explain the motivation behind this work, the first background subsection gives a brief overview of units of reuse for software design and the kind of interfaces that these units define. The next subsection introduces aspect-oriented modelling in general and the *Reusable Aspect Models* approach in particular, and how it can be used to express crosscutting software design concerns. The last subsection illustrates the ambiguity that a software developer faces when reusing aspect models, and highlights the need for flexible instantiation policies.

2.1 Interfaces

Units of reuse, e.g., units used in software design such as classes, components, frameworks, design patterns [9], software product lines [18], etc..., typically either explicitly or implicitly define *interfaces* that detail *how* the unit is supposed to be reused. [3] classifies these interfaces into three kinds: *usage, customization,* and *variation interfaces.*

Usage Interface: The *usage interface* is the interface that is most common. For units that are used in software design, it *specifies the design structure and* *behaviour that the unit provides* to the rest of the application. In other words, the usage interface presents an abstraction of the functionality encapsulated within the unit to the developer. It describes *how* the application can trigger the functionality provided by the unit.

For instance for classes, the usage interface is the set of all *public* class properties, i.e., the attributes and the operations that are visible and accessible from the outside. For components, the usage interface is the set of services that the component provides (i.e., the *provided interface*). For frameworks, design patterns, and SPLs, the usage interface is comprised of the usage interfaces of all the classes that the framework/pattern/SPL offers.

Customization Interface: Typically, a unit of reuse has been purposely created to be as general as possible so that it can be applied to many different contexts. As a result, it is often necessary to tailor the general design to a specific application context. The *customization interface* of a reusable software design unit *specifies how to adapt the reusable unit to* the *specific needs* of the application under development.

For example, the customization interface of generic classes (also called template classes) allows a developer to customize the class by instantiating it with application-specific types. For components, the customization interface is comprised of the set of services that the component expects from the rest of the application to function properly (i.e., the *required interface*). The developer can use this information at configuration time to plug in the appropriate application-specific services. The customization interface for frameworks and design patterns is often comprised of interfaces/abstract classes that the developer has to implement/subclass to adapt the framework to perform application-specific behaviour.

Variation Interface: The *variation interface* of a reusable software design unit describes the available design variations and the impact of the different variants on high-level goals, qualities, and non-functional requirements. A variation interface typically takes the form of a *feature model* [12] that specifies the individual features that the unit offers. The impact of choosing a feature can be specified with goal models [11].

A reusable software design unit needs a variation interface only if it encapsulates several different design alternatives. In this paper, the focus is on improving reuse of a single design, and hence the variation interface is out of scope.

2.2   Aspect-Oriented Modelling

Aspect-orientation adds a new dimension to modularization, because the structure and functionality that aspects define can have a crosscutting effect on the rest of the application. In aspect-oriented modelling (AOM), aspect models encapsulate structural and behavioural elements related to a particular concern. Typically, the different elements within an aspect model need to interact closely with each other, i.e., invoke each other's behaviour or consult each other's state. The potentially crosscutting nature of the concern also requires that the

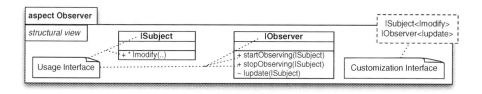

Fig. 1. Observer RAM Model Interface (Customization and Usage)

structure and functionality provided by the model can be applied several times within the same application.

To make aspect models reusable, interfaces are key. In software design modelling, having an explicit model interface makes it possible to apply proper information hiding principles [17] by concealing internal design details from the rest of the application. Because of aspect-oriented techniques, this is possible even if the encapsulated design details crosscut the rest of the application design. This is exemplified by our own *Reusable Aspect Models* approach (RAM)) [14], where each model has well-defined *usage* and *customization interfaces* [2].

The *usage interface* of a RAM model is comprised of all the *public* model elements, i.e., the structural and behavioural properties, that the classes within the design model expose to the outside. To illustrate this, the usage interface of the RAM design of the *Observer* design pattern is shown in Fig. 1. The *Observer* design pattern [9] is a software design pattern in which an object, called the *subject*, maintains a list of dependents, called *observers*. The functionality provided by the pattern is to make sure that, whenever the subject's state changes, all observers are notified. The structural view of the *Observer* RAM model specifies that there is a |Subject class that provides a public operation that modifies its state (|modify) that can be called by the rest of the application. In addition, the |Observer class provides two operations, namely startObserving and stopObserving, that allow the application to register/unregister an observer instance with a subject instance.

The *customization interface* of a RAM model specifies how a generic design model needs to be adapted to be used within a specific application. To increase reusability of models, a RAM modeller is encouraged to develop models that are as general as possible. As a result, many classes and methods of a RAM model are only partially defined. For classes, for example, it is possible to define them without constructors and to only define attributes relevant to the current design concern. Likewise, methods can be defined with empty or only partial behaviour specifications. The idea of the customization interface is to clearly highlight those model elements of the design that need to be completed/composed with application-specific model elements before a generic design can be used for a specific purpose. In RAM, these model elements are called *mandatory instantiation parameters*, and are highlighted visually by prefixing the model element name with a "|", and by exposing all model elements at the top right of the RAM model similar to UML template parameters. Fig. 1 shows that the customization

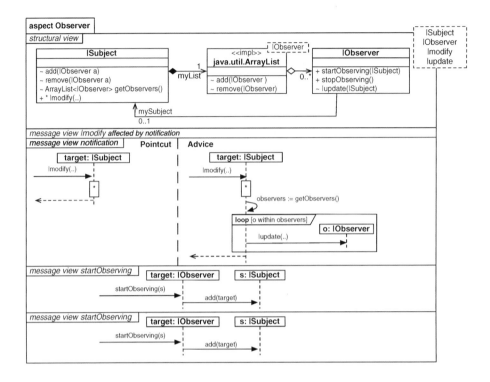

Fig. 2. Internal Design of Observer Aspect

interface for the *Observer* model comprises the class |Subject with a |modify operation, and the class |Observer class with an |update operation.

Fig. 2 shows a possible internal design for the *Observer* aspect. The subject maintains an ArrayList of Observers referenced by myList. The *notification* message view states that the behaviour of |modify is augmented to invoke |update on all registered observer instances after the behaviour of |modify completed execution.

2.3   Instantiation Ambiguities

In the object-oriented world, where classes are the main modularization unit, generic designs are encapsulated within generic classes (also called template classes). The customization interface of a generic class clearly specifies what information the programmer who wishes to reuse a generic class needs to provide in order for the class to be usable. For instance, the Java class ArrayList<E> requires the user to specify the type of the elements that are to be stored within the array. If the user needs two different kinds of ArrayLists in his design, she can simply instantiate the generic class twice with different element types.

In RAM, when a modeller wants to reuse an already existing, generic RAM model within her current design, she must also use the customization interface to

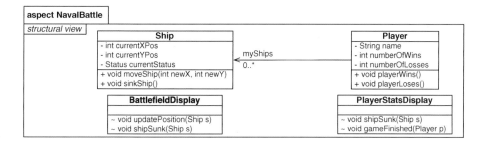

Fig. 3. Simplified Naval Battle Base Model

adapt the generic model to her specific design. This is done by providing *instantiation directives* that map every model element in the customization interface to a model element in the current design model. If desired, *TouchRAM* [1], the modelling tool for the RAM approach, can compose the structure and behaviour of the two models using the instantiation directives to yield the complete software design model.

In some way, the reuse process in RAM is therefore similar to the one of generic classes in programming languages. However, in contrast to generic classes, RAM models typically encapsulate more than one design class, and the functionality provided by the aspect results from interacting instances of several different classes. Just like with classes, a modeller might want to reuse the functionality provided by an aspect once or multiple times in his design. However, since the functionality of the aspect is split over several classes, the user might need parts of the structure or functionality provided by an aspect model multiple times, but not all of it.

Fig. 3 illustrates such a situation. The model shows parts of the design of a turn-based naval battle game, where players control ships that move around on a battlefield. Lets assume that there is a `BattlefieldDisplay` class that takes care of visualizing the battlefield on the screen, and there is also a `PlayerStatsDisplay` class that shows the list of all players together with statistics about their game performance, e.g., how many games they won, and how many ships they sunk.

In such a design, the modeller may want to reuse the *Observer* concern shown in Fig. 1 to notify the display classes whenever the state of the ships or players change. An instantiation directive such as:

```
Subject  → Ship
    modify → moveShip
Observer → BattlefieldDisplay
    update → shipMoved
```

would make sure that whenever a ship moves (because someone invokes the `moveShip` method on a ship), the `updatePosition` method of any `BattlefieldDisplay` instances that previously registered with the ship would be called.

In this situation, however, one could imagine more complex reuses of the *Observer* design that are not trivial to express. For instance, when a ship sinks (because someone invokes the `sinkShip` method on a ship), all registered `BattlefieldDisplay` instances and registered `PlayerStatsDisplay` instances should be notified by a call to their respective `shipSunk` methods. The modeller might be tempted to multi-map the *Observer* class, i.e., to write an instantiation directive such as:

```
Subject   → Ship
   modify → sinkShip
Observer  → BattlefieldDisplay, PlayerStatsDisplay
   update → shipSunk
```

to achieve the desired effect. Unfortunately, the implementation of the *Observer* design shown in Fig. 2 does not support such a multi-mapping, since the generic `java.util.ArrayList` class can only be parameterized with one type. To solve this problem, and in order to be able to reach both `BattlefieldDisplay` and `PlayerStatsDisplay` with a call to `shipSunk`, a superclass needs to be introduced and `shipSunk` must be transformed into a polymorphic call.

Without these changes, the only way to achieve the desired effect is to reuse *Observer* twice, i.e., to map `Observer` in one instantiation directive to `BattlefieldDisplay`, and to map `Observer` in the second instantiation directive to `PlayerStatsDisplay`. This will achieve the desired effect, but internally we then get two array lists, one containing `BattlefieldDisplay` instances, and the other one containing `PlayerStatsDisplay` instances. The `sinkShip` method is also advised twice, i.e., after updating the ship status, a first loop notifies all `BattlefieldDisplay` instances, and then a second loop notifies the `PlayerStatsDisplay` instances. Although this works, using two array lists (and looping through the observers in two separate loops) is not elegant, increases memory use and maybe even decreases performance.

In general, the need for fine-grained control over how many instances of a specific element defined in an aspect model should be created when the aspect model is reused multiple times within the same target model has been already highlighted in [16]. The authors define four so-called introduction policies. By default, new instances of the element are created each time the aspect model was reused (named *PerPointcut-Match* in [16]). It is also possible to specify that only a single instance is created regardless of how many times the aspect model is reused (referred to as *Global*). Finally, the authors also provide the possibility to specify that new instances should be created only for a given matched set or tuple of model elements in the target model (*PerMatchedElement* or *PerMatchedRole*).

3   Instantiation Cardinalities

This section introduces an extension to the customization interface that addresses the issues introduced in subsection 2.3: it solves the reuse ambiguity that the model user currently experiences in RAM and similar AOM approaches. At the same time, this extension makes it possible for the model designer to

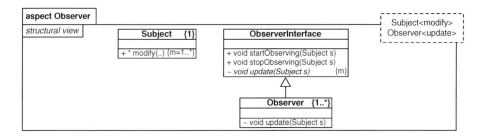

Fig. 4. Observer Model with Instantiation Cardinalities

have fine-grained control about how many instances of a specific model element defined in an aspect model are introduced into the target model.

We propose to augment the customization interface of a reusable unit by allowing the model designer to specify *instantiation cardinalities* for each model element. *The instantiation cardinality* of a model element *declares how many times, minimally and maximally, the model element can be mapped* to model elements of the target model within one instantiation, i.e, within one reuse. The instantiation cardinality is shown in curly brackets to the right of the name of the model element.

Fig. 4 shows a design of the *Observer* pattern with instantiation cardinalities. It is meant to be used for one Subject and potentially several Observers, clearly specified by the instantiation cardinalities {1} for Subject and {1..*} for Observer. To achieve the problematic reuse mentioned in subsection 2.3 (to notify both BattlefieldDisplay and PlayerStatsDisplay when a ship is sunk), the modeller uses the following instantiation directive[1]:

```
Subject → Ship
    modify → sinkShip
ObserverInterface → DisplayInterface
    update → shipSunk
Observer<1> → BattlefieldDisplay
Observer<2> → PlayerStatsDisplay
```

With instantiation cardinalities, there is no need anymore for using the "|" notation to designate mandatory instantiation parameters. Any model element that has a non-zero minimum instantiation cardinality must be mapped. To simplify the notation we also define a default cardinality, i.e., {0..1}.

In order to express the situation where the number of instantiations of one model element must be equal to the number of instantiations of another model element, it is possible to define variables within the instantiation cardinality specification. For example, Fig. 4 states that there must be at least one modify method within the Subject class, but there can be more than one. However, for every modify method there should be a corresponding update method in the ObserverInterface class. By assigning the number of instantiations to the

---

[1] The notation "model_element<x>" is used within an instantiation to refer to the xth instantiation of the corresponding model element.

variable m in the `Subject` class (by specifying {m=1..*}), we are able to express this constraint on the `update` method of the `ObserverInterface` (by specifying {m}).

In this case it is possible to write an instantiation directive such as:

```
Subject  →  Player
    modify<1>  →  playerWins
    modify<2>  →  playerLoses
ObserverInterface  →  DisplayInterface
    update<1>  →  gameCompleted
    update<2>  →  gameCompleted
Observer  →  BattlefieldDisplay
```

to specify that whenever `playerWins` *or* `playerLoses` is called on a `Player` instance, `gameCompleted` of the registered `PlayerStatsDisplay` instances is invoked.

4   Weaver Considerations

In the presence of instantiation cardinalities, the weaver can easily determine how many instances of each model element from the reused aspect should be created in the target model. For model elements that are explicitly mapped, the number of instances is determined by the instantiation directive. Classes, operations and attributes that are not explicitly mapped are created once, except for classes that are contained in another class. In that case, the number of instances of the class is equal to the number of instances of the containing class.

Handling of relationships between classes, i.e., associations, aggregations, compositions and generalization-specialization, are more interesting. Assuming that class A and class B are related with relationship r, the different cases are handled as follows:

- If the instantiation multiplicity of class A is {0}, {0..1} or {1}, and the instantiation multiplicity of B is {0}, {0..1} or {1}, then one single instance of r is created in the target model.
- If the instantiation multiplicity of class A is {q=1..*}, and the multiplicity of B is {0}, {0..1} or {1}, then q instances of the relationship r are created in the target model.
- If the instantiation multiplicity of class A is {q=1..*}, and the multiplicity of B is {q}, then we are in a situation where the number of instances of B is derived from the number of instances of A. In other words, every instance of A has its corresponding instance of B, and hence, 1 instance of the relationship r is created in the target model.
- If the instantiation multiplicity of class A is {q=1..*}, and the multiplicity of B is {p=1..*}, then we are in a situation where the number of instances of A and B are completely independent. Hence, p*q instances of the relationship r are created in the target model.

4.1   Automated Call Forwarding

The rules of object-orientation dictate that in a subclass, the name for a method that overrides a method defined in a superclass must remain the same. In AOM, where sub- and superclasses may happen to be defined in separate aspect models, this constraint hinders true separation of concerns. It requires a designer to chose the method names in one concern based on name definitions of another concern.

To remedy this situation, we allow overridden methods in subclasses to optionally be mapped to methods that do not necessarily have the same name as the superclass method (or any of the method names in the sibling classes). The only constraint is that the method's parameter number and types must match.

If the model user specifies such a mapping, then the model weaver automatically inserts an additional method with the name defined in the superclass, that directly forwards all calls to the mapped method. As a result, it is possible in the aspect model that defines the superclass to make a call that polymorphically dispatches to a differently named method of a subclass defined in a different aspect model.

This feature is not only convenient, it becomes essential when a high-level aspect reuses several generic aspect models or existing implementation classes. For instance, in the *Navalbattle* example from above, if the player statistics are kept on a remote web server, then one might want to reuse the *Observer* aspect model defined in Fig. 4 as follows:

```
Subject  → Ship
    modify → sinkShip
Observer<1> → BattlefieldDisplay
    update → refreshWindow
Observer<2> → PlayerStatsDisplay
    update → sendStatsToServer
```

5   Design Patterns Revisited

Section 3 introduced instantiation cardinalities by means of the *Observer* behavioural design pattern. This case study section applies our ideas to two additional design patterns, the structural design pattern *Composite* [9] and the creational design pattern *Abstract Factory* [9], in order to demonstrate the elegance of instantiation cardinalities.

5.1   Composite

The *Composite* design pattern is a well-known structural design pattern that allows individual objects and collections of objects to be treated uniformly [9]. Operations are defined in a common interface, and invoking such an operation on a collection of objects results in applying the operation to each element in the collection.

Fig. 5 shows that the RAM structural view of the *Composite* pattern is similar to the classic OO UML diagram found in [9]. Instantiation cardinalities

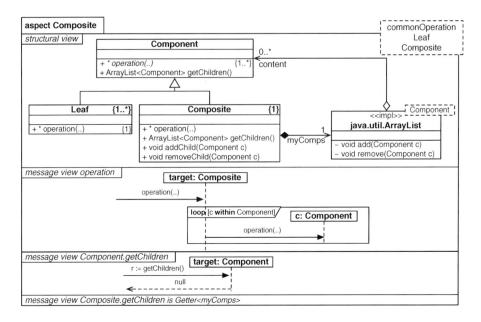

Fig. 5. The *Composite* RAM Model

have been added to each class that clearly show how the classes are intended to be mapped. While there need to be {1..*} Leaf classes, there has to be exactly {1} Composite class. The common Component interface is optional to map, but at least one operation must be specified {1..*}. Mapping it multiple times allows the model user to expose multiple leaf operations.

For example, suppose a higher-level aspect Jukebox reuses the *Composite* aspect as follows:

```
Component → Media
    operation<1> → playMedia
    operation<2> → stopMedia
Leaf<1> → Song
    operation<1> → playSong
    operation<2> → stopSong
Leaf<2> → Video
    operation<1> → playVideo
    operation<2> → stopVideo
Composite → PlayList
    operation<1> → playPlayList
    operation<2> → stopPlayList
```

In the message view for Composite.operation, we define the behaviour that loops through all the children and calls operation on each child. Note that we need to and are allowed to define only one message view for this method, irrespective of the number of times operation is going to be mapped in a higher-level aspect.

The mappings in the Jukebox aspect also nicely illustrates the advantage of automated call forwarding. The designer of Jukebox is not bound to use identical

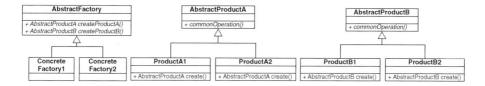

Fig. 6. Abstract Factory in UML

method names for the common operations defined in the different leaf classes. This allows for a great amount of flexibility while modelling. For instance, a user might have started creating the *Jukebox* aspect with the `Song` and `Video` classes together with the `playSong` and `playVideo` operations. Only later, when designing `PlayList`, she realizes that the *Composite* pattern is useful in this context. Because of automated call forwarding, she can simply map the methods to `operation` defined in *Composite* without the need to modify any existing method names. When the two aspects are woven together by the *TouchRAM* tool, the weaver will create a `playMedia` methods in `Song` and `Video` that forward calls to `playSong` and `playVideo`, respectively. That way, the polymorphism exploited in the `Composite.operation` message view is maintained.

5.2   Abstract Factory

Abstract Factory is a creational design pattern that provides an interface for creating families of related or dependent objects without specifying their concrete classes [9].

The pattern can be best described by an example. Consider two vehicle factories: `Toyota` and `Honda`. Each factory produces three types of vehicles: `Car`, `Motorcycle` and `Truck`. `Toyota` produces exactly one vehicle of each type: `ToyotaCar`, `ToyotaMotorcycle` and `ToyotaTruck`. The same is true for `Honda`.

Abstract Factory allows a modeller to instantiate a factory when the application is initialized (`VehicleFactory fact = new Toyota()`). Subsequently, whenever a specific type of vehicle is needed, it can be instantiated (`Car newcar = fact.createCar()`) without having to know if the application uses `ToyotaCars` or `HondaCars`. This decouples the creation of the products from the specific factory that actually produces them.

Figs. 6 and 7 highlight the difference between a standard *Abstract Factory* UML diagram (taken from [9]) and the *Abstract Factory* RAM model. The advantages of using instantiation cardinalities are obvious:

- The RAM model with instantiation cardinalities is a lot more *compact*, while it still clearly visualizes how the model is intended to be used. It captures the essence of *Abstract Factory completely*. The standard OO diagram shows only two `ConcreteFactories` and two `AbstractProducts`. In OO design pattern diagrams that depict multiple subclasses of a common supertype, it is typically shown by two classes with similar names and adding a numeric suffix to the names

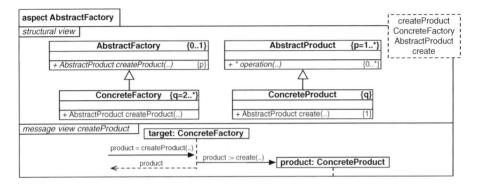

Fig. 7. Abstract Factory with Instantiation Cardinalities

(e.g., `ConcreteFactory1`, `ConcreteFactory2`). In RAM, the fact that there can be one or more `AbstractProducts` {1..*} whereas there need to be at least two `ConcreteFactories` {2..*} is clearly shown in the notation.

- Similarly, since the maximum cardinality can be *, the RAM notation is *scalable*. The OO diagram relies on different suffix types (numerical and alphanumerical) to show the independence of the number of subclasses of `AbstractProduct` and `AbstractFactory`. This technique becomes problematic in case a third set of independent subclasses needs to be specified. In RAM, a designer simply needs to introduce a different variable for every class that can exist independently multiple times, e.g., {q=1..*}.

- The RAM model shows the relationships between the number of classes *unambiguously*. In the standard OO diagram, the same kind of suffix is used to highlight the fact that the same number of subclasses is needed. For instance, there are subclasses `ConcreteFactory` and two subclasses `ProductA`. However, it is not clear whether from a design point of view the number of `ConcreteFactories` is determined by the number of `ProductAs`, or if it is the other way round. In RAM, since instantiation cardinalities allow the possibility of *declaring* and *using* variables, it is clear that:

  - The number of different `AbstractProducts` {p=1..*} (variable p is declared) determines the number of constructor methods in the `AbstractFactory` class {p} (variable p is used).
  - For each `AbstractProduct`, there must be as many `ConcreteProduct` subclasses {q} (variable q used) than there are `ConcreteFactories` {q=2..*} (variable q is declared).
  - There is no direct relation between the number of `ConcreteFactories` {q=2..*} and `AbstractProducts` {p=1..*} (they *declare different variables* p and q).

- In one message view it is possible to define the behaviour for all `createProduct` operations of all `ConcreteFactories`, i.e., for p*q methods! Because of the different variable declarations, the weaver knows that when generating the message view for *createProduct¡i,j¿*, it is supposed to call the `create` method of the jth mapping of the `ConcreteProduct` subclass of the ith mapping of the `AbstractProduct` class. For example, given the instantiation in Fig. 8, the weaver can, for example, generate the message view `ToyotaFactory.createTruck` that calls `ToyotaTruck.create`.

```
AbstractFactory → VehicleFactory
      createProduct<1> → createCar
      createProduct<2> → createTruck
ConcreteFactory<1> → Toyota
ConcreteFactory<2> → Honda
AbstractProduct<1> → Car
      operation → drive
AbstractProduct<2> → Truck
      operation<1> → drive
      operation<2> → load
ConcreteProduct<1,1> → ToyotaCar        (the first mapping dimension refers to
      create → buildToyotaCar            the mapping of the superclass)
ConcreteProduct<1,2> → HondaCar
      create → buildHondaCar
ConcreteProduct<2,1> → ToyotaTruck
      create → buildToyotaTruck
ConcreteProduct<2,2> → HondaTruck
      create → buildHondaTruck
```

Fig. 8. Example Instantiation of *AbstractFactory*

6 Related Work

To the best of our knowledge, none of the well-known AOM approaches provide customization interfaces for aspect models that expose information equivalent to what instantiation cardinalities provide.

For example, in Theme/UML [6], the models that contain crosscutting structure and behaviour are called themes. A theme is a parameterized UML package, and it exposes the generic model elements that must be bound to application specific elements in the form of UML template parameters. Just like in RAM before the introduction of instantiation cardinalities, it is not obvious for a modeller to know if she can bind a parameter to several model elements (similar to multi-mapping in RAM), or rather bind a theme multiple times to elements in a target model.

MATA [20] is a graph-based approach for composing UML diagrams that supports pattern matching to determine where an aspect model is to be applied. If in the aspect model a model element is tagged with the stereotype <<create>>, it means that this model element is created in the target model whenever the pattern matches. This is equivalent to the instantiation policy *PerPointcut-Match* described in [16]. [5] later extended the notation with additional stereotypes <<create++>> for introducing new model elements into a package common to all aspect models (equivalent to the *Global* policy described in [16]), <<create+>>

to introduce new model elements into a package common to all pattern matches, and `<<create->>` to introduce new model elements into a new package that is specific to each parameter binding. Although this allows for more fine-grained control over how many times model elements are introduced when an aspect is applied, it does not help the model user decide on whether to write one complex pattern match or several specific ones.

We believe that the AOM approaches presented above, and even others such as HiLA [10], GeKo [15] or the Motorola WEAVR [7], could benefit from adding instantiation cardinalities to their models in a way that is similar to how we extended RAM.

At a programming level, some aspect-oriented programming languages have introduced features that give the programmer fine-grained control over the number of instantiations of aspects. In *AspectJ* [13] for example, an aspect has per default only one instance that cuts across the entire program. Consequently, because the instance of the aspect exists at all join points in the running of a program (once its class is loaded), its advice is run at all such join points. However, *AspectJ* also proposes some elaborate aspect instantiation directives, such as: 1) *perthis(pointcut)* aspects, meaning that an instance of the aspect is created for every different object that is executing when the specified pointcut is reached; *pertarget(pointcut)*, meaning that an instance of the aspect is created for every object that is the target object of the join points matched by pointcut; 3) *percflow(pointcut)*, meaning that an instance of the aspect is created for each flow of control of the join points matched by the specified pointcut. These elaborate aspect instantiations are all dynamic, i.e., they are based on the execution of a program, and might become relevant in future AOM approaches that support execution of models.

Many other AOP approaches, such as package templates [4], provide means to instantiate crosscutting aspects/modules/templates multiple times and to resolve arising inconsistencies by specifying renamings/mappings. However, this does not solve the problem in the context of reuse, where the designer needs to communicate to the user how and how many times the elements in the reusable aspect were intended to be applied.

7   Conclusion

In this paper we have presented *instantiation cardinalities*, a new concept useful in the context of aspect-orientation in general and aspect-oriented modelling in particular. It allows the designer of a reusable aspect that comprises multiple structural entities to a) specify the customization interface of the module, i.e., highlight which entities are generic and need to be completed with application-specific structure in order for the reusable aspect to be usable in a specific context, and b) clearly specify maximally how many times each structural entity can be mapped to application-specific entities. By declaring and using variables within the instantiation cardinality specification, dependencies between the number of mappings of structural entities can be expressed in a precise way.

This solves the inherent ambiguity that model users face with most aspect-oriented approaches when it comes to reusing existing aspects within an application, and gives the model designer fine-grained control over how many instances of each model element are created in the target model when it is applied. As a result, the designer of the reusable aspect is able to specify all the instantiation policies identified in [16].

In order to allow for true separation of concerns, we have proposed to extend the TouchRAM weaver with automated call forwarding. As a result, it is possible to maintain polymorphic treatment of a set of subclasses in one aspect, while not requiring uniform naming of polymorphically related operations in each individual subclass.

For illustration purpose, the paper presented how instantiation cardinalities integrate with the *Reusable Aspect Models* approach. Furthermore, the practicality and elegance of the approach was demonstrated by showing the detailed aspect-oriented design models of a behavioural design pattern (*Observer*), a structural design pattern (*Composite*) and a creational design pattern (*Abstract Factory*).

References

1. Al Abed, W., Bonnet, V., Schöttle, M., Yildirim, E., Alam, O., Kienzle, J.: TouchRAM: a multitouch-enabled tool for aspect-oriented software design. In: Czarnecki, K., Hedin, G. (eds.) SLE 2012. LNCS, vol. 7745, pp. 275–285. Springer, Heidelberg (2013)
2. Al Abed, W., Kienzle, J.: Information hiding and aspect-oriented modeling. In: 14th Aspect-Oriented Modeling Workshop, Denver, CO, USA, Oct. 4th, 2009, pp. 1–6, October 2009
3. Alam, O., Kienzle, J., Mussbacher, G.: Concern-oriented software design. In: Moreira, A., Schätz, B., Gray, J., Vallecillo, A., Clarke, P. (eds.) MODELS 2013. LNCS, vol. 8107, pp. 604–621. Springer, Heidelberg (2013)
4. Axelsen, E.W., Sørensen, F., Krogdahl, S., Møller-Pedersen, B.: Challenges in the design of the package template mechanism. T. Aspect-Oriented Software Development **7271**, 268–305 (2012)
5. Barreiros, J., Moreira, A.: Reusable model slices. In: 14th Aspect-Oriented Modeling Workshop, Denver, CO, USA, Oct. 4th, 2009, October 2009
6. Carton, A., Driver, C., Jackson, A., Clarke, S.: Model-driven theme/UML. In: Katz, S., Ossher, H., France, R., Jézéquel, J.-M. (eds.) Transactions on Aspect-Oriented Software Development VI. LNCS, vol. 5560, pp. 238–266. Springer, Heidelberg (2009)
7. Cottenier, T., van den Berg, A., Elrad, T.: Motorola WEAVR: Aspect and model-driven engineering. Journal of Object Technology **6**(7), 51–88 (2007). http://dx.doi.org/10.5381/jot.2007.6.7.a3
8. Cottenier, T., Berg, A.V.D., Elrad, T.: The motorola weavr: model weaving in a large industrial context. In: AOSD 2006 Industry Track. ACM, March 2006
9. Gamma, E., Helm, R., Johnson, R., Vlissides, J.: Design Patterns. Addison Wesley, Reading, MA (1995)

10. Hölzl, M., Knapp, A., Zhang, G.: Modeling the car crash crisis management system using HiLA. In: Katz, S., Mezini, M., Kienzle, J. (eds.) Transactions on Aspect-Oriented Software Development VII. LNCS, vol. 6210, pp. 234–271. Springer, Heidelberg (2010)
11. International Telecommunication Union (ITU-T): Recommendation Z.151 (10/12): User Requirements Notation (URN) - Language Definition, October 2012
12. Kang, K., Cohen, S., Hess, J., Novak, W., Peterson, S.: Feature-oriented domain analysis (FODA) feasibility study. Tech. Rep. CMU/SEI-90-TR-21, Software Engineering Institute, Carnegie Mellon University, November 1990
13. Kiczales, G., Hilsdale, E., Hugunin, J., Kersten, M., Palm, J., Griswold, W.G.: An overview of AspectJ. In: Lindskov Knudsen, J. (ed.) ECOOP 2001. LNCS, vol. 2072, pp. 327–354. Springer, Heidelberg (2001)
14. Kienzle, J., Al Abed, W., Klein, J.: Aspect-Oriented Multi-View Modeling. In: AOSD 2009. pp. 87–98. ACM Press, March 2009
15. Kramer, M.E., Klein, J., Steel, J.R.H., Morin, B., Kienzle, J., Barais, O., Jézéquel, J.-M.: Achieving practical genericity in model weaving through extensibility. In: Duddy, K., Kappel, G. (eds.) ICMB 2013. LNCS, vol. 7909, pp. 108–124. Springer, Heidelberg (2013)
16. Morin, B., Klein, J., Kienzle, J., Jézéquel, J.-M.: Flexible model element introduction policies for aspect-oriented modeling. In: Petriu, D.C., Rouquette, N., Haugen, Ø. (eds.) MODELS 2010, Part II. LNCS, vol. 6395, pp. 63–77. Springer, Heidelberg (2010)
17. Parnas, D.L.: On the criteria to be used in decomposing systems into modules. Communications of the Association of Computing Machinery **15**(12), 1053–1058 (1972)
18. Pohl, K., Böckle, G., van der Linden, F.J.: Software Product Line Engineering: Foundations, Principles and Techniques. Springer-Verlag New York Inc, Secaucus, NJ, USA (2005)
19. Reddy, Y.R., Ghosh, S., France, R.B., Straw, G., Bieman, J.M., McEachen, N., Song, E., Georg, G.: Directives for composing aspect-oriented design class models. In: Rashid, A., Akşit, M. (eds.) Transactions on Aspect-Oriented Software Development I. LNCS, vol. 3880, pp. 75–105. Springer, Heidelberg (2006)
20. Whittle, J., Jayaraman, P., Elkhodary, A., Moreira, A., Araújo, J.: MATA: a unified approach for composing UML aspect models based on graph transformation. In: Katz, S., Ossher, H., France, R., Jézéquel, J.-M. (eds.) Transactions on Aspect-Oriented Software Development VI. LNCS, vol. 5560, pp. 191–237. Springer, Heidelberg (2009)

A Model-Based Approach for the Integration of Configuration Fragments

Azadeh Jahanbanifar[1(✉)], Ferhat Khendek[1], and Maria Toeroe[2]

[1] Concordia University, Montreal, Canada
{az_jahan,khendek}@encs.concordia.ca
[2] Ericsson Inc., Montreal, Canada
Maria.Toeroe@ericsson.com

Abstract. A complex system configuration often consists of different fragments developed separately and integrated later to relate them in a consistent manner. The integration process follows certain rules, which relate the elements from the different fragments and ensure certain properties for the complete system configuration. In this paper we propose a model driven approach based on the concept of model weaving. It integrates the configuration fragments into a system configuration while targeting some specific system properties. Our approach is discussed and illustrated within the context of the Service Availability Forum (SA Forum) middleware, where we integrate the Availability Management Framework (AMF) configuration of an application that provides services to the users with the Platform Management Service (PLM) configuration of the platform, which represents the lower layer entities such as the operating systems, virtual machines, hypervisors and hardware elements.

Keywords: Configuration fragments · System configuration · Model integration · Model weaving · Constraints · SA Forum middleware · Availability

1 Introduction

The utilization of reusable commercial off-the-shelf (COTS) components promises a reduction in time and cost of software development as well as higher quality, more reliable and maintainable software. A system (e.g. new composite applications or a system of systems such as in the cloud architectures) is built by putting together such independently developed COTS components. Each of these components/sub-systems may have its own perspective of the system described as a configuration. This configuration specifies the organization and the characteristics of the resources the component/sub-system is aware of and potentially manages. Thus, the composite system is described through various independently developed partial configurations - also known as configuration fragments. One of the main challenges of such composite systems is the integration of these configuration fragments in a consistent manner that reflects the relations and constraints between the elements of the different fragments and ensures that the resulting system meets the required properties such as availability, performance and security. The complexity of this integration task stems from the

© Springer International Publishing Switzerland 2015
G. Taentzer and F. Bordeleau (Eds.): ECMFA 2015, LNCS 9153, pp. 125–136, 2015.
DOI: 10.1007/978-3-319-21151-0_9

overlapping elements of the different configuration fragments (i.e. different logical representation of the same physical entity) and from the complex relationships among the elements of the different configuration fragments. We tackle these challenges in this paper.

We propose a model driven approach which is based on model weaving [1] to integrate the configuration fragments. Model weaving allows one to interrelate different models – in our case representing configuration fragments – by defining links between their elements. These links form a weaving model, which itself conforms to a weaving metamodel. To extend the generic core weaving metamodel special link types can be defined that capture the relations between the elements of the different models [1]. The definition of these abstract links is a design decision and depends on the application domain. Model weaving has been widely used for model integration, model transformation, model merging, etc. [2, 3, 4, 5], however so far it has focused primarily on the static mapping of elements without considering the semantics of these relations. In our approach we take into account the semantics of these relations and target some desired properties of the resulting system configuration. We illustrate our integration approach in the context of the Service Availability Forum (SA Forum) middleware [6], which has been developed by a consortium of telecommunication and computing companies to support the development of Highly Available (HA) systems. It consists of several services and frameworks, which represent and control specific aspects of the system and collaborate with each other [6, 7]. Many of these services and frameworks that we refer to as services in the rest of this paper, require a configuration that specifies the organization and the characteristics of the system and/or application resources under their control. We focus on the configurations of two SA Forum services: the Availability Management Framework (AMF) [8], which manages the redundant software entities for maintaining the service availability, and the Platform Management (PLM) service [9] which is responsible for providing a logical view of the platform entities (hardware and low level software entities) of the system. Thus, they represent different aspects of a system and should be considered as fragments of the system configuration. The configurations for these services are described using UML profiles. We capture the structure and semantics of the relations between these profiles in a weaving model, which is later used to generate the system configuration. Defining the relations between the profiles at a higher level of abstraction through a weaving model has several advantages such as reusability of the link types, increasing the extensibility (by allowing more models to be added) and automating the integration process [1, 14].

The rest of this paper is organized into five sections. In Section 2 we review AMF and PLM services, their respective configurations and configuration metamodels. Section 3 introduces our approach for integrating configuration fragments (configuration models) and its application. In Section 4 we briefly discuss the implementation and results. Related work is reviewed in Section 5 before concluding in Section 6.

2   SA Forum Middleware for Service High Availability

The SA Forum middleware is a standardized solution defined and developed by a consortium of computing and telecommunications companies to enable the development of highly available applications from COTS components and ensure their portability [6]. As mentioned earlier, in this paper we focus on the AMF and PLM services and their respective configurations.

2.1   Availability Management Framework (AMF)

AMF is responsible for maintaining the availability of application services by managing and coordinating the redundant software entities that compose the application under its control [8]. This management is based on the AMF configuration of the application. A simplified example of an AMF configuration of an application is shown in the left side of Fig. 1. In an AMF configuration a component is the smallest service provider entity. A combination of collaborating components forms a Service Unit (SU) and the workload provisioned by an SU is represented as a Service Instance (SI). A group of redundant SUs capable of providing the same SIs forms a Service Group (SG). An application may consist of a number of SGs. At runtime to protect each SI, AMF assigns it in the active and standby roles to the SUs of the SG. In case of the failure of the SU with the active assignment AMF dynamically moves the active assignment from the faulty SU to the standby. Each SU is instantiated on an AMF Node, which is a logical container of the AMF components and SUs. SUs (and SGs) can be configured to be hosted on a particular group of AMF nodes referred to as a Node Group (NG). This means that such SU/SG (the SUs of the SG) can be instantiated only on the Nodes of that Node Group [7, 8]. An AMF configuration consists of these entities, their types and their attributes.

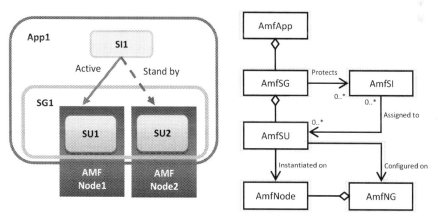

Fig. 1. A simplified AMF configuration and a portion of the AMF configuration metamodel

128   A. Jahanbanifar et al.

A complete description of AMF configurations is out of the scope of this paper, we only introduced the elements required for the rest of the paper. Accordingly, the components and the workload they can protect also have been omitted from the example of Fig. 1 for the sake of simplicity as they will not be used in our approach. More information on AMF configurations can be found in [8].

The concepts in an AMF configuration, their relationships, and the related constraints have been captured in an AMF configuration metamodel. A portion of this metamodel is shown in the right side of Fig.1. Subsequently, an AMF UML profile has been defined by mapping the AMF configuration metamodel to the UML metamodel [11]. The complete definitions of the AMF configuration metamodel and the respective AMF UML profile are discussed in [12].   In our configuration integration approach we use this AMF UML profile as an input.

2.2   Platform Management (PLM)

The PLM service is responsible for providing a logical view of the platform entities of the system, which includes the Hardware Elements (HEs) and the low level software entities also known as the Execution Environments (EEs) [9]. A PLM configuration represents their logical view. The PLM service manages the platform entities and acts as a mediator between the low level software and the hardware part of the system. A simple example of a PLM configuration is shown in the left side of Fig. 2.

In a PLM configuration PLM EEs represent software environments that can execute other software. A PLM EE can be an Operating System (OS), a Virtual Machine Monitor (VMM) or a Virtual Machine (VM) [7, 9]. A PLM HE with computational capabilities can host a VMM or an OS. An OS can be parent of other PLM EEs, e.g. VMMs and VMs can be hosted on VMMs.

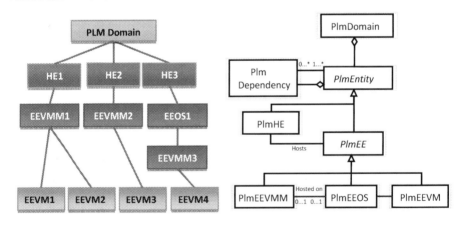

Fig. 2. A simplified PLM configuration and a portion of the PLM configuration metamodel

As for the AMF we have defined a PLM metamodel, which captures the PLM configuration concepts, their relationships and their constraints. The PLM metamodel is based on the PLM specification in [9], but further refines the standard PLM concepts and their relationships. For instance, the PlmEE is specialized into PlmEEVM,

PlmEEVMM, and PlmEEOS. The relationship among these concepts has also been redefined: The relationship between the PlmEEVM and the PlmEEVMM is now defined through the PlmDependency. The PlmEEVM has an association with its PlmEEOS. The PlmEEOS may have an association with a PlmEEVMM, i.e. host it.

These refinements are required to handle appropriately virtualized environments and cloud architectures. A portion of the PLM configuration metamodel is shown in the right side of Fig. 2. Following the same approach as for the AMF UML profile, we defined the PLM UML profile by mapping the PLM configuration metamodel to the UML metaclasses, with the closest semantics.

2.3   Overlapping Elements in Multiple Configurations

The configuration fragment defined for each service (such as AMF or PLM) represents a logical view of the physical entities of the system used/managed by that service. In this sense multiple services may use or manage the same physical entity and therefore different logical representations of this same entity will exist in multiple configuration fragments. For instance the virtual machine (VM) as a physical entity in the system is represented in both AMF and PLM configurations by different logical entities. In the AMF configuration it is known as an AMF Node while in the PLM configuration it is seen as EEVM. In a cloud architecture where a cloud controller such as OpenStack [24] is used for providing and managing platform services, the same VM is also managed by the cloud controller service (e.g. Nova in OpenStack) and represented in its configuration (Nova database).

Different logical representations of the same physical entity will certainly lead to inconsistency if they are handled and modified independently in the different configuration fragments. In order to avoid any inconsistency in the system, the relation between the configuration fragments need to be defined according to the requirements of the domain (or aspect) such as security, availability, performance, etc. These relations should be further captured during the integration of the configuration fragments to guarantee a consistent view of the system i.e. the system configuration.

3   Generation of System Configuration through Weaving

In this section we describe our approach for the integration of configuration fragments (represented as models) using model weaving [1]. We illustrate our approach through the integration of AMF and PLM configurations. Our goal is to integrate these two fragments in such a way that it ensures certain properties for the system configuration.

A weaving model captures the mapping between the elements of the source profiles (the AMF, and PLM UML profiles) and the target profile, i.e. the system configuration UML profile. The system configuration profile at this stage is a combination (union) of the AMF and PLM profiles without any relationship between the elements of these two profiles.

The weaving model should also conform to a weaving metamodel, which describes the types of mapping (link types) that are valid in the weaving model. Once the weaving model is defined with the mappings between the elements of the source and target profiles, to be able to apply it, it needs to be translated into an executable format.

This translation can be achieved using a Higher Order Transformation (HOT) [10], which translates the weaving model into a "Final Transformation" model. The system configuration model is then generated by executing the "Final Transformation" with the AMF and PLM configuration models as input. Fig. 3 shows the overall process of the system configuration generation. In the following we summarize these steps.

3.1   The Relation between the AMF and PLM Configurations

According to the SA Forum specifications [8, 9], each AMF Node is eventually hosted on (mapped to) a PLM EE so that the software entities of the AMF Node can be executed and provide services. This is basically the connection point between the two configuration fragments. In this paper we assume that this PLM EE is an OS instance installed on a VM instance. Therefore, an AMF Node is mapped to a VM, and this is how the two configurations are put into relation. The question that arises here is whether any mapping between the AMF Nodes and the PLM EEs is adequate in an HA system?

Let us consider the AMF and PLM configurations introduced in the previous section and let us assume that AMFNode1 and AMFNode2 from the AMF configuration are mapped to PLM EEs EEVM1 and EEVM2, respectively. These two VMs are running on the same PLM HE (HE1). At this point the PLM HE as well as the VMM will be single points of failure. If this HE crashes both service providers, SU1 and SU2, will be lost and service outage will be inevitable. So, to avoid the single point of failure due to the hosting hardware, we need to make sure that the service providers (SUs) of an SG will never be hosted on the same PLM HE.

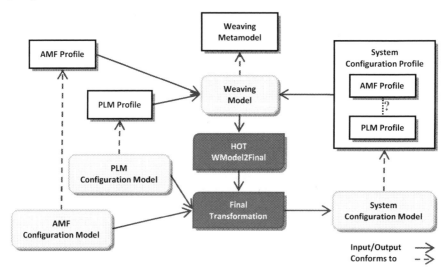

Fig. 3. The system configuration model generation through model weaving

This simple example shows that the distribution of redundant software entities on the hardware elements requires a more elaborated mapping between the elements of these configuration fragments. One would like to relate these configuration fragments in such a way that the AMF nodes on which the SUs of an SG are deployed are never mapped to PLM EEs that may be hosted on the same PLM HE.

To solve this problem we proposed a method [13] that classifies the VMs into hardware-disjoint VM Groups (VMGs). The VMs inside each VMG can be hosted on a set of HEs and this HE set has no intersection with the HE sets of other VMGs. Mapping these VMGs to AMF NGs and selecting an AMF NG for each SU of the SG will guarantee that those SUs will never end up on the same PLM HE. This way we are not only protecting the service by redundant software entities, but we also guarantee the hardware redundancy for these redundant software entities.

This feature of ensuring hardware redundancy in the system configuration is an example of a property that one can target using our approach. Other properties can be considered as well, such as the affinities between SUs of different SGs, which target the optimization of communications between resources.

3.2   Extending the Generic Weaving Metamodel

The identified mappings between the elements of the configuration fragments should be formally represented. They are captured in a weaving model [1]. This consists of a set of links, which depict the relationship (or mappings) between the elements of the source and target metamodels (UML profiles). The links may carry different meanings based on their types. The link types and their linked element types are defined in the weaving metamodel. To introduce the link types required for the integration of the configurations (e.g. AMF and PLM) we extended the AMW generic weaving metamodel [14]. The extended elements are shown in darker color in Fig. 4.

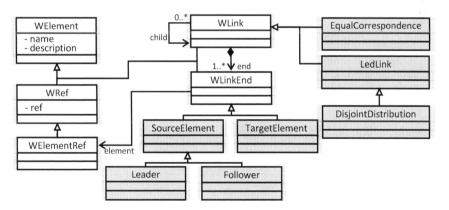

Fig. 4. AMW generic metamodel extended with new LinkTypes and LinkEnds

The first link type required in our work is called "EqualCorrespondence". This link type, inspired by [4], represents the mapping of elements of the source metamodels to the identical element of the target metamodel since many elements from the source models are just copied to the target model. The "EqualCorrespondence" link can do this task by simply mapping the identical elements of these metamodels.

The second link type we added to the generic weaving metamodel is called "LedLink". This link type is used when more than one source elements are involved in a mapping and some of these source elements can influence the other source elements. In other words, some source elements (called "Leader" elements) affect or lead other source elements (called "Follower" elements). Therefore, the *SourceElement* (which is itself an extension of the WLinkEnd) is extended to the "Leader" and "Follower" elements. "DisjointDistribution" link type is an extension of the "LedLink". "DisjointDistribution" link type captures the hardware-disjointness property we are aiming at for the target system configuration.

3.3   Creating the Links in the Weaving Model and Transformation Generation

Once the required link types have been defined in the weaving metamodel, they can be used in the weaving model for relating elements of the source metamodels (UML profiles) to the elements of the target metamodel (UML profile).

The "EqualCorrespondence" is used to map all the elements of the source profiles to the elements of the target one. As mentioned earlier the UML profile of the system configuration is a union of the elements of the PLM and AMF UML profiles, therefore both link end elements of this link type have the same name. Some semi-automated methods such as the technique introduced in [5] can be applied for optimization and thus semi-automate the creation of the mappings based on the similarity (such as string or type similarity) of the elements.

The "DisjointDistribution" link type of the weaving metamodel is used to represent the HW-disjointness mapping between the relevant elements of the AMF and PLM UML profiles. We assumed that we have a fixed PLM configuration and according to the information we have about the platform entities (such as VMs and HEs) we force AMF entities to keep the HW-disjointness for its software entities (i.e. AMF SUs). Thus, in this mapping the PlmEEVM is the Leader source element and the AmfNode is the follower source element and AmfSU is the target element. The application of this link type for mapping the AmfNode, and PlmEEVM as source elements to the AmfSU as the target element is as follows:

```
<<WLink>> DisjointDistribution HEDisjointSUs
  <Source>
      <<Right>>  Leader    PlmEEVM
      <<Left>>   Follower  AmfNode
  <Target>
      <<Target>> TargetElement AmfSU
```

In more details this link will group the elements of the Leader *SourceElement* of the right profile, i.e. the PlmEEVMs, based on the HW-disjoint algorithm in [13]. Based on the established groups, the elements of the Follower *SourceElement* of the left profile are affected (grouped) and mapped to the *TargetElement*, i.e. the AmfSU. These groups are set for the different SUs of an SG therefore guaranteeing hardware redundancy.

The translation of a weaving model into an executable format is done using an HOT, which itself is a transformation model. Basically, each defined link in the weaving model will be translated to one or more transformation rules of the "Final Transformation" model. The "WModel2Final" of Fig.3 is the HOT, which takes the weaving model as input and transforms it into an executable transformation model represented as Final Transformation.

In our case we defined the HOT for the two new link types (i.e. "EqualCorrespondence" and "DisjointDistribution") to generate the "Final Transformation". It takes the AMF and PLM configuration models as input and generates the system configuration model as the output. The generated configuration will have all the elements of both input models and also the mapping between the AMF Node and PLM EE that captures the HW-disjointness property.

4   Implementation and Discussion

We have implemented our approach of integrating configuration fragments using the Atlas Model Weaver (AMW) [14, 15, 16], which is being developed as a plugin for the Eclipse Modeling Framework (EMF) [17]. We extended the generic weaving metamodel of the AMW defined in KM3 [18] with the extensions discussed in Section 3. We used ATL [19] for the implementation of the HOT. The "Final Transformation" generated automatically from the HOT includes the implementation of the algorithm defined in [13].

Although we explained our approach in the context of the SA Forum middleware configuration fragments, we believe it is applicable to other domains where the integration of configuration fragments is required. Our approach is based on the model weaving technique and focusses on the semantics of the relations in the weaving such as the HW-disjointness property to ensure hardware redundancy for redundant software entities to increase the availability of the system. Other properties such as HW-affinity, performance or security may be targeted using the same technique.

Moreover defining special link types in the weaving metamodel allows for the development of more abstract mappings. Abstracting concepts is an intrinsic feature of metamodeling, which is discussed widely in the literature. This advantage becomes bolder in the case of configuration integration from two perspectives: First it increases the reusability of link types since the defined link types can be used in future mappings when other configuration fragments need to be added. As those configuration fragments belong to the same system, there is a fair chance that they require similar link types for their mappings (e.g. using the "EqualCorrespondence" link type). The second advantage of the abstract definition of link types is that it allows for the selection of the desirable interpretation and implementation for the mapping. This means that the declarative definition of the link types can be translated according to the features of the system. Let us consider again the "DisjointDistribution" link type. We interpreted this link with the assumption that we have a predefined PLM configuration with specific elements that are fixed and cannot be modified; on the other hand we forced the AMF to use the newly defined VM groups by changing the AMF configuration. While another interpretation of the "DisjointDistribution" may consider the AMF configuration as fixed and unchangeable model and using other heuristics try to change the PLM configuration in a way to still provide hardware redundancy for redundant software entities.

The fact that model transformation is eventually used to translate the weaving model into an executable format does not fade away the benefits of the weaving model. The reason is that the links of the weaving model help us to capture the transformation patterns and reuse them rather than defining all the rules manually. Another reason for selecting the model weaving technique over the direct model transformation is the extensibility of the weaving for integrating additional models with less manual effort. With model weaving we can simply add more models as input into the weaving process and the respective transformation rules will be generated automatically, while adding more models directly into a transformation requires considerable time and effort to develop the new transformations rules.

5   Related Work

The idea of data mapping and data integration has been widely investigated in the literature [21, 22, 23]. Defining the mapping between the models and model integration can be seen as the successor of the data mapping research. A number of approaches have defined model management operations (such as merging, subtracting, integration, etc.) focusing on the mapping definition between the models and proposing the operations for manipulating the model mappings and the models for different scenarios.

In Rondo [20] the model management operators, such as merge, match, extract, are defined for solving the mapping problem of metadata in XML schemata format. However the defined operators can only create mappings with respect to fixed semantics and they are not flexible enough to represent domain specific mappings. A set of generic model management operations are introduced in [3] and the author explains how these operations can be applied to the models and their mappings for different application scenarios. The operations are defined in algebra, while the implementation and execution of the abstract operators are left to the users. A more specific study on defining model management operations for model integration is discussed in [2]. The authors consider a set of operators for integrating heterogeneous models with the possibility of specifying integration constraints that are considered as pre/post conditions for dealing with overlapping concepts.

Model weaving [1], our choice for model integration, in contrast to the previously mentioned work allows for the definition of the extensible mappings which can then be executed with model transformations. In [4, 5], model weaving is used for integrating software architecture models. The mapping links between the elements of the models are created and then filtered based on some similarities, such as type or name, between the linked elements. Basically the links are used to map similar elements. In our work the links between model elements are more complex and target system properties such HW-redundancy for redundant software entities in the case of AMF and PLM configuration models. The links not only define the structural relationships between the elements, but also complex properties of the target system configuration.

6   Conclusion

In component based systems the system is developed by putting together COTS components from different vendors, each of which may have its own configuration reflecting the organization and the characteristics of the system resources from the component's perspective. This results in having multiple partial configurations (or configuration fragments) for the system that were developed independently even though they are now interrelated as they represent and potentially act on the same system entities. Therefore, these configuration fragments need to form together a consistent system configuration to be able to ensure different system properties such as availability, performance. The integration of these configuration fragments is a challenging task because of the overlap and the complex relations that may exist.

We tackled this problem with a model driven approach using model weaving. We used the SA Forum middleware to illustrate our approach. This middleware consists of several services among which we focused only on AMF and PLM. The proposed approach to integrate configuration fragments takes into account the properties of the target system configuration. We used the weaving model to capture the mapping between the elements of the different configuration profiles. We introduced new link types to capture the special relationship between the elements of these profiles in a weaving model, i.e. they were added to the weaving metamodel. Using a set of ATL transformations we can generate a system configuration from the weaving, AMF and PLM configuration models.

Our approach for integrating configuration fragments allows for the reuse and the extension of the system configuration generation process as the link types were defined once and reused for the mapping of different elements of the configuration fragments. In the future other profiles can also be added to the process using the same or new link types. The automated generation of system configurations from different input configurations is another advantage, which results in saving time and efforts needed for the task. The work reported in this paper is part of a larger project aiming at the integration of configuration fragments and maintaining the properties of the integrated model through auto-adjustments in the face of runtime modifications.

Acknowledgment. This work has been partially supported by Natural Sciences and Engineering Research Council of Canada (NSERC) and Ericsson.

References

1. Del Fabro, M.D., M., Bézivin, J., Jouault, F., Valduriez, P.: Applying generic model management to data mapping. In: Journées Bases de Données Avancés (BDA) (2005)
2. Reiter, T., Kapsammer, E., Retschitzegger, W., Wimmer, M.: Model integration through mega operations. In: Workshop on MDWE 2005 (2005)
3. Bernstein, P.A.: Applying model management to classical meta data problems. In: The Conference on Innovative Data Systems Research (CIDR) (2003)

4. Jossic, A., Del Fabro, M.D., Lerat, J.P., Bezivin, J., Jouault, F.: Model integration with model weaving: a case study in system architecture. In: The International Conference on Systems Engineering and Modeling (ICSEM), pp. 79–84. IEEE CS Press (2007)
5. Del Fabro, M.D., Valduriez, P.: Semi-automatic model integration using matching transformations and weaving models. In: ACM SAC, pp. 963–970 (2007)
6. Service Availability Forum, http://www.saforum.org
7. Toeroe, M., Tam, F.: Service Availability: Principles and Practice. Wiley and Sons (2012)
8. SA Forum, AIS, Availability Management Framework, SAI-AIS-AMF-B.04.01, http://www.saforum.org/HOA/assn16627/images/SAI-AIS-AMF-B.04.01.pdf
9. SA Forum, AIS, Platform Management Service, SAI-AIS-PLM-A.01.02, http://www.saforum.org/HOA/assn16627/images/SAI-AIS-PLM-A.01.02.pdf
10. Tisi, M., Jouault, F., Fraternali, P., Ceri, S., Bézivin, J.: On the use of higher-order model transformations. In: Paige, R.F., Hartman, A., Rensink, A. (eds.) ECMDA-FA 2009. LNCS, vol. 5562, pp. 18–33. Springer, Heidelberg (2009)
11. Object Management Group: Unified Modeling Language – Superstructure Version 2.4.1, formal/2011-08-05, http://www.omg.org/spec/UML/2.4.1/
12. Salehi, P., Hamou-Lhadj, A., Colombo, P., Khendek, F., Toeroe, M.: A UML-Based Domain Specific Modeling Language for the Availability Management Framework. In: 12th IEEE International High Assurance Systems Engineering Symposium, San Jose (2010)
13. Jahanbanifar, A., Khendek, F., Toeroe, M.: Providing Hardware Redundancy for Highly Available Services in Virtualized Environments. In: 8th IEEE International conference on Software Security and Reliability (SERE), San Francisco (2014)
14. Del Fabro, M.D., Bézivin, J., Jouault, F., Breton, E., Gueltas G.: AMW: a generic model weaver. In: The 1ère Journée sur l'Ingénierie Dirigée par les Modèles (2005)
15. Del Fabro, M.D., Bézivin, J., Valduriez, P.: Weaving models with the eclipse AMW plugin. In: Eclipse Modeling Symposium, Eclipse Summit Europe (2006)
16. Atlas Model Weaver (AMW), http://www.eclipse.org/gmt/amw/
17. Eclipse Modeling Framework, EMF, http://www.eclipse.org/emf
18. Jouault, F., Bézivin, J.: KM3: a DSL for metamodel specification. In: Gorrieri, R., Wehrheim, H. (eds.) FMOODS 2006. LNCS, vol. 4037, pp. 171–185. Springer, Heidelberg (2006)
19. Jouault, F., Allilaire, F., Bézivin, J., Kurtev, I.: ATL: A Model Transformation Tool. Sci. Comput. Program. **72**(1–2), 31–39 (2008)
20. Melnik, S., Rahm, E., Bernstein, P.: Rondo: A programming platform for generic model management. In: SIGMOD conference, pp 193–204 (2003)
21. Omelayenko, B.: A mapping meta-ontology for business integration. In: The workshop on Knowledge Transformation for the Semantic Web (KTSW 2002) at the 15th European conference on artificial intelligence. Lyon, France, pp. 76–83 (2002)
22. Maedche, A., Motik, B., Silva, N., Volz, R.: MAFRA—A MApping FRAmework for Distributed Ontologies. In: 13th International Conference on Knowledge Engineering and Knowledge Management, pp. 235–50 (2002)
23. Spaccapietra, S., Parent, C.: View Integration: A Step Forward in Solving Structural Conflicts. IEEE Transactions on Data and Knowledge Engineering **6**(2), 258–274 (1994)
24. Open Stack Cloud Software, http://www.openstack.org/

Towards Incremental Updates in Large-Scale Model Indexes

Konstantinos Barmpis[✉], Seyyed Shah, and Dimitrios S. Kolovos

Department of Computer Science, University of York,
Heslington, York YO10 5DD, UK
{kb,s.shah,dkolovos}@cs.york.ac.uk

Abstract. Hawk is a modular and scalable framework that supports monitoring and indexing large collections of models stored in diverse version control repositories. As such models are likely to evolve over time, responding to change in an efficient manner is of paramount importance. This paper presents the incremental update process in Hawk and discusses the efficiency challenges faced. The paper also reports on the evaluation of Hawk against an existing large-scale benchmark, focusing on the observed efficiency benefits in terms of update time; it compares the time taken when using this approach against the naive approach used beforehand, and discusses the benefits of combining the two, gaining improvements averaging a 70.7% decrease in execution time.

1 Introduction

As discussed in [9,11], the ability of modelling and model management tools to scale up in a collaborative development environment is essential for the wider adoption of MDE. This paper contributes to the study of scalable techniques for collaborative modelling, by presenting and empirically evaluating an incremental approach for indexing evolving models stored in file-based repositories (such as Git or SVN). Section 2 introduces the rationale behind model indexing and provides a brief overview of an existing model indexing framework (Hawk [1]). Section 3 presents a naive and an incremental approach for updating model indexes in response to changes to models stored in file-based repositories that Hawk monitors. Section 4 evaluates their performance on various mutants of models from an existing large-scale benchmark. Section 5 discusses related work and Section 6 concludes the paper and identifies directions for further work.

2 Background

This section overviews model indexing, providing motivation for using it in this domain, and introduces the reader to Hawk, our model indexing framework.

G. Taentzer and F. Bordeleau (Eds.): ECMFA 2015, LNCS 9153, pp. 137–153, 2015.
DOI: 10.1007/978-3-319-21151-0_10

2.1   Model Indexing

In a collaborative environment, models need to be version-controlled and shared among many developers. The default approach for doing this is to use a file-based version control system such as Git or SVN. This has certain advantages as such version control systems are robust, widely-used and orthogonal to modelling tools, the vast majority of which persist models as files. On the downside, since such version control systems are unaware of the contents of model files, performing queries on models stored in them requires developers to check these models out locally first. This can be particularly inefficient for global queries (e.g. is there a UML model in my repository that contains a class named "Customer"?) that need to be executed on a large number of models. Also, file-based version control systems do not provide support for model-element level operations such as locking or change notifications. To address these limitations, several open-source and proprietary model-specific version control systems such as CDO, EMFStore and MagicDraw's TeamServer have been developed over the last decade. As discussed in detail in Section 5, while such systems address some of the limitations above, they require tight coupling with modelling tools, they impose an administration overhead, and they lack the maturity, robustness and wide adoption of file-based version-control systems.

In what can be seen as a happy medium between the two approaches to model version control, *model indexing* is an approach that enables efficient global model-element-level queries on collections of models stored in file-based version control systems. To achieve this, a separate system is introduced which monitors file-based repositories and maintains a fine-grained read-only representation (graph) of models of interest, which is amenable to model-element-level querying. Previous work [2,3] has demonstrated promising results with regards to query execution times, with up to 95.1% decrease in execution time for querying model indexes [2], compared to direct querying of their constituent EMF XMI-based models, and up to a further 71.7% decrease in execution time, when derived (cached) attributes were used [3]. This motivates us to improve upon this technology by improving the efficiency of handling model evolution in such model indexes.

2.2   Hawk

Hawk is a model indexing system that can work with diverse file-based version control systems (VCS) and model persistence formats whilst providing a comprehensive API through which modeling and model management tools can issue queries. Hawk needs to be scalable so that it can accommodate large sets of models, and non-invasive (the VCS repositories, where the primary copies of the monitored models are stored, should not need to be modified or configured). In order for Hawk to be able to index heterogeneous models in a back-end agnostic manner, it provides two abstraction layers:

– **Model Abstraction Layer** This layer provides a set of abstractions for representing heterogeneous models and metamodels in memory. Inspired by EMF's respective abstractions, *metamodel resources* contain types/meta-classes (grouped in packages), which have typed attributes and references, as well as annotations. *Model resources* contain objects representing model elements, which have values for the attributes and references of their type.

- **Graph Database Abstraction Layer** Extensive benchmarking showed that graph databases such as Neo4J and OrientDB perform significantly better than other technologies (e.g. relational databases) [2,14] for the types of queries of interest to a system like Hawk. To avoid coupling with a specific graph database, this layer aims at providing a uniform interface for querying and manipulating graph databases in an implementation-independent manner. It is worth noting that implementations of this layer can conceptually be used to connect to any back-end technology, but will suffer in performance if the data model is not similar with the graph model used here.

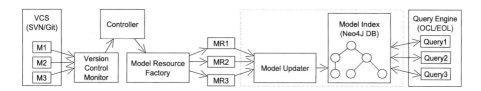

Fig. 1. Overview of the relevant Hawk architecture

Hawk comprises components which can monitor a set of version control repositories, parse and index models of interest stored in them. Figure 1 shows some of the key components of Hawk and their interactions; in the figure, M1–M3 represent model files and MR1–MR3 represent in-memory *model resources* obtained by parsing M1–M3. Below is a brief description of these components:

At the center of Hawk lies the *Controller* of the system, which knows which Hawk components are currently active and is responsible for synchronizing with any changes made to monitored files.

Resource Factories are used to parse metamodel and model files and create the relevant metamodel and model *resources* described above, which are given to the *Controller* to be propagated to the index. They know which files they can parse and also provide a way to give any statically available metamodels to the *Controller* (such as a UML metamodel – without them having to be manually registered).

Version Control Managers are used to poll monitored version control systems in order to get any changes (deltas) to model files of interest. If any such delta is found, it passes it on to the *Controller* so that the changes can be propagated to the model index.

Metamodel Updaters are used to insert *metamodel resources* to the index. As Hawk does not currently deal with metamodel evolution, only the first version of a metamodel is indexed. Model *Updaters* are used to update the index with a new version of a model. In the sequel we examine how such updates can be optimized, focusing on the components found inside the dashed box of Figure 1.

Prototype implementations of the various components exist as Java plugins[1] and support: XMI EMF, BIM[2] EMF and Modelio[3] UML models and meta-models, monitoring of folders on the local machine and on SVN version control repositories, using Neo4J (version 2) Graph NoSQL database for persistence and using Epsilon's EOL [10] as a query engine.

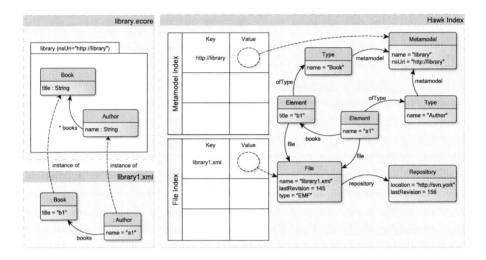

Fig. 2. High-level overview of the contents of a library model index (persisted in a NoSQL graph database), adapted from [3]

Overview of a Hawk Model Index. An example of a Hawk index, containing a simple library metamodel and a model that conforms to it, is illustrated in Figure 2. In general, a model index typically contains the following entities [3]:

- **Repository nodes**. These represent a VCS repository and contain its URL and last revision. They are linked with relationships to the *Files* they contain.
- **File nodes**. These represent files in a repository and contain information on the file such as the path, current revision and type. They are linked with relationships to the *Elements* they contain.
- **Metamodel nodes**. These represent metamodels and contain their names and their unique namespace URIs (in EMF, these would be *EPackages*[4]). They are linked with relationships to the (metamodel) *Types* they contain.
- **Type nodes**. These represent metamodel types (*EClasses* in EMF terminology) and contain their name. They are linked with relationships to their (model) *Element* instances.

---

[1] https://github.com/kb634/mondo-hawk
[2] http://www.openbim.org/
[3] http://www.modelio.org/
[4] We choose to draw parallels with concepts from EMF as they are well-understood.

- **Element nodes**. These represent model elements (*EObjects* in EMF terminology) and contain their attributes (as properties) and their references (to other model elements) as relationships to them.
- **Database Indexes**. Metamodel nodes and File nodes are indexed[5] in the store, so that their nodes can be efficiently accessed for querying (commonly used as starting points for complex graph traversal queries).

It is worth noting that a model index such as the one presented above may end up being a full copy of the actual models found on the relevant version control system but it does not have to be. In principle, if some contents of the model are not deemed useful they can be omitted in order to gain an improvement in injection and possibly query time.

2.3   Updating Model Indexes

As models can evolve over time, appropriate mechanisms need to be in place for efficiently synchronizing the index with any changes in models it monitors. Two alternative approaches that can be used for this:

Naive Synchronization. In this approach, when a model file changes in a repository, Hawk propagates this change by removing all its model elements in the model index and then re-inserting them.

This approach, while seeming inefficient, has various potential benefits:
- The overhead of comparing the contents of the two versions (in two different formats) is avoided. In order to perform an incremental update an element-by-element comparison of the old and new versions of the models has to be performed, which can be very costly.
- The index is expected to be capable of performing massive naive inserts efficiently (such "mass inserts" are used by various database technologies in order to rapidly store an initial version of the data, they may make the model index unavailable during this process). When performing changes to elements in the index (such as when performing an incremental update), this cannot happen, so the time for each individual change to be propagated can substantially increase.

The drawbacks of this approach are:
- The lack of knowledge about changes means that even a change in a single element will require all elements in the model file to be removed and re-inserted into the index. This gets more costly the smaller the change and the larger the model file gets.
- The act of performing a "mass insert" into the index will require heavy usage of its resources and may also limit its availability for use while the update happens. Furthermore, if the index is inefficient in deleting elements, then deleting such large contents may become a bottleneck.

---

[5] http://components.neo4j.org/neo4j-lucene-index/snapshot/

Incremental Synchronization. In this approach, model changes are identified on a model element level by performing a comparison of the old version found in the index with the new version found in the repository. As such, only affected elements (added, removed, changed) have to be updated in the index for achieving synchronization.

The benefits of this approach are:
– As each change is identified on a model element level, avoiding having to delete and insert the entire model file into the index can potentially compensate for the overhead of performing a full model comparison. Hence it can be more efficient both in terms of time as well as resources and availability, as only the relevant subsets of the index will be touched.

The drawbacks of this approach are:
– The overhead of model comparison may be larger than the gain of a fine-grained update if the update is relatively large when compared to the model.
– Such updates impose various requirements on the model files, in order to enable the required comparison (such as the need for model elements to have a unique (non-volatile per file) identifier), which may not be satisfied by some model representation formats.

3   Updates in Hawk

This section presents the process used for updating Hawk model indexes when monitored models change, a combination of naive insertion and incremental updates (using model element signatures – described below), and discusses how this improves the efficiency of updates performed in large model indexes.

3.1   Overview of Hawk Updates

Hawk performs Algorithm 1 every time it finds a changed (added, removed, updated) model file from any of its monitored repositories. As demonstrated in the sequel, using this incremental updating when a model file is already indexed provides a large performance gain when compared to naively deleting and re-indexing it every time it is modified.

3.2   Signature Calculation

In order to update a model, an efficient way to determine whether a model element has changed is needed. A signature of a model element is a lightweight proxy to its current state. In order to calculate a meaningful signature for model elements indexed in Hawk (in order to enable support for incremental updates of the model index, as models in it evolve), every mutable feature of the element needs to be accounted for. As such, the following features are used to calculate the signature of each element:

if *model file already indexed* **then**
  | **if** *change of type added/updated* **then**
  | | incremental update (see Section 3.4)
  | **else if** *change of type removed* **then**
  | | delete indexed elements of *file*, keeping cross-file references to these
  | elements as proxies
  | **end**
else
  | **if** *change of type added/updated* **then**
  | | naive insertion (see Section 3.3)
  | **end**
end

Algorithm 1. Hawk Update Overview

– all of the names and values of its attributes
– all of the names and the IDs (of the target elements) of its references

This works under the assumption that model elements cannot be re-typed during model evolution, which is the case for the popular modeling technologies such as EMF, as well as that model elements have immutable and unique IDs.

A signature can be represented as either a String containing the concatenation of the values listed above or as a hash-code of this String. The String representation ensures that a unique signature exists for any model state, but suffers in terms of comparison performance as potentially very long Strings will have to be compared. On the other hand, the hash-code (Integer) representation allows for rapid comparisons but has a chance (albeit small) for clashes, which show different model states as having the same signature. We decided to use the integer representation as this identifier, to allow rapid comparisons. This signature is used to efficiently find changes in model elements, as detailed below.

3.3 Naive Insertion

For a naive insertion of a model file into Hawk a process outlined in Algorithm 2 is followed. In this process, the elements of the model file are firstly loaded into memory as a *model resource*. Then, for each such element a node is created in the index graph with its attributes as properties, and linked (using relationships) to its file and type/supertypes. Finally, for each element its references are used to link the node with other nodes in the graph.

As this process often requires intense resource consumption, the batch mode of Hawk's back-end is used (if the specific back-end used supports it). This mode makes the database unavailable until the process is completed, but Neo4J has at least an order of magnitude better performance in terms of execution time when compared to on-line (transactional) updating.

3.4 Incremental Updating

For incremental updating of a model file into Hawk, the process outlined in Algorithm 3 is followed. In this process the signatures of each element are used to

use relevant factory to parse the file into a *model resource*
foreach *element in the model resource* **do**
| create model element node in graph
| create signature attribute in node
| create a relationship from this node to its file node
| create a relationship from this node to its type node (and relationships to
| all its supertype nodes)
end
foreach *element in the model resource* **do**
| **foreach** *reference in the references of the element* **do**
| | **if** *reference of element is set* **then**
| | | **foreach** *referenced element* **do**
| | | | **if** *referenced element is not a proxy* **then**
| | | | | create relationship from this node to the node of the
| | | | | referenced element
| | | | **else**
| | | | | add new proxy reference
| | | | **end**
| | | **end**
| | **end**
| **end**
end

Algorithm 2. Naive (batch) insertion algorithm

efficiently determine which elements have changed. Then, for each new element a node is created, for each changed element its properties and relevant references are updated (keeping dangling cross-file references as proxies in Hawk for consistency), and for each removed element its node is deleted. The complexity of this algorithm is $\mathcal{O}(m + n + d \times r)$ where m is the number of model elements in the updated model file, n is the number of model nodes in the model index linked to the (previous version of the) updated file, d is the number of changed elements and r is the number of target elements referenced by the changed element.

This process only alters the part of the model index which has actually changed and as such, it does not need to use more resources than required by the magnitude of the change, potentially saving on memory and execution time.

3.5 Derived Attributes

Derived attributes are used in Hawk in order to speed up certain types of queries [2]. Such attributes are computed using expressions formed in the expression language of a known *Query Engine*. A query engine in Hawk allows for expression languages (such as OCL or Epsilon's EOL [10]) to be used as a query mechanism for a Hawk model index. Such derived attributes are hence pre-computed and cached at indexing time and need to be maintained as the model index evolves.

A simple example is shown in Figure 3; here, the number of books each author has published (named *numberOfBooks*) is pre-computed (using the EOL expression *return self.books.size()*) and stored in a new *DerivedAttribute* node[6] with the attribute name as the relationship linking it to its parent *Element* node.

---

[6] A new node is used for overcoming a limitation found during incremental updating of derived attributes; further information on this can be found in Section 3.6.

let *nodes* be the set containing the ids and pointers to all the nodes (in the model
   index – linked with the updated file)
let *signatures* be the set containing the ids and signatures of the *nodes*
let *delta* be the set containing changed elements
let *added* be the set containing new elements (to be added to the model index)
let *unchanged* be the set containing elements which are the same
foreach *node from all nodes in the model index that are linked with the updated file* **do**
   | add *node* to *nodes*
   | add signature of node to *signatures*
end
foreach *element in elements of model resource* **do**
   | **if** *element id exists in signatures* **then**
   | | **if** *element signature not equal to current signature* **then**
   | | | add element to *delta*
   | | **else**
   | | | add element to *unchanged*
   | | **end**
   | **else**
   | | add element to *added*
   | **end**
end
`/* add new nodes to model index                                  */`
foreach *element in added* **do**
   | add this new element in model file to model index
end
`/* delete obsolete nodes and change altered node attributes       */`
foreach *node in nodes* **do**
   | **if** *node id exists in delta* **then**
   | | remove current properties of node
   | | set all model attributes of node as properties
   | **else if** *node id does not exist in unchanged* **then**
   | | de-reference node (keeping dangling cross-file references as proxies)
   | | delete node
   | **end**
end
`/* change altered references                                      */`
foreach *element in delta* **do**
   | **foreach** *reference in references of element* **do**
   | | **if** *reference is set* **then**
   | | | **foreach** *referenced element in referenced elements of reference* **do**
   | | | | **if** *referenced element is not proxy* **then**
   | | | | | add id of referenced element to *targetIds*
   | | | | **else**
   | | | | | add new proxy reference to model index
   | | | | **end**
   | | | **end**
   | | | **foreach** *relationship in relationships of node linked with the element* **do**
   | | | | **if** *relationship target has id which exists in targetIds* **then**
   | | | | | remove target from *targetIds*
   | | | | **else**
   | | | | | delete relationship as new model does not have it
   | | | | **end**
   | | | **end**
   | | | **foreach** *id in targetIds* **do**
   | | | | add new relationship to model index
   | | | **end**
   | | **else**
   | | | **foreach** *relationship in relationships of node, with the same name as the*
   | | | *reference name* **do**
   | | | | delete this relationship
   | | | **end**
   | | **end**
   | **end**
end

Algorithm 3. Incremental update algorithm

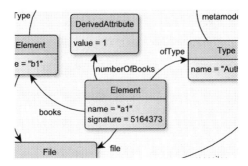

Fig. 3. Pre-computing the number of books of each author

This derived attribute is handled seamlessly with regards to querying, hence an
EOL query used to get the number of books of a specific author a would change
from $a.books.size()$ to $a.numberOfBooks$ (in both cases returning an integer).

Expressions of arbitrary complexity are expected to be used in practice so
that pre-caching the results of such expressions is actually worthwhile. A more
realistic example (but one too complex to present in detail) would be to calculate
(for each author) the names of the authors which have co-written at least three
books with the author in question. This query can be presented in EOL as:

```
var coauthors = self.books.collect(a|a.authors.name);
var authormap = coauthors.flatten.excluding(self.name).asSet().mapBy(
    a|coauthors.select(s|s.contains(a)).size());
var atLeastThreeBooks : Sequence;
for(a in authormap.keySet()){
    if(a>=3) atLeastThreeBooks.add(authormap.get(a)); }
return atLeastThreeBooks.flatten();
```

This would return a Sequence of names of the other authors in question. Caching such complex expressions during inserts/updates can significantly
reduce query execution time of relevant queries, as shown in [2].

3.6   Updating of Derived Attributes

A naive approach for maintaining such attributes would involve having to fully
re-compute each one, every time any change happens to the model index. This
is due to the fact that any such attribute can potentially depend upon any
model element in the index, thus any change can potentially affect any derived
attribute. Such an approach would be extremely inefficient and resource consuming.

As such, an incremental approach for updating derived attributes in Hawk
has been used. In this approach, which is an adaptation of the incremental OCL
evaluation approach discussed in [5], only attributes affected by a change made
to the model index are re-computed when an update happens. In order to know
which elements affect which derived attributes, the scope of a derived attribute
needs to be calculated. The scope of a derived attribute comprises the current
model elements (and/or features) in the model index this attribute needs to

access in order to be calculated. When a derived attribute is added/updated in the model index, the query engine used to calculate this attribute also publishes an *AccessListener* to Hawk, providing the collection of *Accesses* this attribute performed. By recording these accesses (element and/or feature accesses), Hawk updates only the derived attributes which access an element altered during an incremental update. As the incremental update changes the minimal number of elements during model evolution, the updating of derived attributes can be seen to be as efficient as possible with respect to the magnitude of the change.

In more detail, every time an update process happens in Hawk, it records the changes it has made to the model index. A change can be one of the following:

– A model element has been created / deleted
– A property of a model element has been altered
– A reference of a model element (to another one) has been created / deleted
• Note: complex changes (like *move*) are broken down to these simple changes.

Furthermore, every time a derived attribute is added or updated, it records the accesses it requires in order to be computed. An access can be one of:

– Access to a property / reference of a model element
– Access to the collection of model elements of a specific *type / kind*

By having recorded the above mentioned changes and accesses, Hawk can calculate which derived attributes need to be re-computed during a model update using Algorithm 4. As the derived attribute is a node itself, it can be directly referenced and updated if necessary; if the derived attribute was located inside its parent *Element* node, that node would have to be referenced instead and hence all derived attributes in it would have to be updated, as there would not be a way to distinguish which ones need updating and which ones do not.

In the example above, for the derived attribute *numberOfBooks* of node *a1*, the access would read as follows: The derived attribute *numberOfBooks* needs to access node *a1* for its feature *books*. Hence anytime the feature *books* changes for node *a1* (ie: if a member of this reference is added or removed), the derived attribute *numberOfBooks* will have to be recomputed (and only then). As demonstrated by [6], this approach works for expressions of arbitrary complexity as long as they are deterministic (they do not introduce any randomness using random number generators, hash-maps or other genuinely unordered collections). As EOL defaults to using Sequences for collections and does not inherently use random number generators, as long as the expressions provided do not specifically introduce non-determinism, this approach is sound [6].

4 Evaluation

In this section, an existing large-scale benchmark is used to conduct performance tests for updating a Hawk model index. The sample models are mutated in order to simulate changes that are picked up by Hawk.

let *nodesToBeUpdated* be the set containing the derived attribute nodes which
will have to be updated – initially empty

foreach *change in the collection of changes* **do**
    if *the change is a model element change* **then**
        add any derived attribute which accesses this element (or any of its
        structural features) to *nodesToBeUpdated*
    else if *the change is a structural feature change* **then**
        add any derived attribute which accesses this structural feature to
        nodesToBeUpdated
    end
end
foreach *node in nodesToBeUpdated* **do**
    re-compute the value of the (derived attribute) *node*
    update the accesses to the new elements/features this *node* now requires
end

Algorithm 4. Derived attribute incremental update algorithm

4.1 The GraBaTs 2009 Case Study

For evaluating query execution performance in Hawk we use large-scale models
extracted by reverse engineering existing Java code. The updated version of the
JDTAST metamodel used in the *SharenGo Java Legacy Reverse-Engineering*
MoDisco use case[7], presented in the GraBaTs 2009 contest [7] described below,
as well as the five models provided in the contest, are used for this purpose.
In JDTAST *TypeDeclarations* are used to define Java classes and interfaces,
MethodDeclarations are used to define methods and *Modifiers* are used to define
modifiers (e.g static, synchronized) for Java classes and methods. Figures of the
relevant subset of the JDTAST metamodel are found in works like [2,12].

The GraBaTs 2009 contest provided five models, Set0–Set4 (of progressively
larger models, with 70,447, 198,466, 2,082,841, 4,852,855 and 4,961,779 model
elements, respectively), conforming to the JDTAST metamodel. These models
are injected into Hawk and then mutated using various heuristics in order to
test and evaluate its update procedure. In the following sections we use this case
study as a running example to illustrate the implementation and to evaluate it.

4.2 Execution Environment

Performance figures that have been measured on a PC with Intel(R) Core(TM)
i5-4670K CPU @ 3.40GHz, with 32GB of physical memory, a Solid State Drive
(SSD) hard disk, and running the Windows 7 (64 bits) operating system are presented. The Java Virtual Machine (JVM) version 1.8.0_20-b26 has been restarted
for each measure as well as for each repetition of each measure. In each case,
20GB of RAM has been allocated to the JVM (which includes any virtual memory used by the embedded Neo4J database server running the tests).

---

[7] http://www.eclipse.org/gmt/MoDisco/useCases/JavaLegacyRE/

4.3   Model Manipulation

In order to perform model manipulation operations, we used Epsilon's EOL language [10]. EOL is an imperative OCL dialect which supports model modification. We decided to perform five model mutations (changes), which are representative of modifications performed in Java code. These mutations are performed by five EOL operations (available online[8]). By using these operations in an EOL script we can change the model it is run on in a realistic[9] yet sufficiently random manner[10].

4.4   Model Update Execution Time

Table 1 shows the average time taken to complete an update for the models produced by performing the model mutations presented in Section 4.3 on the original GraBaTs models. M(INS) represents the initial insert of the original GraBaTs models into an empty Hawk index (using the naive insert process) and M(0%)–M(50%) represent the update time (from the original model) to one containing 0% to 50% content mutations. These mutations contain an equal degree of each mutation operation found in Section 4.3 so that the total change to the model ends up being $N\%$ of the original model contents. As such, each of the five mutation operations performs changes equal to $\frac{N}{5}\%$ of the original model elements; since some changes are addition/removal operations on model elements, the size of the resulting model is not the same as that of the original.

Table 1. Update Execution Time Results

| Mutation | Execution Time (in seconds) | | | | | | | | | |
| | Set0 | | Set1 | | Set2 | | Set3 | | Set4 | |
	Naive	Inc.	Naive	Inc.	Naive	Inc.	Naive	Inc.	Naive	Inc.
M(INS)	9.96	n/a	18.69	n/a	118.19	n/a	291.06	n/a	346.46	n/a
M(0%)	16.61	2.70	45.72	6.07	-	63.96	-	162.52	-	224.85
M(10%)	16.82	3.94	47.71	10.45	-	94.59	-	247.94	-	292.86
M(20%)	17.76	4.71	48.22	11.53	-	115.86	-	364.94	-	417.50
M(30%)	18.93	5.66	50.60	15.04	-	145.56	-	440.78	-	622.51
M(40%)	21.84	7.04	54.73	18.79	-	165.48	-	781.35	-	-
M(50%)	22.09	7.97	60.21	20.92	-	193.41	-	-	-	-

For each case both the incremental and naive updates were tested and compared with one another. The naive update follows the process described in the prequel for naive insertion, after having had the currently indexed elements

---

[8] https://github.com/kb634/mondo-hawk/blob/master/model_manipulations.eol
[9] Operations often used in manipulation of Java code, such as deleting a Java class
[10] For example, by randomizing which Java class is deleted each time.

deleted from the index. As the naive update process failed to terminate for the larger sets (Set2–Set4), figures for these models are not presented for the naive update process. The reason for this failure is that the Neo4J back-end runs out of memory when trying to delete the entire contents of the model index. This is an unforeseen limitation in the Neo4J database, as we require of it to perform a single transaction to delete the entire contents (as it does not support nested transactions but only flattened nested transactions, which only commit when the top-level transaction is closed) in order to maintain consistency between model versions. We also note that the incremental update fails to complete for 50% of Set3, 40% of Set4 and 50% of Set4. This is due to the fact that the magnitude of the change is so large that not enough memory is available for Neo4J to be able to fit this change in a transaction. The aim is to test the limits of Hawk, as such a system typically aims at collecting a large amount of fragmented models and not large monolithic ones; in the former case memory would not be an issue as it can be flushed after each file is updated. Furthermore, a 40% or 50% change on a model with millions of elements is not an expected use-case and again is presented to test the limits of the system.

These results suggest that the incremental update process is substantially faster than the naive approach, while also not compromising availability of the index[11]. This can be largely attributed to there being no support for "mass deletes" in the index, which ends up taking the majority of time needed for a naive update. The actual time taken for the incremental updates is promising as it scales linearly with the magnitude of the change in the model, giving us improvements of up to 78.10% decrease in execution time for a 10% model change and up to 65.25% for a 50% model change, averaging a 70.7% decrease in execution time over all of the comparable results[12].

4.5   Derived Attribute Update Execution Time

Results for the execution time of altering derived attributes are not presented as they would have to be compared to a baseline. Such a baseline would have been to use a naive approach whereby all derived attributes in the model index would have to be updated any time any model element or feature gets updated. As this approach would have been inefficient compared to the incremental one, it was never implemented so a meaningful comparison cannot be made.

4.6   Threats to Validity

There are five observed threats to the validity of this approach:

– The model mutations performed may have influenced the results. We tried to limit this by performing multiple mutations in each case, all of which contain a random factor in them.

---

[11] As it does not block any incoming queries which may need to be performed.

[12] The 10 results from set0 and set1 that both naive and incremental approaches completed, disregarding the 0% change values as they are presented as a baseline.

- The percentage change of each model may not be indicative of real model change. We tried to limit this by exploring a large variety of changes ranging from zero to fifty percent of the original model.
- The model sizes used for empirical evaluation may not be indicative. Hawk aims at handling large fragmented models, thus we anticipate that the size of each fragment will not be orders of magnitude greater than the test models.
- Using an integer representation for the signatures has a chance for collisions; this chance tends to 1 in 4.29 billion for non-trivial Strings. In all of the empirical tests performed no clashes have been observed, which gives us some confidence that the approach should be used for performance reasons.
- The last one is regarding the correctness of the incremental algorithm. While this is not formally proven, empirical tests comparing the index state after an incremental update with that of the original naive update, previously used in Hawk (for the same changes), provided the same results for all of the mutated models where both the incremental and naive updates completed.

5   Related Work

Aiming at tackling versioned collaborative development of models, proprietary model repositories such as MagicDraw's TeamServer[13] have been developed; they allow for model-element-level versioning, comparison and querying and support multiple concurrent users. Nevertheless, such systems are highly-coupled with the respective vendors' modelling tools and hence have limited flexibility as they bind the user to a specific technology.

Similarly, open-source model repositories such as CDO[14] and EMFStore [8] have arguably gained little traction while commonly supporting a wide variety of back-end technologies. In our view, there are several valid reasons for this. From a practitioner's point of view, choosing a model-specific version control system supported by a small open-source community over a robust and widely-used and supported file-based version control system for storing business-critical models is not a straightforward decision. Also, using two version control systems in parallel (e.g. Git for code and CDO for models) can introduce fragmentation as models and code changed in the context of the same conceptual *commit*, will need to be manually distributed over two unconnected version control systems.

Various model persistence mechanisms have been developed in the past few years as a scalable alternative to the XMI file-based model persistence used in popular modeling technologies such as EMF. Many of these, such as NeoEMF [4], Morsa [12], MongoEMF[15] and EMF fragments [13] use NoSQL databases like Neo4J or MongoDB as a back-end and deliver promising results with respect to model traversal and querying. On the other hand such systems do not handle version control of models stored in them.

---

[13] http://www.nomagic.com/products/teamwork-server.html
[14] http://www.eclipse.org/cdo/documentation/index.php
[15] https://github.com/BryanHunt/mongo-emf/

6   Conclusions and Further Work

In this work we presented an incremental approach to updating model indexes, using lightweight model element signatures. From the empirical data collected we can conclude that incremental updates seem to outperform a naive approach to achieving synchronization in model indexes. As availability can be important in this context, the fact that the solution which does not compromise availability is the most performant is noteworthy. We also discussed an incremental approach for updating derived attributes which uses model changes and accesses to only update derived attributes affected by a model change.

Obtaining these results motivates us to further this work by investigating the use of derived references in model indexes, by providing better support for meta-model evolution, and by providing support for scoping queries to limit results to elements found in specific files in an efficient manner.

Acknowledgments. This research was part supported by the EPSRC, through the Large-Scale Complex IT Systems project (EP/F001096/1) and by the EU, through the MONDO FP7 STREP project (#611125).

References

1. Barmpis, K., Kolovos, D.S.: Hawk: towards a scalable model indexing architecture. In: Proceedings of the Workshop on Scalability in Model Driven Engineering, pp. 6:1–6:9. BigMDE 2013, ACM, New York, NY, June 2013
2. Barmpis, K., Kolovos, D.S.: Evaluation of contemporary graph databases for efficient persistence of large-scale models. Journal of Object Technology **13–3**(3), 1–26 (2014)
3. Barmpis, K., Kolovos, D.S.: Towards Scalable Querying of Large-Scale Models. In: Cabot, J., Rubin, J. (eds.) ECMFA 2014. LNCS, vol. 8569, pp. 35–50. Springer, Heidelberg (2014)
4. Benelallam, A., Gómez, A., Sunyé, G., Tisi, M., Launay, D.: Neo4EMF, a scalable persistence layer for EMF Models. In: Cabot, J., Rubin, J. (eds.) ECMFA 2014. LNCS, vol. 8569, pp. 230–241. Springer, Heidelberg (2014)
5. Egyed, A.: Instant consistency checking for the uml. In: Proc. of the 28th International Conference on Software Engineering, pp. 381–390. ICSE 2006. ACM (2006)
6. Egyed, A.: Automatically detecting and tracking inconsistencies in software design models. IEEE Transactions on Software Engineering **37**(2), 188–204 (2011)
7. GraBaTs: 5th Int. Workshop on Graph-Based Tools (2009). http://is.tm.tue.nl/staff/pvgorp/events/grabats2009/
8. Koegel, M., Helming, J.: Emfstore: a model repository for emf models. In: Proceedings of the 32nd ACM/IEEE International Conference on Software Engineering-vol. 2, pp. 307–308. ACM (2010)
9. Kolovos, D.S., Paige, R.F., Polack, F.A.: Scalability: The Holy Grail of Model Driven Engineering. In: Proc. Workshop on Challenges in MDE, collocated with MoDELS 2008. Toulouse, France (2008)
10. Kolovos, D.S., Paige, R.F., Polack, F.A.C.: The epsilon object language (EOL). In: Rensink, A., Warmer, J. (eds.) ECMDA-FA 2006. LNCS, vol. 4066, pp. 128–142. Springer, Heidelberg (2006)

11. Mougenot, A., Darrasse, A., Blanc, X., Soria, M.: Uniform random generation of huge metamodel instances. In: Paige, R.F., Hartman, A., Rensink, A. (eds.) ECMDA-FA 2009. LNCS, vol. 5562, pp. 130–145. Springer, Heidelberg (2009)
12. Pagán, J.E., Cuadrado, J.S., Molina, J.G.: A repository for scalable model management. Software & Systems Modeling, 1–21 (2013)
13. Scheidgen, M., Zubow, A.: Map/reduce on emf models. In: Proceedings of the 1st International Workshop on Model-Driven Engineering for High Performance and Cloud Computing, pp. 7:1–7:5. MDHPCL 2012 (2012)
14. Shah, S.M., Wei, R., Kolovos, D.S., Rose, L.M., Paige, R.F., Barmpis, K.: A framework to benchmark nosql data stores for large-scale model persistence. In: Proc. 15th Conf. on Model-Driven Engineering Lang, and Systems, Models 2014 (2014)

A Model Management Imperative: Being Graphical Is Not Sufficient, You Have to Be Categorical

Zinovy Diskin[1,2]([✉]), Tom Maibaum[1], and Krzysztof Czarnecki[2]

[1] NECSIS, McMaster University, Hamilton, Canada
{diskinz,maibaum}@mcmaster.ca
[2] University of Waterloo, Waterloo, Canada
{zdiskin,kczarnec}@gsd.uwaterloo.ca

Abstract. Graph-based modeling is both common in and fundamental for Model Driven Engineering (MDE). The paper argues that several important model management (MMt) scenarios require an essential extension of graphical models. We show that different versions of model merge and sync, including many-to-many correspondences between models, can be treated in a uniform, compact and well-defined mathematical way if we specify graphical models as directed graphs with associative arrow composition and identity loops, that is, as categories.

1 Introduction

Graph-based modeling is common in and fundamental for MDE. Such graphical models as Class and ER-diagrams in structural modeling, and Labeled Transition Systems (LTSs) and Sequence Diagrams in behavioral modeling, are real assets to software engineering. The goal of the paper is to argue that several important model management scenarios require an essential extension of graphical models. We show that different versions of model merge and sync (choice and parallel composition in the context of behavior modeling), including many-to-many correspondences between models, can be treated in a uniform, compact and well-defined mathematical way if we specify graphic models as directed graphs with associative arrow composition and identity loops, i.e., as categories.

This is *not* the first call for categories from the model management (MMt) domain. Formalizing model merge as colimit in the respective categories of models and mappings is well known [3,19,22,26], the category-theory based graph transformation framework for model transformations is in active development [14,17,18,21], and a broad categorical view of MMt can be found in [10,24]. In these papers, MMt operations are formalized as operations over (typed attributed) graphs, and MMt scenarios thus live within a suitable category of graphs. We can say that this work advocates the use of *categories-in-the-large*. In contrast, in the present paper we show that an accurate mathematical modeling of complex MMt scenarios, like merging LTSs modulo complex many-to-many correspondences between them, or synchronized parallel composition of LTSs,

© Springer International Publishing Switzerland 2015
G. Taentzer and F. Bordeleau (Eds.): ECMFA 2015, LNCS 9153, pp. 154–170, 2015.
DOI: 10.1007/978-3-319-21151-0_11

require models themselves to be considered as categories—we refer to this idea as to the use of *categories-in-the-small.*. Importantly, categories we need may be subject to non-trivial commutativity constraints and thus are *not free* categories generated by the respective graphs. That is, they are "real" categories rather than categorical completions of graphs. We thus show that a full realization of the known categories-in-the-large framework needs categories-in-the-small.

The paper makes three contributions to the literature. The first one is methodological as described above. The second is technical: we propose a novel extension of the classical notion of LTS based on ideas of the *enriched* category theory. Our LTSs as categories carry an additional structure of partial order between "parallel" (having the same source and target) transitions. Moreover, this order is actually a semi-lattice carrying OR (and perhaps partially defined AND) operations on transitions. Third, we explain how model merge and composition can be specified using (co)limits in a tutorial-like manner, and specially focus on adequacy of the mathematical models we build for the subject matter: constructs included into the models are motivated by the domain to be modelled rather than by mathematical completeness.

Our plan for the paper is as follows. In Sect. 2 we consider several scenarios of LTS merge, and motivate the necessity to include into the LTS formalism sequential and *or/and*-parallel composition of transitions. In Sect. 3 we show that adding to the LTS formalism identity (idling) loops allows us to treat synchronized parallel composition of LTSs via a limit operation. In these sections, considerations are accurate but not formal. In Sect. 4 we formally define an LTS as a functor from a category of states and transitions (enriched over the category of posets) to a category of labels (similarly enriched). This defines a category in which our merge-as-colimit and sync-as-limit scenarios are unravelled. Section 5 presents a summarizing discussion, and Section 6 concludes.

2   Model Merge and Colimit

We use *model merge* to refer to the following scenario. Several models expressing *local* views of the system are first *matched* by linking elements of the models that correspond to the same system element. Then models are integrated into a single *global* model, which includes all data from the local models but without redundancy, in accordance with the match. We will consider three typical cases of intermodel relationships and show that if the complexities of intermodel relationships are properly modeled, then the merge procedure as such is given by the same simple colimit operation. However, the universe in which the merge-as-colimit idea works well for complex intermodel correspondences is a category of graphs with a suitable *additional structure* of sequential and parallel arrow composition, i.e., the universe of enriched categories.

2.1   Getting Started: Simple Match and Merge

Figure 1 presents two consumption models. Model M_1 states that buying an apple is a wise way of spending your dollar, but first you need to work and earn it. Model M_2 suggests spending the dollar earned on buying a cake.

Suppose we want to merge the two models into an integrated model U without data redundancy and loss. For this, we first specify correspondences between the models by bidirectional links r_x $(x = 0, \$, w)$ connecting (we also say *matching*) elements considered to be "the same" as shown in Fig. 1(a). Then we (disjointly) merge the two graphs and glue together matched elements (and only them). Such merge is easily performed "by hand", resulting in model $U = (M1 + M2)/R$ in Fig. 1(b) (read "merge of models $M1$ and $M2$ modulo correspondence $R = \{r_0, r_w, r_\$\}$").

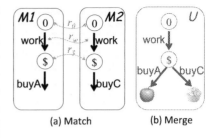

(a) Match   (b) Merge

Fig. 1. Model-based merge (case 1)

The merge procedure can be formally specified as calculating the *colimit* of the *correspondence span* in the category of graphs as shown in Fig. 2. In this figure, the correspondence links r_x $(x = 0, \$, w)$ from Fig. 1(a) are reified as, resp., states (for $x = 0, \$$) and transitions $(x = w)$, which constitutes LTS R. The special nature of R's elements is formalized by two projection mappings $r_i \colon R \to M_i$, $i = 1, 2$.[1] Thus, matching models results in a correspondence span (in the sequel, *corr-span*) (r_1, R, r_2). Taking the colimit of the corr-span results in a model U together with two mappings $u_i \colon M_i \to U$, $i = 1, 2$, specifying how local models are embedded into the merge.

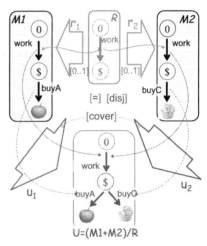

Fig. 2. Map-based merge (case 1)

For Fig. 2 and subsequently, we use the following shading/color schema. Given models and mappings are shaded, while algebraically computed ones are blank (and additionally blue with a color display; the blue color is assumed to recall mechanical computation). Although the elements of the corr-span are produced by the procedure of model matching, this procedure cannot be considered a formal algebraic operation taking two models and returning a corr-span between them. Indeed, correspondences are derived using various contextual and heuristic information *about* the models rather than immediately contained *in* them; moreover, model matching may require an input from the user. Thus, speaking algebraically, the corr-span is a given datum and hence shaded. However, its color is green rather than black to recall the special nature of the

---

[1] To avoid clutter in Fig. 2 and other our figures, in order to specify a mapping between graphs, we only show links between arrows and assume that their sources and targets are linked respectively, and those links are omitted.

heuristics-based model match quasi-operation. Constraints are shown in red; if a constraint is a postcondition of an operation, its name is typed in blue but enclosed by red brackets.

Thus, the colimit operation takes a span and produces a *cospan* (two mappings with a common target). Importantly, the colimit cospan can be uniquely defined (up to isomorphism) by a set of constraints (postconditions) $\{C1, ..., C4\}$ it must satisfy. Moreover, these constraints well correspond to natural requirements for model merging. Constraint $C1$ requires mappings u_1, u_2 to be total: nothing from models M_i is lost in the merge U. In our diagrams, all mappings are assumed to be total (and single-valued) by default, and the corresponding multiplicity constraints are omitted. Constraints $C2, C3$ specify properties of the quadruple (r_1, r_2, u_1, u_2). Constraint $C2$ is *commutativity* [=]: $x.r_1.u_1 = x.r_2.u_2$ for any element $x \in R$ (note the closed contours formed by links starting at R in Fig. 2), which ensures that elements linked by the corr-span are glued in U. On the other hand, constraint $C3$ (*disjointness*) requires *non*-linked elements *not* to be glued: if an element $x \in M_1$ is outside the range of mapping r_1, then element $x.u_1 \in U$ must be outside the range of u_2, and if $x.u_1 = x'.u_1$ then $x = x'$. Similar conditions are required for any $y \in M_2$ outside the range of r_2. Finally, constraint $C4$ states that two mappings u_i jointly *cover* the graph U, and hence every element in U has come from either $M1$, or $M2$, or both. It can be proven [8] that in the universe of graphs and graph mappings, given a corr-span (R, r_1, r_2), there is one and only one (up to isomorphism) cospan (U, u_1, u_2) satisfying the four constraints above. This cospan is called the *colimit* of the span, and it can be computed by a simple algorithm (see, e.g., [1] or [8]). Thus, the colimit operation in the category of graphs accurately captures the requirements for merge in the case of simple one-one correspondences between the models.

Our next goal is to analyse whether the simple pattern above works for more complex cases of intermodel relationships.

2.2   Complex Match and Merge via Derived Transitions

Practical intermodel relationships are often more complex than the one-to-one matches considered above. A simple *one-to-many* match is shown in Fig. 3(a). Model M_1 says you can convert a dollar into a smile by either buying and eating an apple, or by buying and eating a cake. Model M_2 is more abstract and says you can convert a dollar into a smile by fir-

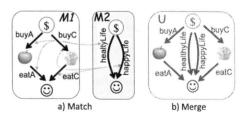

Fig. 3. Model-based merge (case 2)

ing either *healthyLife* or *happyLife* transitions, but is not specific about details of what should be done. Suppose we know that by *healthyLife* model M_2 actually means buying and eating an apple, so that transition *healthyLife* matches two transitions in M_1. Similarly, transition *happyLife* matches buying and eating a cake. Hence, corr-links in Fig. 3(a) must be accompanied with equations (E1) *healthyLife = buyA; eatA* and (E2) *happyLife = buyC; eatC* specifying details of the relationships. Such constraints are often called *(correspondence) expressions* in the literature on model match and merge [2].

The merge can easily be produced by hand Fig. 3(b), but now LTS *U* as shown is underspecified: constraints (E1), (E2) are not shown. To take such expressions into account, the merge algorithm has to be more intelligent and actually more complicated than for one-to-one matching. Managing corr-expressions was declared as one of the big problems of model management in [2].

Let us see how the problem can be treated categorically. A key observation is that a one-to-many relationship is replaced by a one-to-one relationship to a respective *derived* transition, *buyA; eatA* for *healthyLife* and *buyC; eatC* for *happyLife*, as shown in Fig. 4. Derived transitions are shown by dashed arrows (blue with a color display), and the respective triangle diagrams are marked with symbol [;] referring to the operation of arrow composition. The left marker [;] says that the left unnamed transition is *buyA; eatA*, and analogously for the right [;].

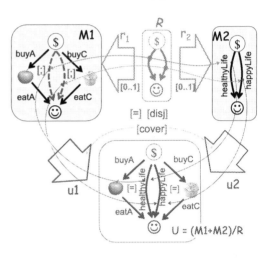

Fig. 4. Map-based merge (case 2)

Use of derived transitions allows us to reduce *one-to-many* to *one-to-one* matching, and then the simple merge algorithm described above can be directly applied and produces the result shown in the lower part of Fig. 4. The main merge principle of copying all data from original models into the merge is realized, and operation labels [;] are copied to *U* as well, but as derived transitions are named in *U* and hence appear there as basic rather than derived elements, their *definitions* in M_1 amount to equational *constraints* [=] in *U*. Thus, constraints $E1, E2$ specified above for the match, are now transferred to the merge. Note that disjointness [disj] of (r_1, r_2, u_1, u_2) amounts to injectivity of u_1 and u_2.

The same idea is applicable for other operations on transitions, e.g., their AND (parallel) or OR (choice) composition, as the example below demonstrates. Suppose that model M_2 has only one transition *beHappy*, which can mean either buying and eating an apple, or, perhaps, buying and eating a cake. With the naive

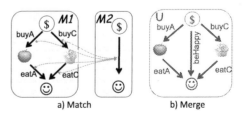

a) Match   b) Merge

Fig. 5. Model-based merge (case 3)

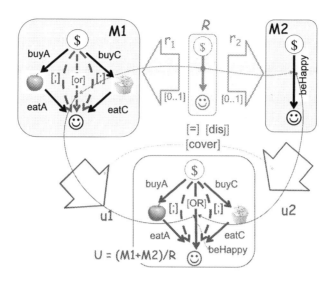

Fig. 6. Map-based merge (case 3_1)

expression-based approach, we would have a match in Fig. 5(a) accompanied with expression (E) specifying the relationship:

(E) $beHappy = buyA; eatA$ or $buyC; eatC$.

We can specify this relationship by a one-to-one match as shown in Fig. 6. We first derive two composed transitions in model M_1 as above, and then apply to them the binary choice operation [or]. The result is the vertical transition in M_1, which is matched to the $beHappy$-transition in M_2. Now we apply the same simple colimit procedure as above, and produce model U as shown in the figure. As the middle transition now has a name, we replace its *definition* in model M_1 by a *constraint* [OR] specified by the expression E above. Similarly, if transition $beHappy$ in M_2 assumes, in terms of model M_1, buying and eating both apples and cakes, we introduce a binary operation [and] on transitions, and match $beHappy$ with derived transition $buyA;eatA$[and]$buyC;eatC$. The result is again a one-one match involving derived transitions.[2]

2.3   Non-injective Match and Merge

There is a different interpretation of the naive match in Fig. 5. We may assume that transition $beHappy$ in M_2 is not a choice between *healthyLife* and *happyLife*, but rather their abstraction that simply does not distinguish between them. A direct way of modeling this interpretation is specified by the corr-span in Fig. 7, in which the right leg r_2 maps two transitions to the same target. The colimit

---

[2] To make operation [and] feasible, we need to interpret state $ as providing enough money for the concurrent execution of all transition leaving the state, and similarly the smile-state means a holistic happiness rather than a number of "happiness units".

of this span is shown in the lower half of the figure; note that two different transitions in model M_1 are glued together in the merged model U.

At first sight, this gluing in the merge can seem bizarre, but let us consider the case in more detail. The match says that transition *beHappy* is "equal" to *buyA;eatA* and to *buyC;eatC* as well. Hence, $buyA;eatA=buyC;eatC$, so that the match reveals a new constraint on model M_1 not initially declared in model M_1.

This is not a rare situation: some properties of an object are only revealed (*emerge*) when this object is related to other objects (and this is what category theory is about). As model merge should preserve all input information, the constraint about M_1 stated by the corr-span is to be respected in the merged model U, and this is exactly what the colimit does. Note how accurately this situation is treated categorically: neither of the original models is changed, but everything needed is captured by a properly specified corr-span.

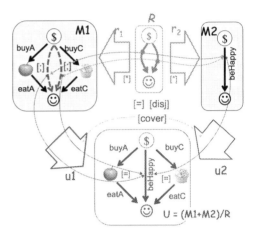

Fig. 7. Map-based merge (case 3_2)

3   Parallel Composition and Limits

Parallel composition of executable components (or behaviors) is a fundamental operation of behavior modeling. It assumes that several (local) components run simultaneously so that global states and transitions are tuples of local states and transitions. Some local transitions from different components may be synchronized, i.e., be always executed simultaneously (as a *handshake*). We will show that parallel composition can be specified categorically by an operation called *limit*, or else *synchronized product*, which places it into the realm of categorical methods and ideas. In particular, as limits are dual to colimits in some precise sense, model merge and parallel composition appear as dual scenarios; we will often call the former *additive*, and the latter *multiplicative (or parallel) merge*.

Suppose that the two models from Sect. 2.1 specify behaviors of two consumers acting in parallel (following a similar example in the textbook [20, p.42], we call them Ben and Bill). We assume that Ben and Bill work together on a joint project to earn their dollars, but buy their snacks separately and independently, i.e., concurrently. In our case, a concurrent composition can be easily constructed by hand, and is often described by diagrams like in Fig. 8 explaining the name *interleaving concurrency*.

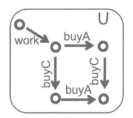

Fig. 8. Interleaving

To consider the example in more detail, we add to both models *idle-loop* transitions as shown in Fig. 9 (ignore links to and from the models for a moment). That is, every state in a LTS is endowed with a loop denoting the do-nothing transition from the state to itself. Independence of Ben's and Bill's buying can now be expressed precisely: irrespective of what Ben is doing (idling or buying), Bill can idle or buy. The joint behavior is shown by LTS U in the right-lower corner of Fig. 9 (Expression $U = (M_1 \times M_2) \setminus R$ refers to

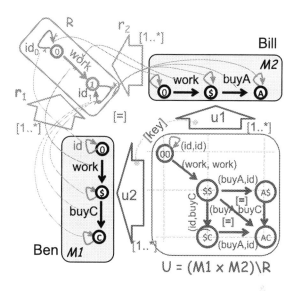

Fig. 9. Synchronized parallel composition

U as a product of M_1 and M_2 modulo correspondence R, which we will consider later.) States in U are pairs of local states, and transitions are pairs of local transitions. Horizontal and vertical transitions in U are those in which one component is idling, whereas diagonal transitions combine two non-idle actions (and idle loops in the product are pairs of idle loops, only one such loop is shown). Thus, idle transitions are fundamental for modeling parallel composition. Note also that both triangle diagrams are declared to be commutative: from the global viewpoint, it does not matter how the system transitions from two dollars to two snacks—all paths are equal. This commutativity appears to be a precise formal counterpart of Ben's and Bill's independence in buying snacks.

As U's elements are pairs, each of them is supplied with a pair of links to the respective elements in M_1 and M_2. To avoid clutter, these links are not shown but can be easily restored as horizontal and vertical projections of U's elements; they constitute a pair of mappings $u_i \colon U \to M_i$, and the constraint [key] states that any element $e \in U$ is uniquely identified by pair $[u_1(e), u_2(e)]$. Both mappings $u_i \colon U \to M_i$ are surjective. This captures simultaneity of the parallel composition: any local element (state or transition) must become a component of a global element.

So far, we have built the composed behavior U by reasonable "physical" considerations. Remarkably, the same LTS U can be automatically computed by an operation called *limit*, if synchronization between the models is properly specified. This specification is given by mappings $r_i \colon M_i \to R$, $(i = 1, 2)$ from the local models to a common model R representing the *global (synchronized)* view of the behavior. We call the triple (r_1, R, r_2) a *synchronizing cospan*. The global view should evidently contain a global transition *work*, composed of two local instances of *work* acting in parallel (note the corresponding links in the r_i). Further, there are two global idle loops. The first, id_0, is a pair of local idle transitions, shown by the respective links in the cospan (r_1, r_2). The second, id_1, is much more interesting. It is the common target of several local transitions from both sides, meaning that, from the global viewpoint, the differences between the respective states are non-essential, and all actions are globally considered as idling, i.e., changes they cause are abstracted away in the global view.

Now the desired result of synchronized composition can be formally defined by a simple formula: $U \stackrel{\text{def}}{=} \{(e_1, e_2) \in M_1 \times M_2 : r_1(e_1) = r_2(e_2)\}$, which gives exactly the LTS U in Fig. 9 motivated "physically"; mappings u_1, u_2 are canonic projections. Note the commutativity of square (r_1, r_2, u_1, u_2): paired local transitions should be globally indistinguishable. The operation producing span (U, u_1, u_2) specified by the formula above from a cospan (R, r_1, r_2) is called the *limit* (in the category of LTSs). We denote the result by expression $U = (M_1 \times M_2) \setminus R$ (read "product of M_i modulo sync-cospan R"), and also call it the *synchronized product*. Thus, the MMt operation of LTS parallel merge can be formally defined as the LTS sync-product, but the latter requires having in the LTS formalism sequential composition of transitions and idle transitions.

4   LTSs: From Graphs to Categories to Enriched Categories

We formalize constructions described above in a categorical way. We first motivate state labels and make labeling a *functor* from a category of transitions to a category of labels; then we specify model merge and parallel composition as operations over functors (Sect. 4.1 and 4.2). We then consider how to model OR- and AND-composition of transitions as operations over arrows, and come to the notion of an *enriched LTS* (Sect. 4.3). We assume that elementary notions of category theory are known to the reader (see, e.g., [1]), but to fix notation and terminology, we provide several basic definitions in the footnotes.

4.1   Labeling as a Functor

A *(directed) graph* G comprises a set $G^\bullet$ of *nodes*, a set $\vec{G}$ of *arrows*, and two functions, so: $\vec{G} \to G^\bullet$ and ta: $\vec{G} \to G^\bullet$. Given nodes X, Y, we write $a: X \to Y$ if $X = \text{so}(a)$ and $Y = \text{ta}(a)$, and denote the set of all arrows from X to Y by $\vec{G}(X, Y)$. We write $e \in G$ to say that $e \in G^\bullet \cup \vec{G}$ is an element of graph G.

A classical LTS is a graph T whose nodes are called *states* and arrows are *transitions*; the latter are labeled via a function $\lambda: \vec{T} \to L$ into a predefined set L of *(action) labels*. As our examples of LTS merge and sync showed, we need to have in the LTS formalism sequential composition of transitions and idle transitions. Moreover, in the behavioral modeling context, associativity of composing transitions, and identity equations for idling, are very natural conditions.

In other words, the transition graph should be a category.[3] However, labels form a set and, thinking categorically, mapping a category (even a graph) to a set is not natural. Hence, we assume that states also have labels. Indeed, as a rule, applying a transition to a state requires the latter to satisfy some pre-conditions, and the result of transition execution satisfies some post-conditions. These pre- and post-conditions can be encoded by *state labels*, which together with transition labels form a graph, even a category, and labeling should be compatible with those categorical structures. Thus, an LTS becomes a triple $M = (T, \lambda, L)$ with T a category of (states and) transitions, L a category of labels, and labeling $\lambda\colon T \to L$ a mapping of categories, i.e., a functor.[4] For example, the category of labels for our model of buying and eating apples and cakes could consist of three nodes \$, *snack*, and $\smile$ (see model $L1$ in Fig. 10); two arrows *buy*: \$→*snack* and *eat*: *snack*→$\smile$, their composition *life*, and three idle loops (omitted in Fig. 10).

Fig. 10 also shows an accurate specification of labeling: in model $T1$, elements' names before colons refer to states and transitions, while names after colons refer to their labels. The latter can be considered as types, and the former as their instances. Importantly, labeling preserves arrow composition and idle loops. Similarly, for model $M2$, the category of labels could be taken to be a single arrow *life*: \$ →$\smile$ (plus two idle loops), while the transition category has two non-trivial arrows *healthy* and *happy*. Note that the classical LTS notion is subsumed if we require the set $L^\bullet$ of state labels to be a singleton: then there is only one state label, and a transition can be always applied to a state.

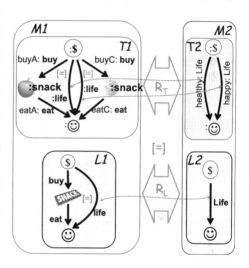

Fig. 10. Labeling

An important property of the transition category $T1$ of model $M1$ in Fig. 1 is that it is *freely* generated by the respective base graph by adding to it all idle loops and all possible arrow compositions (subject to associativity and identity equations). This is how we specified this category in Fig. 4: the basic transitions

---

[3] A *category* is a graph with (i) an associative arrow composition and (ii) identity loops. Point (i) means that for any pair (a, b) of consecutive arrows, an arrow $a; b$ is defined, and $(a; b); c = a; (b; c)$. Point (ii) means that every node $X \in G^\bullet$ is assigned with *identity* arrow $\mathrm{id}_X\colon X \to X$, and $\mathrm{id}_X; a = a = a; \mathrm{id}_Y$ for any $a\colon X \to Y$.

[4] Given categories C_1, C_2, a *functor* $f\colon C_1 \to C_2$ is a graph morphism that preserves composition and identity loops. That is, $f(a; b) = f(a); f(b)$ for any pair of consecutive arrows a, b in C_1, and $f(\mathrm{id}_X) = \mathrm{id}_{f(X)}$ for any node X in C_1. In its turn, being a graph *morphism* provides preservation of incidence between nodes and arrows: $\mathrm{so}(f(a)) = f(\mathrm{so}(a))$ and $\mathrm{ta}(f(a)) = f(\mathrm{ta}(a))$ for any arrow $a \in C_1$.

are shown by black solid arrows while derived composed transitions are dashed (and blue with a color display); idle loops were omitted.

Importantly, even if local transition categories are freely generated, LTS merge can result in categories with non-trivial equations. Consider, for instance, our example in Fig. 7: even if we ignore the name of the middle transition in the merged LTS, and hence can remove it from the model (it can be restored by composition if needed), the commutativity constraint $buyA;eatA = buyC;eatC$ must be kept. Thus, the universe of LTS merge is the universe of "real" categories rather than graphs and freely generated categories. This discussion motivates the following definition.

Definition 1. An *LTS* is a triple $M = (T, \lambda, L)$ with T and L categories of transitions and labels resp., and $\lambda\colon T \to L$ a functor.   □

4.2   Model Management for LTSs

Our examples in Sections 2 and 3 show that the notion of LTS morphism is fundamental for LTS model management. As an LTS is a two-layer structure, their morphisms are also two-layered.

Definition 2. An *LTS morphism* $m\colon M \to M'$ is a pair of functors, $m_T\colon T \to T'$ and $m_L\colon L \to L'$, which commute with labeling: $m_T; \lambda' = \lambda; m_L$.   □

For example, matching LTSs results in two corr-spans, between labels and between transitions, such that commutativity between matches and labeling holds as shown in Fig. 10, where we use bidirectional arrows as a succinct notation for triples (left link, corr-object, right link). Our diagrams in Sections 2 and 3 were not quite accurate by leaving labels implicit. An accurate description would be to leave diagrams as is, but provide the possibility to zoom-in and reveal the two-layer picture shown in Fig. 10. Correspondingly, operations over LTSs we considered are also two-layered: they begin with a two-layer (parallel) match followed by a two-layer (parallel) merge. As we argued, it makes sense to formally define these operations as colimit (for merge) and limit (for parallel merge/composition). After that, category theory provides the respective machinery roughly sketched below.

Let Cat denote the category of all (small) categories. Then, according to our formal definitions of LTSs and their morphisms, the category of all LTSs is nothing but the arrow category $\mathsf{Cat}^{\to}$ over Cat: its objects are Cat-arrows, i.e., functors, and their morphisms are commutative squares described in Definition 2. It is well known that such an arrow category has all (two-layer) limits and colimits with well known simple algorithms computing them [1]. (A simple description of these algorithms can be found in our TR [8].)

4.3   Parallel Composition of Transitions

The most immediate way to formalize OR- and AND-parallel composition motivated in Sect. 2 is to enrich the set of transitions $T(X, Y)$ for any pair of states X, Y with a partial order $\sqsubseteq_{XY}$ (we will often omit the subindex), and define binary OR and AND operations as taking the least upper bound (LUB) and the greatest lower bound (GLB) of two transitions w.r.t. $\sqsubseteq$. A natural "physical" interpretation of relation $\sqsubseteq$ is that stating $t1 \sqsubseteq t2$ means that transition $t1$ is a specialization of transition $t2$, for example, stating *happy* $\sqsubseteq$ *healthy* (both of type *Life*) means that *happy:Life* assumes *healthy:Life* (but needs more than that). Particularly, firing transition $t1\colon X \to Y$ automatically implies transition $t2\colon X \to Y$ (but not necessarily the converse). Categorically, specialization can be seen as a special *2-arrow* between transitions (*1-arrows*); in structural modeling, such arrows are often called *isA*-arrows. Now OR-composition of transitions $t1, t2\colon X \to Y$ is defined to be their LUB: firing any of ti automatically means firing $t1 \vee t2$. Similarly, we could define AND-composition of transitions (true concurrency) as taking their GLB wrt. $\sqsubseteq$: firing $t1 \wedge t2$ means firing both $t1$ and $t2$. This operation makes perfect sense in our context if we interpret state \$ as having as much money as necessary for buying all snacks, and correspondingly state $\smile$ as happiness provided by eating any number of snacks.

There is an essential difference between OR and AND compositions. It is reasonable to assume that any two transitions can be OR-composed—this is an explication of the fact that choice is inherited in the notion of LTS. In contrast, AND-composition (which means the concurrent execution) may exist for some transitions, but may not exist for others (which cannot run concurrently).

An immediate formalization of these ideas is provided by the notion of a category *enriched* over the category of posets Pos.[5]

Definition 3. An *OR-enriched* LTS is a triple (T, λ, L) with T and L categories of transitions and labels resp. enriched over Pos^+, and $\lambda\colon T \to L$ an Pos^+-enriched functor. The notion of an *(OR,AND)-enriched* LTS is defined similarly.

Specifically if we have transitions $t1$ and $t2$ with labels $l1$ and $l2$ resp., then OR-composition of $t1$ and $t2$ must be labeled by OR-composition of $i1$ and $l2$; and similarly for AND (because we require functor λ to be enriched). Note that the category of labels can be trivially enriched: $t1 \sqsubseteq t2$ iff $t1 = t2$. Then enrichedness of the labeling functor λ implies that only transitions with the same label can be OR- or AND-composed. In this way enriched labeling brings a strict type discipline to modeling with LTSs.

Colimits of enriched LTSs are computed componentwise: objects, arrows, 2-arrows. For instance, if in our merge scenario in Fig. 4, model $M2$ would have a 2-arrow from happyLife to healthyLife (i.e., we state *happy* $\sqsubseteq$ *healthy* over label *Life*), then the merged LTS would also have this 2-arrow, which together with commutativity constraints implies $buyC;eatC \sqsubseteq buyA;eatA$. This is yet another

---

[5] A category C is *enriched* over Pos if for any two objects $X, Y \in C^\bullet$, collection of all arrows $C(X, Y)$ from X to Y is a poset. Moreover, arrow composition $\_;\_\colon C(X, Y) \times C(Y, Z) \to C(X, Z)$ is a poset morphism (i.e., an order-preserving mapping) for all triples X, Y, Z. A functor $f\colon C_1 \to C_2$ between Pos-enriched categories is *Pos-enriched*, if $f_{XY}\colon C_1(X, Y) \to C_2(f(X), f(Y))$ is a poset morphism for all pairs X, Y. In a similar way we can define enrichedness over category Pos^+ of all posets with finite LUBs, or $\mathsf{Pos}^\times$ of all posets with finite GLBs, or category $\mathsf{Pos}^{+\times}$ of all lattices by requiring preservation of, resp., LUBs, GLBs, or both.

illustration of how one model ($M2$ in this case) imposes a constraint on another model ($M1$). Also note that even if local LTSs are freely enriched over Pos^+ (OR-compositions are added for all pairs of transitions), their colimit can be enriched non-freely. For example, in Fig. 6, the merged model U satisfies constraint $beHappy = buyA;eatA \lor buyC;eatC$ denoted by [OR].

5   Observations, Discussions, Future and Related Work

We will first discuss briefly several possible practical and theoretical applications of the framework, and then consider related work.

Universality of (co)limits and Specifications for MMt Tools. Categorical formalization of merge as colimit, and parallel composition as limit, reveals a remarkable duality between these two types of model management scenarios. The general patterns of the two operations are shown in Fig. 11. Colimit takes a corr-span and produces a cospan, while limit takes a sync-cospan and produces a span: the diagrams are mutually convertible by inverting directions of all arrows. Importantly, both operations can be uniquely defined by the respective post-conditions. We discussed them for colimit in Sect. 2.1, and similar conditions can be formulated for limit as well. In addition to constraints [=] and [key], we need to require the limit span to be *maximal* in some precise technical sense, which ensures that *all* globally indistinguishable pairs are collected in U. Dually, properties [cover] and [disj] provide *minimality* of the colimit cospan. Thus, the existence of (co)limits is a property of the universe of models and mappings rather than a user-defined superstructure (details can be found in any category theory textbook, e.g., [1]).

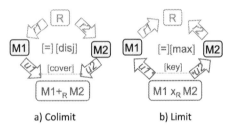

a) Colimit   b) Limit

Fig. 11. Duality

In the categorical literature, defining (co)limits via their postconditions (minimality or maximality) is referred to as their *universality*.

Universality of (co)limits may be important for the proper design and use of MMt tools. As shown in [16], miscommunication between tool users and tool builders can be a major problem in MDE practice (see [9] for a detailed discussion). The possibility of defining model merge and parallel composition via (co)limit operations, which in their turn can be defined universally via postconditions, opens the door for specifying semantics of MMt tools in an unambiguous and precise way. We do not want to say that, e.g., any model merge scenario can be reduced to colimit, but colimit is a core concept of model merge to which specific merge scenarios and tools should be related. Considering a particular model merge scenario as either a particular case of an incomplete colimit, or the complete colimit, or a particular way of postprocessing the colimit (e.g., to resolve conflicts produced by the colimit), can guide the tool design, and facilitate communication between the tool users and tool builders. We plan a comparative study of model merge tools w.r.t. the colimit "yardstick" for future work.

MMt Colors and Tools. Either type of model merge consists of two stages: the green and the blue. The former is model match, which requires heuristics, contextual analysis, and often some user input. After models are matched and a corr-(co)span is produced, their merge is a routine and fully automatic (blue) operation (colimit or limit). The green and the blue stages of model merge are different both methodologically and technologically, and it makes sense to strictly separate concerns in the architecture of MMt tools. For example, in [6] we argue that schema and data integration algorithms mixing match and merge become unnecessarily complicated; the same is true for model merge tools. In [10], we show that the green vs. blue divide appears in other MMt scenarios, e.g., model transformation, and in [7] we argue that mixing green and blue leads to the inflexible architecture of model synchronization tools.

Modeling Concurrency. LTSs are considered to be well suited for modeling sequential behavior and choice, while their expressiveness for modeling concurrent behavior is limited and reduces concurrency to interleaving. Our categorical elaboration of LTSs brings new ideas to the subject. First, we distinguish between *external* concurrency via parallel composition of LTSs, and *internal* concurrency modeled with AND-compositions of transitions within the same LTS. In either case, commutativity is fundamental. Second, our notions of internal OR/AND compositions of transitions modify the understanding of what an LTS is. An LTS appears to be a signature of basic transitions from which different behaviors can be composed by applying OR and AND operations. In particular, an LTS enriched over the category $\mathsf{Pos}^{\times}$ (posets with GLBs) allows the concurrent execution of any finite set of transitions, but a more practical notion would be an LTS with only partially defined AND-composition. Applications of enriched LTSs for modeling true concurrency can be interesting future work.

Related Work. An LTS is a classical behaviour model defined as a transition relation $T \subset S \times L \times S$ over sets S of states and L of labels. Adding to the formalism composition of labels, thus making L a monoid or even a category, was considered by several authors: references and discussion can be found in [27]. Categorization of LTSs in these works is mainly motivated by mathematical reasons of unification and elegance. In contrast, we motivate categorical constructs by practical MMt scenarios and carefully discuss adequacy of our mathematical models. We are not aware of viewing commutativity between sequences of transitions as a major construct for the interleaving model of concurrency.

The notion of order-enriched LTS fits in the general paradigm of STS (*structured transition systems*) [5] stemming from an influential paper "Petri nets are monoids" (PNAM) [23], but there is an essential difference. For PNAM, applying AND to transitions assumes applying AND to their source and target states (to buy a one-dollar apple and a one-dollar cake, you need two dollars, and eating both snacks results in two smiles). The corresponding categorical structure is a monoidal rather than enriched category. The PNAM ideas were generalized in STSs by adding two different (but related) superstructures to LTSs: one for states and one for transitions, and the former is typically not poorer than the latter. In contrast, we do not assume any superstructure for states (other than that given by labeling). Also, the PNAM approach does not consider the OR-monoidal structure, which for LTSs is even more fundamental than AND. Categories combining AND- and OR-monoidal structures [4] were studied as categorical models of linear logic—a resource-sensitive version of propositional logic. Our order-enriched LTSs are not resource-sensitive.

Using colimits for modeling various operations of "putting widgets together" can be traced back to Goguen's pioneering work [13], and has often been used in computer science, databases, and ontology engineering; annotated references relevant to MDE can be found in [3,11]. Our use of colimits for merging behavioral models with complex correspondences via derived transitions is novel (usually more complicated methods are employed for such cases, see, e.g., [25]); its relation to semantic merge developed in [3] needs further research.

Using limits for synchronized parallel composition is less well known [15]; the closest to our setting is, probably, in [12], where they use limits for parallel composition of alphabets seen as pointed sets. But for us, an alphabet is a category, an LTS is a functor into this category, and we compose both alphabets (as types) and their "instances" (states and transitions). We are also not aware of the explicitly stated relationships between Model Management and Process Algebra: Merge/colimit is Choice, while Synchronization/limit is Parallel composition.

6   Conclusion

We have analyzed merge and parallel merge of LTSs. The main observation is that the merge procedures as such can be relatively simple (and formalized by the categorical operations of (co)limit), if correspondences between LTSs are properly specified using *derived* transitions. Operations needed for transition derivation are (i) adding idle-loop transitions for all states, (ii) sequential composition of transitions, and (iii) their OR- and AND-parallel composition. Adding (i) and (ii) to the LTS formalisms makes LTSs (mappings between) categories, and adding (iii) enriches them with a 2-arrow structure.

Although in the paper we only considered one class of models, LTSs, constructs we used should be applicable in a much wider context. Indeed, LTSs can be seen as a typical behavioral model and a benchmark for behavior modeling. As for structural modeling, we show in [8] that ideas and constructs we have considered in the paper are directly applicable for structural modeling with class diagrams as well. After all, the very nature of category theory, designed for a proper unification and generalization of different mathematical structures, facilitates "technology transfer" from LTSs to broad model universes.

Acknowledgments. We are grateful to anonymous reviewers for useful comments and suggestions. Financial support was provided by the Automotive Partnership Canada via sponsoring the NECSIS project.

References

1. Barr, M., Wells, C.: Category theory for computing science. Prentice Hall (1995)
2. Bernstein, P.A.: Applying model management to classical meta data problems. In: CIDR (2003)
3. Chechik, M., Nejati, S., Sabetzadeh, M.: A relationship-based approach to model integration. ISSE **8**(1), 3–18 (2012)
4. Cockett, J.R.B., Koslowski, J., Seely, R.A.G.: Introduction to linear bicategories. Mathematical Structures in Computer Science **10**(2), 165–203 (2000)
5. Corradini, A., Montanari, U.: An algebraic semantics for structured transition systems and its applications to logic programs. Theor. Comput. Sci. **103**(1), 51–106 (1992)
6. Diskin, Z., Easterbrook, S., Miller, R.: Integrating schema integration frameworks, algebraically. Tech. Rep. CSRG-583, University of Toronto (2008) http://ftp.cs.toronto.edu/pub/reports/csrg/583/TR-583-schemaIntegr.pdf
7. Diskin, Z., Xiong, Y., Czarnecki, K., Ehrig, H., Hermann, F., Orejas, F.: From State- to Delta-Based Bidirectional Model Transformations: The Symmetric Case. In: Whittle, J., Clark, T., Kühne, T. (eds.) MODELS 2011. LNCS, vol. 6981, pp. 304–318. Springer, Heidelberg (2011)
8. Diskin, Z.: Towards category theory foundations for model management. Tech. Rep. GSDLab-TR 2014-03-03, University of Waterloo (2014). http://gsd.uwaterloo.ca/node/566
9. Diskin, Z., Gholizadeh, H., Wider, A., Czarnecki, K.: A Three-Dimensional Taxonomy for Bidirectional Model Synchronization. J. of Systems and Software (2015), to appear
10. Diskin, Z., Kokaly, S., Maibaum, T.: Mapping-aware megamodeling: design patterns and laws. In: Erwig, M., Paige, R.F., Van Wyk, E. (eds.) SLE 2013. LNCS, vol. 8225, pp. 322–343. Springer, Heidelberg (2013)
11. Diskin, Z., Xiong, Y., Czarnecki, K.: Specifying overlaps of heterogeneous models for global consistency checking. In: Dingel, J., Solberg, A. (eds.) MODELS 2010. LNCS, vol. 6627, pp. 165–179. Springer, Heidelberg (2011)
12. Fiadeiro, J.L., Costa, J.F., Sernadas, A., Maibaum, T.S.E.: Process semantics of temporal logic specifications. In: Bidoit, M., Choppy, C. (eds.) COMPASS/ADT. Lecture Notes in Computer Science, vol. 655, pp. 236–253. Springer, Heidelberg (1991)
13. Goguen, J.A.: A categorical manifesto. Mathematical Structures in Computer Science **1**(1), 49–67 (1991)
14. Golas, U., Lambers, L., Ehrig, H., Giese, H.: Toward bridging the gap between formal foundations and current practice for triple graph grammars. In: Ehrig, H., Engels, G., Kreowski, H.-J., Rozenberg, G. (eds.) ICGT 2012. LNCS, vol. 7562, pp. 141–155. Springer, Heidelberg (2012)
15. Große-Rhode, M.: Semantic Integration of Heterogeneous Software Specifications. Monographs in Theoretical Computer Science. An EATCS Series, Springer (2004)
16. Hutchinson, J., Whittle, J., Rouncefield, M., Kristoffersen, S.: Empirical assessment of mde in industry. In: ICSE, pp. 471–480. IEEE, ACM (2011)
17. Lambers, L., Hildebrandt, S., Giese, H., Orejas, F.: Attribute handling for bidirectional model transformations. ECEASST **49** (2012)
18. Lauder, M., Anjorin, A., Varró, G., Schürr, A.: Bidirectional model transformation with precedence triple graph grammars. In: Vallecillo, A., Tolvanen, J.-P., Kindler, E., Störrle, H., Kolovos, D. (eds.) ECMFA 2012. LNCS, vol. 7349, pp. 287–302. Springer, Heidelberg (2012)

19. Liang, H., Diskin, Z., Dingel, J., Posse, E.: A general approach for scenario integration. In: MODELS, pp. 204–218 (2008)
20. Magee, J., Kramer, J.: Concurrency: state models and Java programs. Wiley (1999)
21. Mantz, F., Taentzer, G., Lamo, Y.: Well-formed model co-evolution with customizable model migration. ECEASST 58 (2013)
22. Marchand, J., Combemale, B., Baudry, B.: A categorical model of model merging. In: Modeling in Software Engineering, pp. 70–76. MISE, ICSE Workshop (2012)
23. Meseguer, J., Montanari, U.: Petri nets are monoids. Inf. Comput. **88**(2), 105–155 (1990)
24. Muller, P., Fondement, F., Baudry, B., Combemale, B.: Modeling modeling modeling. Software and System Modeling **11**(3), 347–359 (2012)
25. Nejati, S., Sabetzadeh, M., Chechik, M., Easterbrook, S.M., Zave, P.: Matching and merging of statecharts specifications. In: ICSE (2007)
26. Sabetzadeh, M., Easterbrook, S.: An algebraic framework for merging incomplete and inconsistent views. In: 13th Int. Conference on Requirement Engineering (2005)
27. Sobociński, P.: Relational presheaves as labelled transition systems. In: Pattinson, D., Schröder, L. (eds.) CMCS 2012. LNCS, vol. 7399, pp. 40–50. Springer, Heidelberg (2012)

Opening the Black-Box of Model Transformation

John T. Saxon[1]([✉]), Behzad Bordbar[1], and David H. Akehurst[2]

[1] University of Birmingham, Birmingham, UK
{j.t.saxon,b.bordbar}@cs.bham.ac.uk
[2] Itemis AG, 44536 Lünen, Germany
dr.david.h@akehurst.net

Abstract. The automated execution of model transformation plays a key role within Model Driven Development. The software that executes a transformation, commonly known as a transformation engine, receives the meta-models of the source and destination, and a set of transformation rules as input. Then the engine can be used to convert instances of the source meta-model to produce a destination model. Transformation engines are often seen as black boxes. In order to be sure of the correct execution, it is crucial to understand how a transformation engine executes a given transformation. This paper presents a method of capturing and analysing the activities carried out within the transformation engine by elaborating on existing tracing mechanisms used by existing engines. We compare the tracing mechanisms involved in four popular, rule-based transformation frameworks and highlight their shortcomings. A new trace meta-model is presented to deal with some of these shortcomings. These processes can be applied to all existing frameworks; as a proof of concept we have extended an existing traceability framework, based on our earlier work, to implement these mechanisms.

1 Introduction

The execution of model-to-model (M2M) transformations is often viewed as a black box process. Transformation engines such as the Epsilon Transformation Language (ETL) [16] and the ATLAS Transformation Language (ATL) [15] require the meta-models of the source, destination and a set of transformation rules as input. Then a transformation engine, behind the scenes, automatically executes the rules and converts a source model to generate the destination model. Even during testing and verification, all existing research focuses on correctness of rules, while treating the transformation engine as a black-box that is assumed to execute correctly. One exception to this "black-box" routine is the process of *tracing* [1,9,18]. Traceability can be supported in transformation engines and gives access to the linkage between source and destination models established by a transformation execution [18]. To the best of our knowledge the first tracing mechanism, within non-graph based transformation engines, was implemented and used by UML2Alloy [21] through the Simple Transformer (SiTra) [2]. UML2Alloy produces Alloy models from a UML class diagram and

© Springer International Publishing Switzerland 2015
G. Taentzer and F. Bordeleau (Eds.): ECMFA 2015, LNCS 9153, pp. 171–186, 2015.
DOI: 10.1007/978-3-319-21151-0_12

OCL statements via a transformation. In Shah et al. [21], the transformation trace was used to convert a counter example produced by Alloy back to UML.

This paper is based on our study of four model transformation frameworks: ATLAS Transformation Language (ATL) [15], Epsilon Transformation Language (ETL) [16], Operational Query/View/Transform (QVT-O) [18], and the Simple Transformer [2]. We have identified a number of shortcomings of the existing frameworks with respect to traceability mechanisms implemented within them. In this paper we focus on three issues: orphan objects, loss of information regarding the ordering of execution and the dependencies between the rules. These shortcomings and their adverse effects, which are common to most frameworks, are described with the help of well-known examples. Then we explain a modification to the design of transformation engines that can eliminate these deficiencies. We present an implementation of the design by extending SiTra. We also describe the changes required to modify ETL to compliment the design. This is to show that other engines can adopt our design easily. Finally we evaluate, the approach by mapping a relational database to Apache HBase [22], a NoSQL database, via a non-trivial transformation. This transformation is different from most transformations specified on the relational databases as both the data is migrated and the schemas are mapped. In particular we report on the execution of the transformation on the so-called employee database provided by MySQL. This dataset contains four million rows over six tables and has been successfully transformed to HBase.

This paper is structured as follows: in section 2 we explain our preliminaries. Section 3 provides some more detail with regards to traceability within M2M transformation. We then illustrate the shortcomings in section 4. In section 5 we present a summary of our solution and in section 6 we fully describe our new version of SiTra. In order to evaluate our work, we present a case study in section 7, specifically looking at transforming a non-trivial model of a relational database into HBase [22] (a NoSQL database). Followed by a couple of important points regarding how this can be implemented within ETL section 8. We then display the current related work in section 9 and conclude in section 10.

2   Preliminaries

2.1   Model Transformation Frameworks

Model transformation software tools, commonly known as model transformation frameworks, are used to execute M2M transformations [2,7,15,16,18,24]. These tools use a wide range of technologies and differ in the degree of support they provide and their complexity. Some model transformation frameworks have strong GUI support for programming, support of persistence and management of models, re-factoring checking, etc. However they all support the *core functionality* depicted in Figure 1 [8]. Each model transformation framework requires meta-models of both the source and destination and a set of transformation rules as input. Then the framework will *execute* the rules on an instance of the source

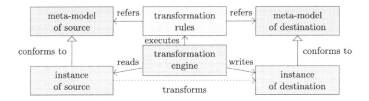

Fig. 1. An Overview of M2M Transformation

meta-model to produce an instance of the destination meta-model. In this paper we focus on this specific core functionality.

2.2 SiTra

The *Simple Transformer* (SiTra) is a Java library that supports the above core functionality. Produced in 2006, it has been used and modified by various groups in numerous projects and tracing activities. Among others, SiTra is used in UML2Alloy [21], AC2Alloy [13], SD2Alloy [3], OWL-S to BPEL [4], state machines to VHDL [26] and sequence diagrams to coloured Petri nets [5]. The emphasis of SiTra, although originally educational, is on using Java so that developers can execute rules in lightweight frameworks. The Java implementation is available online[1]. There are also implementations of SiTra in C# and Python.

```
1   public class ClassToTable implements Rule<Class, Table> {
2     public boolean check(Class source) {
3       return true; }
4
5     public Table build(Class source, Transformer transformer) {
6       return new Table(); }
7
8     public void setProperties(Table target, Class source,
9         Transformer transformer) {
10      List<Column> cols =
11          transformer.transformAll(source.getAttributes());
12      target.setColumns(cols);
13      ... } ... }
```

Fig. 2. A rule for transforming a Class object into a Table object

The framework itself defines two interfaces: *a)* `Rule`; and `Transformer`. The Rule provides an interface to create a particular output given an input and comprises of three simple methods that map to the guard, the instantiation phase

---

[1] http://baserg.github.io/sitra

and the binding phase of a M2M transformation. The `Transformer` interface gives the developer the bare essentials for completing an actual M2M transformation. The prime focus of SiTra is the simplicity of writing rules in an imperative language without a need of specialised tool knowledge. Figure 2 shows the popular transformation of an object orientated class to a relational table. The interface of a rule lends itself to the standard three operations within all M2M transformation engines.

1. The `check` method, line 2, is the *guard* of the rule, i.e. it determines whether the rule is applicable for the given source object.
2. The `build` method, line 5, instantiates the target object for the source that it relates to.
3. The `setProperties` method, line 8, sets the attributes of the resultant target object; from here one may call other transformations to complete the final model.

For further examples we refer the reader to the tutorial section of footnote 1.

3   Traceability within Model Transformation

Traceability is a technique for keeping track of rule invocations [18]. It has been used in many applications and has been discussed at length as an important requirement [6,11,19,23,25,27]. For a survey of traceability see "Survey of Traceability Approaches in Model-Driven Engineering" [12].

The trace instances are stored as a three tuple: $(A, AtoB, B)$. This indicates for each transformation of the source input A, using the transformation rule $AtoB$, the target output B has been created. Thus any other attempt to rerun this specific rule with the same source, the same output will be returned. This happens within popular transformation tools such as the ATL [15], QVT-O [18], the ETL [16] and SiTra.

There are however two levels of traceability: *a) internal*; and *external* as defined by [14]. Internal traceability is a private mechanism used within a transformation engine. It is used to trace what outputs are generated by what inputs. As this is internal, the API is private so the actual trace cannot be persisted and therefore is lost once the transformation is completed. ATL [15], Xtend [10] and Eclipse's implementation of QVT-O follow this mechanism. An external trace however, remains after the transformation has been completed. This enables its users to persist, or use the trace for further analysis and transformations. SiTra and ETL provide a linear trace of what rules and inputs have created what outputs.

4   Challenges of Tracing in Model Transformation

4.1   Orphans

Orphan objects are objects that are created within the M2M transformation but are not recorded within the trace. In hybrid/imperative engines like ETL and

SiTra it is possible to use the **new** keyword to create objects within the rule itself whilst not as part of the definition. Hence orphans are not accounted for within the trace, meaning if one were to attempt to find the source of this object there is no link internally or otherwise.

To see this, consider the well-known example of mapping object orientated models to relational database. This example used by Epsilon's own OO2DB example[2] the rule `Class2Table` has a conditional statement to determine whether it requires a foreign key to reference a parent table. Here it will create a `Column` and a `ForeignKey` object; neither of these are recorded within the trace due to the use of the Java allocation and not by the transformation engine.

Of course, in the above example, the ETL code can be re-factored to avoid using this keyword by using the language's ability to implement inheritance between rules. This would entail three rules: *a)* an abstract rule containing the basic `Class2Table` transformation without the if statement; a concrete, empty, rule for Classes that do not extend another; and another concrete rule for Classes that do, which extends the abstract to include the new elements for the foreign key.

In the case of SiTra, due to the restrictions placed upon in Java, the definition of a rule must only have one input and one output, i.e. `Rule<Input, Output>`. A fix for this could be the use of tuples as the `Output`, for example a `Pair<X,Y>` or `Triple<X,Y,Z>`.

The two solutions we provide here do not stop the developer from using the **new** keyword and both can increase the complexity of the rules themselves. It is not possible to remove the **new** keyword entirely. As a result, there is a clear scope in modifying the execution engines within the transformations frameworks to take good care of the orphans.

4.2   Ordering of Rule Execution

For the maintenance and debugging of a M2M transformation, the developers need to recreate the transformation. Often when a set of transformation rules is executed, there is a possibility that they are executed in a different order. This change of order can be because of the low-level implementation choices such as how a *collection* is implemented or details arising from the scheduling within the execution environment. To demonstrate the variation in the order of executing rules consider the OO2DB example used by various rule engines.

Suppose R_1 and R_2 represent the two rules that map classes and attributes to tables and table columns, respectively:

1. The Class is associated to a collection of Attributes. The overall transformation requires the `ClassToTable` to transform the attributes during its binding phase to generate the columns and assign their parent to the resultant Table object. However not all iterators iterate objects in the same order

---

[2] https://www.eclipse.org/epsilon/examples/index.php?example=org.eclipse.epsilon. examples.oo2db

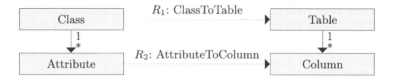

Fig. 3. A sample of rule dependencies

of which they were added. A `HashSet` in Java for example provides no guarantees as to the iteration order of the set. Thus a second execution may result in a contrasting order of elements.

2. The Starting Object: The item that *kicks off* the transformation may also change the resultant model. Given a Class *Person* with three attributes, *name*, *age* and *height* one may not assume the resultant transformation starting with `ClassToTable` would be equal to one starting with the *age* attribute using `AttributeToColumn`. If the `AttributeToColumn` were to set an order attribute within the Column it creates using a global variable which attribute is transformed first makes a difference to the final model.

To study the execution of the transformation it is essential to capture the correspondence between the source and destination elements as a part of tracing. In addition, we propose existing tracing mechanisms to be extended so that the ordering of the execution of the rules can also be captured. This would allow the developers to study the transformation, using the execution traces, and hence know in what order the rules are executed.

4.3   Rule Dependencies

Consider the example in Figure 3, which involves two dependent rules, R_1 and R_2. The execution of the transformation via ETL consists of two stages. The first step, initialisation, matches each rule to a specific source model element and creates the target elements. For example if the source meta-model consists of one class (c_1) associated to five attributes ($a_1, \ldots, a_5$), R_1 is executed once on the class to produce the table and subsequently R_2 is executed five times to produce the columns. Once the destination objects have been created, the second phase, called binding, runs the body of the rule on the objects that have been created. This part sets properties and creates the associations between the, currently disconnected, destination model elements. This is the same for ATL and QVT-O. The procedure for SiTra however is slightly different. All rules are called lazily, i.e. objects are created when they are called by parent transformations and not before. R_1 would iterate through the classes attributes to call R_2 to retrieve columns and would bind them to its table when instructed. Since ordering of the source is arbitrary, it is possible that an attribute object is processed first by R_2. This would result in starting the transformation on the attribute and that rule transforming the class that is associated to it, i.e. the execution of R_1 on the parent class. Then from R_1 the remaining attributes are transformed, i.e. the four remaining executions of R_2.

A linear trace dictates what was created in relation to the execution of the instantiation phase. For instance a trace $T := t_1t_2 \ldots t_n$ explains that the transformation t_2 was instantiated after the transformation t_1 and that is when the targets were created. However it ignores the nested nature of a model transformation. The links between rules are lost, i.e. we don't know what rule depends on the output of another. Did, for example, t_1 require the results of t_3, or in imperative languages did t_1 transform the source of t_3 to get the results. A model transformation is a graph and this graph is lost within the standard trace. Using our example the output of $R_1(c_1)$ invoking $[R_2(a_1), R_2(a_2), \ldots R_2(a_5)]$ may not be the same as $R_2(a_5)$ invoking $R_1(c_1)$, which subsequently invokes $[R_2(a_1), R_2(a_2), \ldots R_2(a_4)]$. In frameworks where a developer may have a global state: it must be part of the engine to assume there is one.

Using M2M transformations to assist in a software development process, i.e. partially generating design models from architecture models, architecture models from analysis models, or generating tests from requirements, would require that the traceability be retained for auditing reasons. This is especially true for safety critical applications and in general compliance matrix generation. There is a clear scope for identifying methods of capturing the ordering of execution and inter-rule dependencies for assisting load balancing, profiling and validation.

5   Sketch of the Solution

In the previous section we have outlined some of the shortcomings of the existing tracing mechanisms in use within M2M transformations. To summarise, we extend an existing framework to deal with:

1. Capturing the nested nature of a transformation
2. Capturing rule dependencies; and
3. Capturing orphan objects created within the transformation.

Our solution involves a new meta-model to capture more information regarding the internals of a M2M transformation and the use of dynamic proxy classes to capture orphan objects. The suggested methods are independent of the model transformation frameworks and with minor alterations can be adopted by all mainstream frameworks. We explain parts of the solution briefly and then demonstrate, by case study, using a non-trivial example of transforming a relational database to HBase.

6   SiTra

6.1   Capturing Rule and Transformation Dependencies

The Simple Transformer (SiTra) is an imperative Java implementation of a M2M transformation [2]. It provides two interfaces that can be used to create a transformation engine and the rules for it. Additionally, the bundle comes with an engine that can be used out of the box. Seyyed M. A. Shah et al. amended this to add traceability [21]. However this, like others, has all of the issues we have discussed in the previous section regarding traceability. In this section we will discuss the changes we have made to solve these issues.

We have already discussed the initialisation and binding phases within M2M transformation engines. In SiTra the initialisation phase is synonymous to the `build` method and binding is the `setProperties` method; however the scheduling differs from more declarative engines as they are called lazily rather than upfront. These two are distinct as they allow nested transformations. If you were to call a transformation which is dependent on itself, the initialised objects need to be available to the lower transformations. For instance the transformation of an *Attribute*, from a object orientated (OO) model, to a *Column*, from a relational database view, would require access to the newly transformed *Table* to set its owner. Without this we would have an infinite loop. We illustrate this inter-rule dependency with our `ClassToTable` rule, shown in Figure 2 and with a cut down `AttributeToColumn` rule shown in Figure 4. Both transformations call upon each other in order to set references.

```
1    public class AttributeToColumn implements Rule<Class, Table> {
2        public void setProperties(Column target, Attribute source,
3            Transformer transformer) {
4            Table parent = transformer.transform(source.getParent());
5            target.setParent(parent);
6        ... } ... }
```

Fig. 4. An example of an inter-rule dependency

Whilst exploring this we also found that SiTra would only transform a source object, A, once. This was because another structure is being queried within the engine, a cache. However the source object was used as the key of the map (`Map<Source, Target>`). This behaviour was found in ETL as well. Using the `equivalent()` method or `::=` operator seemed to return the first item within the transformation trace. You were able to transform a source object multiple times but if a later match was required a manual filtering of transformed objects is needed. Here we found the internal tuple needed to be amended. The map $(A, AtoB) \rightarrow B$ uses the source object, A, and the rule, $AtoB$ as the key, this allowed us to request any transformation of A given a rule with ease.

The largest issue we have found within transformation traces is the verboseness of the trace itself. A lot of information is lost when these elements are created. The current state-of-the-art provides a chronological list of rules; we never get to see the dependencies between rules and transformations. ETL uses an equivalent structure as SiTra's `ITrace` interface [21], inferred from the QVT standard [18]. In which is contained the tuple as described in section 3. This tuple does not take into consideration the nested nature of a transformation, and only concerns the instantiation phase on the first run. It may also be important to

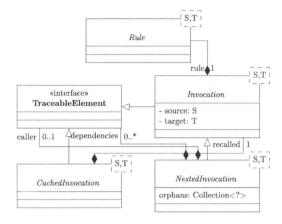

Fig. 5. A new meta-model for a traceable model transformation

see what transformations actually call the `build()` method and which have the object returned from the transformation trace. Fig. 5 shows the new transformation trace within SiTra. Here we have illustrated new types of trace element. `Invocation` is the equivalent of the previous `ITrace`, it simply contains the source, target and the rule responsible. This alone can provide the current state-of-the-art. We have introduced two more types of traceable element within SiTra: *a)* `NestedInvocation`; and `CachedInvocation`. These provide more detail to the actual internals of the transformation. The former provides the same information as the standard however contains two more elements: *a)*the calling transformation trace element (if applicable); and the trace elements generated because of the current transformation. The latter simply provides the trace element that represents the first run of the transformation. In order to maintain this list, and to reduce the effect on performance by traversing it, we amended the internal cache once more: $(A, AtoB) \rightarrow (B, TraceableElement)$. Using this latest implementation we can now see that a source element, A, and a rule, $AtoB$, returns the target object B and is referenced by $TraceableElement$. This can be simplified further as the `TraceableElement` includes B: $(A, AtoB) \rightarrow TraceableElement$.

Our meta model provides solutions to retain the order of execution of transformation rules and the ability to recreate the transformation. This is provided by the nested nature of our meta-model as it explains what rules are completed and what invoked them. The capability to find the actual binding phase, opposed to a recollection, is provided by the new cached invocation type. Allowing the user to recreate the situation at the time of creation. This cached invocation aids in providing a graph of rule dependencies.

6.2   A Dynamic Proxy to Catch Orphans

The process of creation, specifically the binding phase, involves invoking mutator methods to change the state of the destination object. These setters are often passed new objects that need to be traced, particularly in SiTra, newly allocated objects. In order to catch these orphans we need to intercept *all* mutators to check to see if the additional objects are within the trace. For example, when adding a foreign key to a child table, we need to intercept the list of constraints.

For each transformation of source s we get a target t. In order to intercept we make a $Proxy(t)$ that maintains the functionality of the original target however the setters are modified. In each setter we check to see if the additional element is within the trace, and if not we add it the current invocation of the trace. Once this has been completed we then call the *actual* setter of the target object. To ensure traces are added for all orphans, as well as grandchildren of the target, instead of passing the original parameter we pass a proxy of it. This allows the recursion of the orphan tracking.

There are two types of call to intercept:

1. Mutator methods: we define a mutator method as one that has no return type, one parameter and begins with "set". This allows us to catch local attributes to the target.
2. Getter methods that return a collection: we define a getter as a method that has no parameters and returns a collection.

The former we have explained, however the latter is slightly different. Rather than intercepting simple *set* and *get*, we intercept collection mutators like *put*, *add*, *addAll*, etc.

7 Case Study

In order to demonstrate our new framework we have created a non-trivial transformation between a relational database and HBase, involving a transformation of the schema as well as the data. We then applied this to an *instance* of the relational database using the employee database provided by MySQL[3], a widely used test database for benchmarking. This dataset contains four million rows over six related tables.

For the purpose of this case study, and due to space restraints, we shall not delve into the rules in depth for this transformation. Instead we shall use them, partial or otherwise, to demonstrate what happens within the black-box that is SiTra. The M2M transformation itself will be available online[4].

Meta-Model of Apache HBase. The meta-model of Apache HBase, the destination, is shown in Figure 6. Here we can see a very simple representation of the internals of the NoSQL database engine. We have a Namespace, which is synonymous to a Database in relational terms, but that is as far as similarities between HBase and a relational database go. A Table in a NoSQL sense is more of a key-value store, whereas the relational view would view its Tables as a tree

---

[3] https://dev.mysql.com/doc/employee/en/
[4] https://baserg.github.io/sitra

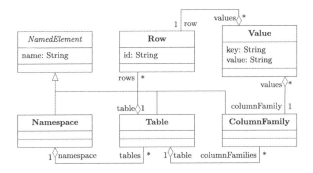

Fig. 6. The meta-model of a Apache HBase

structure. A Table contains a selection of Column Families and Rows. The former enables more structure within the key store whilst the latter is the data itself. A Row contains an id, this is the key for all related data to this Table. Finally we have Values tied to the Rows and Column Families, each value has its own key to differentiate itself from the other values within a Column Family.

This meta-model allows us to realise the structure and the data of Apache HBase. In turn this is used to generate HBase shell to persist our transformation to a real HBase server. In order to do this we use the template engine Xtend.

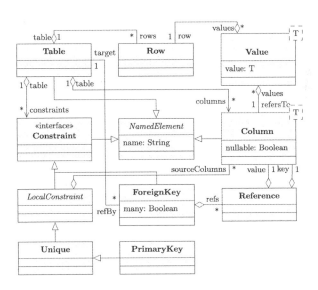

Fig. 7. The meta-model of a relational database

Meta-Model of a Relational Database. Since NoSQL databases generally do not have schemas, we needed a meta-model for a relational database that includes the data itself. Unlike OO2DB where we are purely transforming structure, NoSQL database avoids creating structure unnecessarily. The primitive structures that are created are simple buckets for string or binary data. Therefore in order to properly transform a database we need to access the data within the relational tables.

Figure 7 shows us the meta-model of a relational database, our source meta-model. Here we have a Table with Constraints, Rows and Columns. Where a Constraint is local to the Table, i.e. a Unique index, a Primary Key or a Foreign Key. Those in turn reference Columns to enforce their Constraint and in the case of a Foreign Key provide a mapping of a selection of Columns of one table to another target table. In order to keep the data, we have a Value class, which references the Column it belongs to and the Row it is part of. This latter element allows us to have the data we require for the transformation.

7.1   Catching Orphans

In order to depict the orphan issue we take a subset of the transformation we have created. Specifically the transformation of a *Relational Table* to a *HBase Table*. When creating a HBase Table one must make a *default* column family to hold the primitive data. For example the `employee` would contain a column family called *0* and in there would have values relating to their name, age and gender. In SiTra we would define a rule to be `Rule<db.Table, hbase.Table>`, this would only execute on tables with no or more than two foreign keys, as this would be a *root* table or a complex lookup table (which would need to be referenced).

We can envisage a binding phase as shown in Figure 8. As normal, the `target` would appear in the internal trace of SiTra as it would be added after the instantiation phase, however we have introduced a new element: a column family. This element is disconnected from the transformation trace. However when `setProperties` is called, the `hbase.Table` is in fact a dynamic proxy instance. This instance, as mentioned in subsection 6.2, captures *getters* whereby the return is a collection and in turn returns a collection proxy, which intercepts the lists mutators. Before the addition to the collection is made, the proxy determines whether it has seen the `columnFamily` before and if not adds it to the *orphan* collection in the currently active trace instance (as seen in Figure 5).

```
public void setProperties(hbase.Table target, db.Table source,
    Transformer transformer) {
  ColumnFamily columnFamily = new hbase.ColumnFamily();
  columnFamily.setName("0");
  target.getColumnFamilies().add(columnFamily);
}
```

Fig. 8. A sample of a scenario leading to The creation of an orphan in SiTra

Our transformation of the employee database manually creates columns families in the same fashion as above, both the employee and department tables have this default column family. Relationships however are treated slightly differently. Those lookup tables aren't transformed into different tables, instead are a group of column families attached to the parent table. Therefore each relational child table, the columns are converted to column families and are added to the parent HBase table. This still uses the same mechanism as above, however there is a loop to iterate the new column families. SiTra was able to retain all orphan objects for this transformation.

7.2   The Nested Nature of Model-to-Model Transformation

Continuing the example of a relational table and an HBase table, the transformation will recurse by transforming the rows that the table has, and in turn the values will be transformed. This natural tree structure that happens is captured within the new meta-model. Whereby an invocation *depends* on another, as shown in Figure 5. In order to implement, and retain this information, we use a simple stack. Not unlike a process stack, our *stack frame* is the invocation element as it has access to all components: source, target, orphans and of course dependencies. When an item is *built* a trace element is created to record this transaction, it is then added to the top of the stack. Once the binding phase has completed, it is then popped off the top.

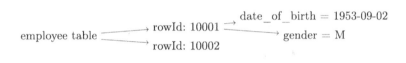

Fig. 9. Depicting the nesting of rules

Figure 9 illustrates a small portion of our output model. Level one is that of a relational table to an HBase table, level two transforms the rows, where the rowId is the primary key of the table. Finally level three is the transformation of the values, for the default column family. The tree for the whole transformation is very large; however we have an implementation that can persist these links into the graph database Neo4j (available at http://www.neo4j.org).

7.3   Deriving Rule Dependencies

Our meta-model retains the information regarding all transactions within the transformation, particularly the recollection of previously transformed elements of the source model, which is currently unavailable from the current state-of-the-art. These two relationships between different transformations can be used to derive the inter-rule dependencies. For example, when transforming a relational table to a HBase table, the rule will attempt to transform its data, i.e. its rows.

Once this is complete it will add the rows to itself. However the rows themselves require the HBase table to add itself to it, its opposite. This cyclic assignment is a must if we do not have a modelling framework to automatically set these links, like ECORE. From this point we can derive that the first rule, in this instance, depends on the second, and vice versus.

To gather this we need only iterate through the trace elements and generate a graph of the rules used. If we move down a level, of `NestedInvocation`, we know that the parent required it, if we find a `CachedInvocation` we know *a)* it has been transformed before; and it has been recalled for this current execution.

8   Epsilon Transformation Language

The mechanisms described in this paper can be applied to other frameworks as well. The meta-model described in Figure 5 can be presented in most frameworks; however a key difference with SiTra and ETL is the scheduling. ETL flattens the model, matches and instantiates all model elements before binding them whereas SiTra is completed on the fly. However ETL can derive the dependency links between transformations by realising the first time the bind is called on an object, and by the way transformations are referenced, using the `equivalent()` methods. The orphan capture can also be completed: if using ECORE one may use its native notification pattern. `EContentAdapter` can be used on either the first transformation or upon the ECORE resource that is tracking the output. Opposed to intercepting calls, as is needed on regular POJOs, one may simply interpret the notification from the change methods.

9   Related Work

Mäder explains that traceability links are rarely re-used in the maintenance of a system despite the ever-increasing complexities that they contain [17]. He puts partial blame to the failure of tools to provide usable functionality for stakeholders to query and capture traceability links. The move to an integrated traceability mechanism with a verbose trace would allow it to be persisted inside a data store such that standard queries can be made in an attempt to solve some of those issues.

Frédérick Jouault argues that traceability need not be part of the overall transformation engine as a High Order Transformation (HOT) can be used, he uses HOT, with an ATL example, to introduce trace link elements into an existing transformation script [14]. Here an instance of ATL is transformed into another version of ATL with additional outputs along with an imperative binding. Iván Santiago et al. also used this in order to add iTrace capabilities to transformations so they can measure the quality degradation that the introduction of trace generation causes [20]. Here we have a decoupled the mechanism used to implement traceability; however this is an additional step for validation. Our approach maintains the implementation within the framework in order to remove the additional burden it places upon the developer.

10   Conclusion

The primary conclusion of this paper is that there is little in terms of built in traceability in rule-based transformation engines. Those that do provide an external trace are unable to provide enough information to relate to the internals of a M2M transformation. Model transformations themselves are relational processes, they relate the parties involved: sources, targets and rules, but also relate to each other and generate a dependency model within rules and executions of rules. The latter is lost in QVT's trace instance.

We have provided a new, independent, trace meta-model that could be used within most M2M transformations engines to maintain the tracing information. In addition we have provided some information on how other engines may implement this functionality, particularly the ability to track orphans. To demonstrate these mechanisms we have implemented it by extending SiTra. These changes to SiTra have brought it up to the current state-of-the art in terms of traceability and provide these mechanisms natively.

References

1. Aizenbud-Reshef, N., et al.: Model traceability. IBM Systems Journal **45** (2006)
2. Akehurst, D.H., Bordbar, B., Evans, M.J., Howells, W.G.J., McDonald-Maier, K.D.: SiTra: simple transformations in java. In: Wang, J., Whittle, J., Harel, D., Reggio, G. (eds.) MoDELS 2006. LNCS, vol. 4199, pp. 351–364. Springer, Heidelberg (2006)
3. Alwanain, M., Bordbar, B., Küster, J., Bowles, F.: Automated Composition of Sequence Diagrams via Alloy. MODELSWARD (2014)
4. Bordbar, B., Howells, G., Evans, M., Staikopoulos, A.: Model transformation from OWL-S to BPEL Via SiTra. In: Akehurst, D.H., Vogel, R., Paige, R.F. (eds.) ECMDA-FA. LNCS, vol. 4530, pp. 43–58. Springer, Heidelberg (2007)
5. Bowles, J., Meedeniya, D.: Formal Transformation from Sequence Diagrams to Coloured Petri Nets. In: 2010 17th Asia Pacific Software Engineering Conference (APSEC) (2010)
6. Briand, L., et al.: Traceability and SysML design slices to support safety inspections: a controlled experiment. ACM Trans. Softw. Eng. Methodol. **23** (2014)
7. Claypool, K.T., Rundensteiner, E.A.: Gangam: a transformation modeling framework. In: 2003. (DASFAA 2003) Proceedings Eighth International Conference on Database Systems for Advanced Applications (2003)
8. Czarnecki, K., Helsen, S.: Feature-based survey of model transformation approaches. IBM Systems Journal **45** (2006)
9. Ebner, G., Kaindl, H.: Tracing all around in reengineering. IEEE Software **19** (2002)
10. Eclipse Foundation. Xtend (2014). URL: http://www.eclipse.org/xtend/ (visited on 03/04/2015)
11. Fritzsche, M. et al.: Application of Tracing Techniques in Model-Driven Performance Engineering. In: 4th ECMDA Traceability Workshop (2008)
12. Galvao, I., Goknil, A.: Survey of traceability approaches in model-driven engineering. In: 2007 EDOC 2007 11th IEEE International Enterprise Distributed Object Computing Conference (2007)

13. Geepalla, E., Bordbar, B., Last, J.: Transformation of spatio-temporal role based access control specification to alloy. In: Abelló, A., Bellatreche, L., Benatallah, B. (eds.) MEDI 2012. LNCS, vol. 7602, pp. 67–78. Springer, Heidelberg (2012)
14. Jouault, F.: Loosely coupled traceability for ATL. In: Proceedings of the European Conference on Model Driven Architecture (ECMDA) Workshop on Traceability (2005)
15. Jouault, F., Kurtev, I.: Transforming models with ATL. In: Bruel, J.-M. (ed.) MoDELS 2005. LNCS, vol. 3844, pp. 128–138. Springer, Heidelberg (2006)
16. Kolovos, D.S., Paige, R.F., Polack, F.A.C.: The Epsilon Transformation Language. In: Vallecillo, A., Gray, J., Pierantonio, A. (eds.) ICMT 2008. LNCS, vol. 5063, pp. 46–60. Springer, Heidelberg (2008)
17. Mäder, P.: Interactive traceability querying and visualization for coping with development complexity. In: CoRR (2013)
18. OMG. Meta Object Facility (MOF) 2.0 Query View Transformation Specification Version 1.1., Jan. 2011. URL: http://www.omg.org/spec/QVT/1.1/PDF/ (visited on 03/04/2015)
19. Paige, R.F., et al.: Building model-driven engineering traceability classifications. In: 4th ECMDA Traceability Workshop (2008)
20. Santiago, I., Vara, J.M., de Castro, V., Marcos, E.: Measuring the effect of enabling traces generation in ATL model transformations. In: Filipe, J., Maciaszek, L.A. (eds.) ENASE 2013. CCIS, vol. 417, pp. 229–240. Springer, Heidelberg (2013)
21. Shah, S.M.A., Anastasakis, K., Bordbar, B.: From UML to alloy and back again. In: Ghosh, S. (ed.) MODELS 2009. LNCS, vol. 6002, pp. 158–171. Springer, Heidelberg (2010)
22. The Apache Software Foundation. Apache HBase (2014). URL: http://hbase.apache.org/ (visited on 03/05/2015)
23. Vara, J.M., et al.: Dealing with traceability in the MDDof model transformations. In: IEEE Transactions on Software Engineering **40** (2014)
24. Varró, D., Balogh, A.: The model transformation language of the VIATRA2 framework. Science of Computer Programming **68** (2007)
25. Willink, E.D., Matragkas, N.: QVT Traceability: What does it really mean? (2014). URL: http://www.eclipse.org/mmt/qvt/docs/ICMT2014/QVTtraceability.pdf (visited on 03/04/2015)
26. Wood, S.K., et al.: A model-driven development approach to mapping UML state diagrams to synthesizable VHDL. IEEE Transactions on Computers **57** (2008)
27. Yie, A., Wagelaar, D.: Advanced Traceability for ATL. In: Proceedings of the 1st International Workshop on Model Transformation with ATL (MtATL 2009) (2009)

Property Access Traces for Source Incremental Model-to-Text Transformation

Babajide Ogunyomi$^{(\boxtimes)}$, Louis M. Rose, and Dimitrios S. Kolovos

Department of Computer Science, University of York, Deramore Lane, Heslington,
York YO10 5GH, UK
{bjo500,louis.rose,dimitris.kolovos}@york.ac.uk

Abstract. Automatic generation of textual artefacts (including code, documentation, configuration files, build scripts, etc.) from models in a software development process through the application of model-to-text (M2T) transformation is a common MDE activity. Despite the importance of M2T transformation, contemporary M2T languages lack support for developing transformations that scale with the size of the input model. As MDE is applied to systems of increasing size and complexity, a lack of scalability in M2T (and other) transformation languages hinders industrial adoption. In this paper, we propose a form of runtime analysis that can be used to identify the impact of source model changes on generated textual artefacts. The structures produced by this runtime analysis, property access traces, can be used to perform efficient source-incremental transformation: our experiments show an average reduction of 60% in transformation execution time compared to non-incremental (batch) transformation.

1 Introduction

Although MDE can reduce systems complexity and increase developer productivity [1], achieving scalability of MDE processes, practices and technologies remains an open research challenge and is important for widespread industrial adoption [2]. The scalability challenges in MDE are numerous, and include: performant persistence of very large models, modularity and reusability in the definition of very large modelling languages, and efficient propagation of change between artefacts (including models). This paper focuses on the latter challenge, in the context of propagating changes from models to textual artefacts (such as source code, documentation, or build scripts).

Our primary motivation for this work stemmed from our participation in an EC FP7 project (INESS, grant #218575) which involved applying model-to-text transformation to generate code that was amenable to model checking. Code generation from UML models supplied by our industrial partners took about 1 hour. Re-generation of code took 1 hour to execute even for small changes to the source model, because all code files were being re-generated even when the changes did not affect the content of some of them. Ideally, the execution

© Springer International Publishing Switzerland 2015
G. Taentzer and F. Bordeleau (Eds.): ECMFA 2015, LNCS 9153, pp. 187–202, 2015.
DOI: 10.1007/978-3-319-21151-0_13

time of the code-generating transformation would have been directly proportional to the magnitude of the change to the source model: small changes to the model would have resulted in significantly reduced execution time of the code-generating transformation. This ideal is realised with a *source incremental* transformation engine [3].

In this paper, we propose *property access traces*, an approach to achieving source incremental model-to-text (M2T) transformation. Property access traces use runtime analysis to capture information about the way in which a transformation accesses its source models. When the source models change, a property access trace provides an efficient means for determining which subset of the transformation must be re-executed to propagate changes to the textual artefacts. Crucially, a property access trace allows the transformation engine to reduce (and ideally eliminate) execution of the parts of the transformation that have not been affected by the changes to the source models, and the M2T transformation scales better as a whole. This paper makes the following contributions:

– A design for computing and querying property access traces in order to perform efficient propagation of changes from models to textual artefacts (Section 3).
– An implementation of property access traces for a contemporary M2T transformation language, EGL [4], including a discussion of its limitations (Sections 3 and 4).
– An empirical evaluation and discussion of the benefits of property access traces for two existing M2T transformations (Section 4).

2   Background: M2T Transformation

This section briefly summarises contemporary approaches to M2T transformations and the different types of incrementality that are needed for effective and efficient M2T transformation.

The majority of contemporary M2T transformation languages use an approach (Listing 1.1), in which M2T transformations comprise several modular templates, whose structure closely resembles the generated text. Any portions of generated text that vary over model elements are replaced with *dynamic (executable) sections*, which are evaluated with respect to one or more source models. Any portions of generated text that remain the same are termed *static sections*. A M2T transformation normally comprises several templates, and co-ordination logic that invokes each template on the relevant part of the source models.

```
1   Hello, [%= person.name %]!
```

Listing 1.1. A template-based M2T transformation, in EGL syntax, which contains a static section ("Hello, "), a dynamic section (that outputs the value of the name attribute of a *person* model element) and another static section ("!").

Incrementality in model transformation – and in general – seeks to react to changes in an artefact (such as a model) in a manner that minimises the need for redundant computations. For M2T transformation, three types of incrementality have been identified: user edit-preserving incrementality, target incrementality, and source incrementality [3]. User-edit preserving incrementality and target incrementality are now widely supported, but source incrementality is not [5]. In this paper, we focus on source incrementality and argue that it is an essential feature for providing scalable M2T transformation capabilities.

Source incrementality is the capability of a M2T transformation engine to respond to changes in its source models in a way that minimises (and ideally eliminates) the need for re-computations that will not eventually have an impact on its output. Our intuition, which we investigate and assess in this paper, is that achieving a high degree of source incrementality can significantly improve the efficiency of complex transformations, especially when they operate on large or complex source models (e.g., with many cross-references between model elements and/or inter-dependencies between source models).

3   Property Access Traces

In this section, we propose *property access traces*, which contain concise and precise information collected during the execution of a M2T transformation and can be used to detect which templates need to be re-executed in response to a set of changes in the input model(s). We demonstrate how property access traces can provide comprehensive support for source incrementality for contemporary template-based M2T transformation engines. In contrast to existing approaches to source incremental model-to-text and model-to-model transformation, property access traces do not rely on model differencing or static analysis (which can be computationally expensive and imprecise).

This section provides an overview of using property access traces for source incremental transformation, discusses the way in which existing template-based M2T languages can be extended with support for property access traces, and briefly describes a prototypical implementation of property access traces for the EGL[4] M2T language.

3.1   Overview

To provide support for source incrementality, a transformation engine must be capable of identifying the subset of the transformation that is sensitive to changes in its input models (impact analysis), and re-executing the subset of the transformation to update the target (change propagation). Performing accurate impact analysis presents arguably the greatest challenge: in a template-based M2T transformation, a template might be sensitive to some types of change to a model element, but not to others. In the example presented in Figure 1, student reports are generated by a template that, clearly, is sensitive to changes to the name of a course (e.g., "SEPR" changes to "Software Project"), but not to the name of the lecturer (e.g., "Mary Johnson" changes to "Mary Johnson-Smith"), similarly, changes to student names should not trigger re-generation of course reports.

Property access traces, as discussed below, provide a lightweight but effective mechanism for recording an M2T transformation's execution information which can be then used to detect relevant changes in the source model, and to determine which parts of the transformation need to be re-executed against which model elements. When a transformation is first executed, property access traces are captured and persisted in non-volatile storage. A *property access trace* records which parts of the transformation access which parts of the source models. In subsequent executions of the transformation, the property access trace is used to detect whether the source models have changed, and to re-execute only those parts of the transformation that are affected by source model changes. Determining which parts of the transformation to re-execute is possible because we require that transformation templates have two characteristics: they must be stateless and deterministic. A stateless template takes its data only from input models, which means that the generated text is dependent only on data that we can observe. A deterministic template is one which when executed twice on the same input performs the same actions and produces the same output, which means that we can always predict which parts of the input models the template will access. Under these conditions, property accesses alone can be used to determine whether or not a re-invocation of a template will produce a different output after the input models have been changed. A similar correctness argument is made for the incremental model consistency checking approach in [6].

3.2   Design

In order to demonstrate the feasibility of *property access traces*, we extend EGL (the Epsilon Generation Language)[4]. EGL is a template-based M2T language. EGX is an orchestration sub-language of EGL which provides mechanisms for co-ordinating template execution.

Before discussing the details of implementing *property access* traces for EGL, we first describe the way in which transformation execution is implemented in the language (Figure 2). An M2T transformation in EGL is specified in the form of an EGX program, which comprises a number of rules and EGL templates. Typically, each rule will also contain a target, which is a specification of the destination of the output of the transformation. In its simplest form, a rule binds an EGL template to a metamodel type and executes the template for each model element of the correct type. The transformation engine starts by loading the input model(s), before executing the EGX program. Transformation execution begins by evaluating each rule in the EGX program, to determine its metamodel type, then invokes the associated *Template* on every model element of its type[1], and writes the output of executing the templates to files.

---

[1] EGX rules also support *guards* which can further limit their applicability

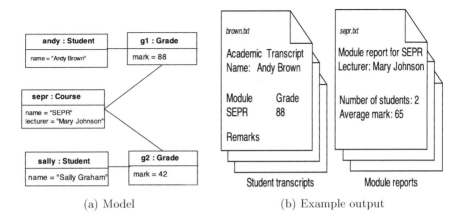

(a) Model   (b) Example output

Fig. 1. Artefacts for a M2T transformation that generates reports

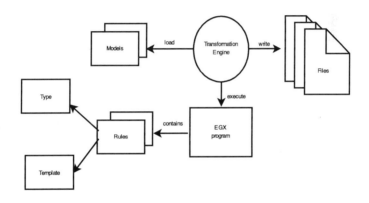

Fig. 2. Overview of transformation execution using EGX

Consider, for example, the M2T transformation in Listing 1.2, which produces student transcripts and course reports of the forms shown on the right-hand side of Figure 1. This EGX program comprises two transformation rules: *StudentToTranscript* (lines 1 -5), *CourseToReport* (lines 7 -11). EGX passes each object of type *Student* to the *studentToTranscript.egl* template (Listing 1.3) and each object of type *Course* to the *courseToReport.egl* template (Listing 1.4). Additionally, in each transformation rule, a target (filename) is defined, whose value is determined at the transformation execution time.

In a typical M2T (batch) transformation engine, execution involves evaluating all templates against all instances of that context type every time a transformation is executed. In a source incremental M2T transformation engine, transformation execution involves identifying only the templates that need to be re-evaluated to propagate changes from the source model to the generated text. In other words, a source incremental M2T transformation engine identifies but,

```
1   rule StudentToTranscript
2       transform aStudent : Student {
3           template : "studentToTranscript.egl"
4           target : aStudent.name + ".txt"
5   }
6
7   rule CourseToReport
8       transform aCourse : Course {
9           template : "courseToReport.egl"
10          target : aCourse.name + ".txt"
11  }
```

Listing 1.2. Example of an EGX M2T program applied to input model in Figure 1(a)

```
1   Student name : [%= aStudent.name %]
2   Course  Grade
3   [% for(grade in aStudent.grades) { %]
4   [%= grade.course.name + " " + grade.mark %]
5   [% } %]
```

Listing 1.3. M2T template for generating student transcripts specified in EGL syntax

crucially, does not re-evaluate templates for which the generated text is known from a previous invocation of the transformation.

3.2.1 Extending M2T transformation languages with Property Access Traces.
Implementation of property access traces involves extending the execution engine of a M2T language with four new concepts. Property access traces comprise transformation information that is derived from model elements and from the templates that are invoked on those model elements. During the execution of a template, a *PropertyAccessRecorder* captures the properties of the accessed model elements. The recorded *PropertyAccess(es)* which make up a *PropertyAccessTrace* are then persisted in non-volatile storage, a *PropertyAccessStore*. Figure 3 illustrates the conceptual organisation of the information contained in a *PropertyAccessTrace*.

– A ***PropertyAccess*** is a triple ¡e, p, v¿, where e is the unique identifier of the model element, p is the name of the property, and v is the current value of the property. The way in which model element identifiers are computed varies, depending on the underlying modelling technology (e.g., XMI IDs or relative paths for EMF XMI models). There are two types of property accesses – *AttributeAccesses* and *ReferenceAccesses* – which vary in the type of value that they store. *AttributeAccesses* store a string value and are used when the property has a primitive type. *ReferenceAccesses* store the unique identifiers of the referenced model elements and are used when the property is a reference.
– A ***PropertyAccessTrace*** (Figure 3) captures which transformation rules are invoked on which source model elements and, moreover, which *PropertyAccesses* resulted from each invocation of a transformation rule (a *RuleInvocation*) in Figure 3).
– A ***PropertyAccessRecorder*** is responsible for recording *PropertyAccesses* during the execution of a template, and updating the *PropertyAccesses* when a

```
1    Course Report for [%= aCourse.name %]
2    Lecturer: [%= aCourse.lecturer %]
3
4    Number of students:[%= aCourse.grades.size() %]
5    Average mark:[%=aCourse.grades.collect(mark).sum()/aCourse.grades.size() %]
```

Listing 1.4. M2T template for generating course reports specified in EGL syntax

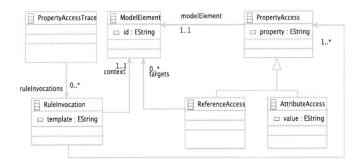

Fig. 3. Overview of Property Access Trace

change in the value of a *PropertyAccess* is detected. It is important to note that since property access traces contains data about input model elements only, any other type of change to the transformation specification is not considered (See section 4.3 for a discussion on known limitations of this approach).

– A ***PropertyAccessStore*** is responsible for storing the *PropertyAccess*es passed on to it by the *PropertyAccessRecorder*. The *PropertyAccessStore* is also responsible for making *PropertyAccess*es (that were stored during a previous transformation execution) available to the transformation engine. We use an embedded RDBMS to store *property access*es, but other options (e.g., graph databases, XML documents, etc.) are also possible. A *PropertyAccessStore* must be capable of persisting, in non-volatile storage, the property access trace information between invocations of a M2T transformation. The main requirement for a *PropertyAccessStore* is performance: any gains achieved with a source incremental engine might be negated if the *PropertyAccessStore* cannot efficiently read and write property access traces.

We now briefly describe the way in which these concepts are used to achieve source incremental transformation, before providing an example. During the initial execution of a transformation, the *PropertyAccessRecorder* creates *PropertyAccess*es from the properties of model elements that are accessed during the execution of each rule. The collected *PropertyAccess*es are organised by *RuleInvocation* by the transformation engine to form a *PropertyAccessTrace* and stored by the *PropertyAccessStore*. At subsequent execution of the M2T transformation, the transformation engine retrieves the previous *PropertyAccessTrace* from the *PropertyAccessStore*. Whenever the transformation engine would ordinarily invoke a transformation rule, it instead retrieves each relevant *PropertyAccess*

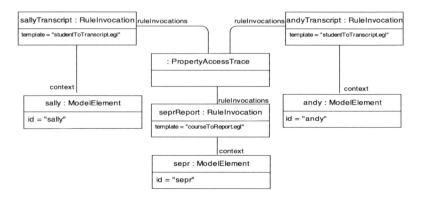

Fig. 4. A partial property access trace for executing *studentToTranscript.egl* on *andy* and *sally*, and *courseToReport.egl* on *sepr*

from the *PropertyAccessTrace* and queries the model to determine if the value of any of the *PropertyAccess*es has changed. Only when a value has changed is the transformation rule invoked. The *PropertyAccessTrace* is updated and stored if any values have changed.

3.2.2 Example. To further demonstrate the way in which property access traces achieve source-incremental M2T transformation, we now consider an example. Our example uses the transformation in Listings 1.3 and 1.4, which generate student transcripts and course reports from a university model. Executing the transformation on the simple university model in Figure 1(a) causes the transcript-generating rule to be invoked once on each student, *andy* and *sally*, and the course report-generating rule once on course *sepr*. As such, the resulting property access trace comprises three rule invocation objects (Figure 4). Each rule invocation object comprises several property accesses, which are recorded during the execution of the templates in Listing 1.3 and 1.4.

Let us consider the properties accessed during the invocation of the template on *sally*. The *sallyTranscript* rule invocation (Figure 5) comprises several attribute and reference access objects and is constructed as follows. Firstly, the template accesses `sally.name` (line 1 of Listing 1.3) and creates the *aa1* attribute access (Figure 5). The template then accesses `sally.grades` (line 3) and this creates the *ra1* reference access. The *grade.course.name* traversal expression in the template (line 4) creates two property accesses: the *ra2* reference access for *grade.course* and the *aa2* attribute access for *course.name*. Finally, the *grade.mark* expression (line 5) creates the *aa3* attribute access. The boxes with a dashed border in Figure 5 reinforce the relationship between property access objects in the trace and the expressions in the template (Listing 1.3). Note that each property access stores a reference to the model element from which its value was obtained.

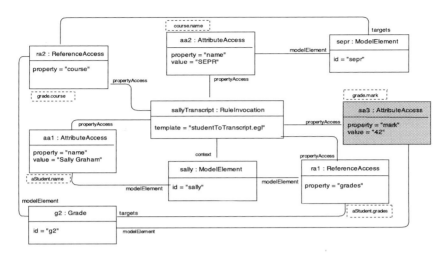

Fig. 5. Expansion of the property access trace for the *sallyTranscript* rule invocation

When the M2T transformation is executed again, the transformation engine retrieves the property access trace (including Figures 4 and 5) and queries the parts of the model that were previously accessed by the transformation, such as the name of each student. Only when the value of any property differs from the value stored in a property access is the containing rule invocation re-executed.

For example, the *sallyTranscript* rule invocation (Figure 5) indicates that if all of the following constraints hold, then the rule invocation need not be re-executed:

1. `sally.name ==` ''Sally Graham'' – due to *aa1*
2. `sally.grades ==` {g2} – due to *ra1*
3. `g2.course ==` sepr – due to *ra2*
4. `sepr.name ==` ''SEPR'' – due to *aa2*
5. `g2.mark ==` ''42'' – due to *aa3*

Suppose that Sally's grade for the SEPR course is changed: the mark attribute of *g2* is changed from 42 to 54. Note that the *aa3* attribute access (highlighted in Figure 4) stores the old value for the mark, 42. When the transformation is re-executed, condition #5 above will no longer hold: *g2.mark* will now evaluate to 54. Consequently, the transformation engine will re-execute the *sallyTranscript* rule invocation.

We have not shown the complete property access trace for the *andyTranscript* rule invocation (due to space constraints), but it is very similar in structure to the *sallyTranscript* rule invocation in Figure 5. The property accesses for *andyTranscript* result in the following constraints:

1. `andy.name ==` ''Andy Brown''
2. `andy.grades ==` {g1}
3. `g1.course ==` sepr

```
4. sepr.name == ``SEPR''
5. g1.mark == ``88''
```

From these constraints, it is clear that the change to *g2.mark* does not require a re-execution of the *andyTranscript* rule invocation as none of the constraints above depend on *g2.mark*. If, on the other hand, our change had been to *sepr.name* rather than to *g2.mark*, then both of the sets of constraints shown above would be unsatisfied and both the *sallyTranscript* and the *andyTranscript* rule invocations would be re-executed.

In general, determining whether or not a rule invocation needs to be re-executed requires the evaluation of $O(n)$ constraints where n is the number of property accesses for that rule invocation.

4   Evaluation and Experience Report

In this section we report on the results of the empirical evaluation of *property access traces*, in which we compare the transformation execution times in incremental and non-incremental modes for two existing transformations. The results of our experiment show that source incremental transformations can be more efficient than non-incremental transformations, particularly for frequent or relatively small changes to models.

4.1   Empirical Evaluation

To assess the performance of *property access traces*, we used two existing EGL transformations: Pongo and GraphitiX. We investigated whether property access traces are effective when used for repeated invocations of code generation over the lifetime of an MDE project (Pongo), and whether property access traces are effective as the proportion of change in the input model increases (GraphitiX). We also investigated the memory and disk usage of *property access traces* (Pongo and GraphitiX) to ensure that resource usage is reasonable.

4.1.1 Pongo. Pongo[2] generates data mapper layers for MongoDB, a non-relational database. Pongo takes as input an Ecore model that describes the types and properties of the objects to be stored in the database, and generates Java code that can be used to interact with the database via the user-defined types and properties (without needing to use the MongoDB API).

We compared the total time taken for incremental and non-incremental code generation over the lifetime of a real MDE project. For this purpose we used Pongo v0.5, and 11 versions of the GmfGraph Ecore model (obtained from the Git repository[3] of the GMF team). To simulate code generation activities in the GMF project, we ran Pongo using non-incremental and incremental EGL on each version of the GmfGraph Ecore model.

---

[2] https://code.google.com/p/pongo/
[3] https://git.eclipse.org/c/gmf-tooling

Table 1. Results of using non-incremental and incremental M2T transformation for the Pongo M2T transformation, applied to 11 historical versions of the GMFGraph Ecore model

Version	Changes (#)	Non-Incremental		Incremental	
		Invocations (#)	Time (s)	Invocations (#)	Time (s; %)
1.23	-	72	1.79	72	2.29 (128%)
1.24	1	73	1.72	6	0.93 (54%)
1.25	1	73	2.01	4	0.69 (34%)
1.26	1	74	2.03	6	0.66 (33%)
1.27	10	74	1.97	44	0.78 (40%)
1.28	10	74	1.95	44	0.67 (34%)
1.29	14	74	1.94	14	0.52 (27%)
1.30	24	77	2.02	41	0.70 (35%)
1.31	1	77	1.86	0	0.40 (22%)
1.32	1	77	1.95	0	0.38 (19%)
1.33	3	79	2.00	8	0.55 (28%)
Total			21.24		8.57 (40%)

The results (Table 1) show the difference in number of template invocations and total execution time between non-incremental and incremental execution modes of execution, for each of the 11 versions of the GmfGraph model. Expectedly, during the first invocation of the transformation (version 1.23) in incremental mode, the execution took slightly longer to execute than the non-incremental mode because the former incurs an overhead as the transformation in addition to evaluating templates, must record and process model element properties that are accessed in each template. However, during subsequent executions of the transformation, the incremental mode of execution required between 19% and 54% of the execution time required by the non-incremental mode. In other words, during the execution of the transformation on all versions of the GmfGraph project, we observed upto an 81% reduction in total execution time. Although the overall reduction in execution time (12.67s) is modest, that is partly explained by the relatively small size of the Pongo transformation (6 EGL templates totalling 329 lines of code), and of the GmfGraph model (averaging 65 classes).

4.1.2 GraphitiX. GraphitiX[4] is a Java code generator for Graphiti-based graphical model editors. GraphitiX takes as input annotated Ecore models, which contain a description of the syntax of a domain-specific modelling language. GraphitiX (23 EGL templates totalling 1689 lines of code) is much larger than Pongo.

As such, we used GraphitiX to investigate whether property access traces are effective as the proportion of change in the input model increases. In particular, we sought to identify how large a change to the input model was necessary in order for incremental transformation to become slower than non-incremental transformation due to the overhead incurred in querying a property access trace.

For this purpose we used GraphitiX (Subversion revision 1) and a synthetic Ecore model. We executed GraphitiX on the model, made a change to the model,

---

[4] https://code.google.com/p/graphiti-x/

Table 2. Results of using non-incremental and incremental M2T transformation for the GraphitiX M2T transformation, applied to increasingly larger proportions of changes to the source model

Changes (Elements #: %)	Non-Incremental		Incremental	
	Templ. Invocations (#)	Time (s)	Templ. Invocations (#: %)	Time (s)
-	4014	14.13	4014	20.63
1 (0.1%)	4014	12.09	9 (0.22%)	7.85
5 (0.5%)	4014	14.44	25 (0.62%)	6.92
10 (1%)	4014	14.09	45 (1.12%)	7.59
20 (2%)	4014	13.86	85 (2.11%)	7.13
100 (10%)	4014	15.01	405 (10.09%)	8.60
300 (30%)	4014	14.83	1205 (30.01%)	11.35
600 (60%)	4014	14.30	2405 (59.92%)	16.30
700 (70%)	4014	14.44	2805 (69.88%)	18.50

and re-executed GraphitiX in incremental and non-incremental modes. We varied the proportion of change made to the model. We changed the model by modifying a subset of all classes (by renaming the class and one of its attributes). We chose this type of modification because, as developers of GraphitiX, we knew that that the transformation would be sensitive to these changes. Table 2 supports this claim: the proportion of template invocations in incremental mode is roughly the same as the proportion of change made to the model. In other words, we selected this type of modification to avoid changing the model in a way that had very little impact on the generated artefacts, or vice versa.

As shown in Table 2, our results suggest that source incremental transformation using *property access traces* requires less computation until a significant proportion (threshold) of the input model is changed. In this case, that threshold was reached when approximately 60% of the input model was changed (see the highlighted row in Table 2). This corresponds to 1200 changes, as 2 changes were applied to each changed model element. The threshold will be different for other transformations, and will depend on factors such as: the amount of *property accesses* in templates, and the complexity of model queries in the templates.

4.1.3 Memory and Disk Utilization. To demonstrate that our approach is feasible with respect to resource usage, we investigated the memory and disk usage of property access traces during our experiments with Pongo and GraphitiX.

With respect to memory usage, we observed that peak memory usage for incremental EGL was slightly higher than for non-incremental EGL. For Pongo, peak memory usage for incremental EGL was 102% of non-incremental EGL (200.1Mb compared to 196.7Mb). For GraphitiX, peak memory usage for incremental EGL was 110% of non-incremental EGL (480Mb compared to 436Mb).

With respect to disk usage, we observed that property access traces have modest requirements particularly for a modern development machine: the average size of the property access trace on disk was 412Kb for Pongo and 6.9Mb for GraphitiX. We have not yet optimised our implementation of property access traces to reduce disk space usage.

It is important to note that the memory and disk usage will vary for different transformations, depending on the size of the input model and in particular the amount of *property accesses* made by the transformation.

4.2   Discussion

Our initial experiments indicate that the use of property access traces for providing source incrementality is promising: we have demonstrated that a reduction in execution time is observed for realistic changes to a model (e.g., the changes made to GmfGraph Ecore model). The results also indicate that source incrementality using our approach is more efficient than non-incremental transformations when frequent, small changes are made to a model throughout the lifetime of a project.

The results of the experiments in our previous work[7], which used *signatures* for source-incremental M2T transformation suggested that source incrementality can be used to realize upto 45% performance gain in transformation execution time. *Property access* traces offer a further 15% reduction in transformation execution time. Overall, a 60% reduction in transformation execution time was observed using *property access* traces.

It is important to note that the example M2T demonstrated in section 3.2.2 was simplified for brevity. The templates (in Listings 1.3 and 1.4) did not contain model-querying statements such as, collection-filtering operations (e.g., `Student.all.select(s|s.name == ''Andy Brown'')`). However, as discussed in [6] and in Section 3.1, the complexity of navigation expressions (as long as they are deterministic) is irrelevant. *The two M2T transformations we used for evaluating our approach make extensive use of complex OCL-like collection navigation and filtering operations.*

Lastly, an incremental M2T transformation is correct if it results in the regeneration of all the required files whose contents were affected by the change(s) to the input model. To verify the correctness of the incremental execution of the two transformations that we used in the evaluation of *property access traces*, we performed tests which compared the output of the transformations in incremental mode with the output of the transformations in non-incremental mode. The outcome of our tests indicate that the contents of the files generated in incremental mode were always the same as the contents of the same files generated in non-incremental mode.

4.3   Limitations of Property Access Traces

Property access traces exhibit some limitations. Some of these limitations relate to our current implementation – and will be addressed in future work – whilst some limitations are inherent to the approach.

Our current implementation of *property access traces* in EGL monitors property accesses only during the execution of templates. However, *property access traces* can become over-sensitive to changes to parameters contained in unordered collections because it cannot distinguish between unordered and ordered collections. Consider a template (e.g., `[%= Student.grades.mark %]`) that only prints out the grades of a student, the *PropertyAccessRecorder* records a property access of *grades* on *Student*, whose value is a collection of *Grades*, and also records a property access of *mark* on each *Grade* in the collection *Student.grades*. If in a change event, a *Grade* is removed and re-added to the collection *Student.grades*, these modification operations will result in the same set of *Student.grades*, albeit with a different order, since the re-added *Grade* is inserted at the back of the collection. This will cause the template to be re-executed unnecessarily. The order of collections are important for accurate comparison of modified structural features of a model element. Our current implementation does a string comparison of the values of *property accesses* recorded from calls that return a collection of structural features, and cannot detect if mere re-ordering of collections is a significant change event. Furthermore, our current implementation does not record the accessing of all model elements of a specific type (e.g. Student.allInstances().size()). We currently have a prototypical implementation that extends our *PropertyAccessRecorder* in order to record accesses of *allInstances* nature.

Inherent limitations of the *property access trace* approach are that the use of non-deterministic programming constructs (e.g., random number generators, hash-sets, hash-maps) in a template prevent source incrementality (because the template must always be invoked to compute an appropriate result), and that property access traces can be pessimistic: it is conceivable that a template might access a property but not use its value in the generated text (e.g., `[% if(aGrade.mark > 70) { //do-nothing } %]`). In these cases, a property access trace would result in an unnecessary re-execution of the template.

5   Related Work

Property access traces follow the model profiling method for model consistency checking by Egyed [6]. However, our approach differs in the sense that *property access traces* detect input model changes at runtime, while Egyed's approach assumes notifications of input model changes (e.g., from the modelling technology). Our approach does not rely on the model editor or the underlying modelling framework, hence it can be readily applied to a new version of an input model to compute model changes, with respect to the transformation, as shown in the running example (Section 3.2).

To the best of our knowledge, Xpand[5] is the only contemporary M2T language that supports source incremental transformation. Incremental generation in Xpand uses a combination of trace links and model differencing techniques. Difference models are used to determine changed subset of input models, and trace links are used to specify how source model elements are mapped to generated files. Once the difference model is constructed, impact analysis is performed to determine which changed model elements are used in which templates. A template is re-executed if it consumes a model element that has changed. The efficiency of the approach to incrementality employed by Xpand is heavily dependent on the effectiveness of the underlying modelling framework in performing model differencing. For instance, calculating model diffs between all the versions of GmfGraph models used for the Pongo transformation took about 1.3 seconds

---

[5] http://eclipse.org/modeling/m2t/?project=xpand

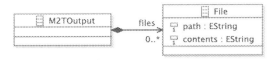

Fig. 6. Example representation of a M2T as M2M metamodel

(average) using EmfCompare which is the same tool that Xpand uses to compute model diffs. This figure represents the time taken to perform only a part of the computation done by Xpand's incremental engine exceeds the time taken to execute each Pongo transformation (see Table 1) all versions of the Gmf-Graph model. As model differencing is integral to Xpand's incremental method, there is no need to conduct a full scale comparison of *property access traces* and model differencing incremental approaches. Furthermore, performance can be impaired because model differencing requires that (at least) two versions of the input model, along with a diff model are loaded, which requires at least three model traversals. This might also be impractical since access to the previous version of the model is needed and may not be available. Property access traces as explained in section 3 do not require model differencing and hence offer a fundamentally different approach to source incrementality.

An M2T transformation could be expressed as an M2M transformation, where the target metamodel resembles Figure 6. As such, a Turing-complete incremental M2M language could be used to express incremental M2T transformations. Song et. al. use model differencing and static analysis to incrementally execute QVTr transformations [8], and as such have the same limitations as Xpand, discussed above. Additionally, static analysis can be too pessimistic to be useful for incremental transformation as discussed in our previous work [7]. More generally, M2M languages may be limited in their ability to handle unique features of M2T languages (e.g., handling protected regions, white spaces, escape direction, etc.). There has been considerable work on incrementality for triple-graph grammars – see [9] for a recent comparison – but TGGs are generally not Turing-complete (although some do provide fallback mechanisms). Additional research is needed to investigate whether the restricted capabilities of incremental TGGs are sufficient to implement complex model transformations.

6   Conclusion

Despite the potential productivity and portability gains of MDE, the inability of MDE tools and techniques to support the building of large and complex systems through processes that scale remains an open research challenge. In this paper, we proposed *property access traces*, an approach to reducing the execution time of M2T transformations in response to changes to source models. We have contributed a design for extending M2T transformation languages with support for *property access traces*, and demonstrated the feasibility of *property access traces* through an empirical evaluation. We have shown that the potential performance gains of source incremental transformation via property access traces are substantial: we observed an average reduction in transformation execution time of 60%. Instead of computing model differences between versions of input models as used by Xpand's incremental transformation technique, *property access traces* employs a technique that only requires the current state of a model, whose efficiency also does not depend on the effectiveness of an underlying modelling framework to calculate model diffs.

In future work, we will improve our implementation of property access traces to address the limitations described in Section 4.3, after which we will extend our empirical evaluation to investigate incrementality for larger and more complicated M2T transformations (such as the INESS M2T transformation described in Section 1).

Acknowledgments. This work was partially supported by the European Commission, through the Scalable Modelling and Model Management on the Cloud (MONDO) FP7 STREP project (grant #611125). The motivating example discussed in this paper was taken from Rose's work on the INESS project, which was supported by the European Commission and co-funded under the 7th Framework Programme (grant #218575).

References

1. Mohagheghi, P., Fernandez, M.A., Martell, J.A., Fritzsche, M., Gilani, W.: MDE adoption in industry: challenges and success criteria. In: Chaudron, M.R.V. (ed.) MODELS 2008. LNCS, vol. 5421, pp. 54–59. Springer, Heidelberg (2009)
2. Kolovos, D., et al.: Scalability: the holy grail of model driven engineering. In: ChaMDE 2008 Workshop Proceedings, pp. 10–14 (2008)
3. Czarnecki, K., Helsen, S.: Feature-based survey of model transformation approaches. IBM Systems Journal **45**(3), 621–645 (2006)
4. Rose, L.M., Paige, R.F., Kolovos, D.S., Polack, F.A.C.: The epsilon generation language. In: Schieferdecker, I., Hartman, A. (eds.) ECMDA-FA 2008. LNCS, vol. 5095, pp. 1–16. Springer, Heidelberg (2008)
5. Ogunyomi, B.: Incremental model-to-text transformation (qualifying dissertation). Technical report (2013)
6. Egyed, A.: Automatically Detecting and Tracking Inconsistencies in Software Design Models. IEEE Transactions on Software Engineering **37**(2), 188–204 (2011)
7. Ogunyomi, B., Rose, L.M., Kolovos, D.S.: On the use of signatures for source incremental model-to-text transformation. In: Dingel, J., Schulte, W., Ramos, I., Abrahão, S., Insfran, E. (eds.) MODELS 2014. LNCS, vol. 8767, pp. 84–98. Springer, Heidelberg (2014)
8. Song, H., Huang, G., Chauvel, F., Zhang, W., Sun, Y., Shao, W., Mei, H.: Instant and incremental QVT transformation for runtime models. In: Whittle, J., Clark, T., Kühne, T. (eds.) MODELS 2011. LNCS, vol. 6981, pp. 273–288. Springer, Heidelberg (2011)
9. Leblebici, E., Anjorin, A., Schürr, A., Hildebrandt, S., Rieke, J., Greenyer, J.: A comparison of incremental triple graph grammar tools. In: Electronic Communications of the EASST, vol. 67 (2014)

Author Index